Baseball's Bonus Babies

ALSO BY BRENT KELLEY
AND FROM McFARLAND

*Voices from the Negro Leagues: Conversations
with 52 Baseball Standouts of
the Period 1924–1960* (1998; paperback 2005)

*"I Will Never Forget": Interviews with
39 Former Negro League Players* (2003)

*The San Francisco Seals, 1946–1957:
Interviews with 25 Former Baseballers* (2002)

*The Pastime in Turbulence: Interviews with
Baseball Players of the 1940s* (2001)

*The Negro Leagues Revisited: Conversations
with 66 More Baseball Heroes* (2000)

*They Too Wore Pinstripes: Interviews with
20 Glory-Days New York Yankees* (1998)

*The Early All-Stars: Conversations with Standout
Baseball Players of the 1930s and 1940s* (1997)

*In the Shadow of the Babe: Interviews with Baseball Players
Who Played With or Against Babe Ruth* (1995)

*Baseball Stars of the 1950s: Interviews with
All-Stars of the Game's Golden Era* (1993)

*The Case For: Those Overlooked by
the Baseball Hall of Fame* (1992)

# Baseball's Bonus Babies

*Conversations with 24 High-Priced Ballplayers Signed from 1953 to 1957*

BRENT KELLEY

McFarland & Company, Inc., Publishers
*Jefferson, North Carolina, and London*

LIBRARY OF CONGRESS CATALOGUING-IN-PUBLICATION DATA

Kelley, Brent P.
 Baseball's bonus babies : conversations with 24 high-priced ballplayers signed from 1953 to 1957 / Brent Kelley.
     p.    cm.
 Includes index.

   ISBN-13: 978-0-7864-2519-8
   softcover : 50# alkaline paper ∞

   1. Baseball players—United States—Salaries, etc.—History.
 I. Title.
 GV880.K46   2006
 796.357092'2—dc22                                    2006004001

British Library cataloguing data are available

©2006 Brent Kelley. All rights reserved

*No part of this book may be reproduced or transmitted in any form or by any means, electronic or mechanical, including photocopying or recording, or by any information storage and retrieval system, without permission in writing from the publisher.*

Cover photograph by Sarah Sanders

Manufactured in the United States of America

*McFarland & Company, Inc., Publishers*
 *Box 611, Jefferson, North Carolina 28640*
   www.mcfarlandpub.com

For Jason and Stephanie and Cathy and Roger.
The kids did well.

# Contents

*Introduction* .................................... 1

**1953** ........................................... 3
    1. Reno Bertoia                                5
    2. Tom Qualters                             10
    3. Mel Roach                                    25
    4. Dick Schofield                            32

**1954** ........................................... 39
    5. Paul Giel                                      41
    6. Harmon Killebrew                     48

**1955** ........................................... 55
    7. Jim Brady                                    57
    8. Tom Carroll                                 64
    9. Wayne Causey                            76
    10. Jim Derrington                        84
    11. Don Kaiser                                 90
    12. Lindy McDaniel                      96
    13. Jim Pagliaroni                       105
    14. Jim Pyburn                                111
    15. Jim Small                                   116

**1956** ........................................... 123
    16. Jerry Kindall                           125
    17. Mike McCormick                   140

**1957** ........................................... 149
    18. Steve Boros                             151
    19. John DeMerit                        161

| | |
|---|---|
| 20. Von McDaniel | 167 |
| 21. Don Pavletich | 174 |
| 22. Buddy Pritchard | 178 |
| 23. Jerry Walker | 185 |
| 24. Frank Zupo | 191 |

*Appendix: Players Signed Under the Bonus Rule of 1953–1957* ............................... 199
*Index* ........................................... 201

# Introduction

After World War II, the United States prospered. Baseball joined in this prosperity. The minor leagues expanded to an all-time high in numbers of teams and leagues. Young talent was being signed to contracts for many dollars—bonuses. This did not sit well with several teams, and the minor leagues, especially, did not like it. They could not compete financially with major league teams. Many minor league clubs were still privately owned and did not have the money available to pursue the better prospects.

In an attempt to control the bonus spending, baseball passed a bonus rule in 1946 setting the maximum that could be paid to a player. Anything over this maximum made him a bonus player and there were restrictions placed on him. He could not be sent to a lower classification and at the end of his first year he had to be promoted to the major leagues.

There were some good players signed under this rule. The Philadelphia Phillies were particularly successful, getting both Robin Roberts and Curt Simmons. However, cheating was widespread and many under-the-table deals were made. The rule was unpopular in both the major leagues and the minor leagues, so in 1950 it was ended.

The next two years, several large bonuses were paid to untried youngsters. The Boston Red Sox alone paid $700,000 in bonuses in 1952 and stocked their San Jose (California League) team with the high-priced players. It was determined that a new rule was needed to control the spending, so in 1953 a second bonus rule was put into effect. This one stated that any player signed for more than a $4,000 bonus must stay two full seasons on the roster of the signing club.

This turned out to be a terrible rule. All major league teams signed players under the rule, some more than others, but there were far more failures than there were successes.

Again, there was cheating on the rule, although today no one knows how extensive it was. And, again, it was a rule that no one liked, but it lived for five years.

The only documented (at the time) case of cheating occurred in 1955. The Baltimore Orioles signed pitcher Tom Borland for a $40,000 bonus and assigned him to the Oakland Oaks of the Pacific Coast League. When it was learned, Borland was set free and Baltimore was fined.

The Yankees, never very active in the signing of Bonus Babies, got around the rule when they signed 18-year-old Clete Boyer. Although it was Yankee money that signed him, he was placed on the roster of the Kansas City Athletics, a team under the control of the Yankees. He played out his two years there and as soon as his bonus time was up, he was "traded" to the Yankees.

When the rule ended after the 1957 season, players who still had time left to spend on the major league roster were allowed to be sent to the minor leagues. No one was sorry to see the rule go. Eventually, the amateur draft still in effect today came about.

I want to thank Jim Rebollini for supplying the minor league statistics of the Bonus Babies interviewed here.

# 1953

The first player signed under the new Bonus Rule was Ohio State All-American football player Vic Janowicz, to whom the Pirates paid $25,000. He hadn't played baseball since high school and it showed. He was gone forever after his two years were up.

Altogether, there were 13 bonuses paid and most are only a line in *The Baseball Encyclopedia,* but there were a few bright spots. The Tigers gave $35,000 to Al Kaline and he proved to be a bargain.

Joey Jay (Milwaukee, $40,000) eventually won 20 games twice, but not for the Braves. Dick Schofield (St. Louis Cardinals, $40,000) became the quintessential utility infielder and enjoyed a long career. Reno Bertoia (Detroit, $23,000) was an everyday player for a few years.

# 1 Reno Bertoia

*Reno Bertoia was one of the first Bonus Babies to be signed, receiving $23,000 from the Detroit Tigers in 1953.*

BRENT KELLEY: *You signed a bonus contract at the age of 18. Who scouted you for the Tigers?*

RENO BERTOIA: Actually, the guys that scouted me and signed me were two different people. The guy that was scouting me was Pete Fox; he was a [former] Tiger outfielder. But the farm director at that time was John McHale and he later became the president of the Milwaukee Braves and Montreal Expos.

*How many teams were after you?*

RB: They tell me all of 'em were after me, but as far as making contact, Chicago [Cubs] was real interested and also the Giants. Once they heard I was going to be signing for a bonus, a lot of teams just stayed away because they were averse to signing bonus ballplayers.

The week after I signed I was supposed to go to Chicago and work out with the Cubs. [Tony] Lucadello was going to bring me in to Chicago, but then I signed a week earlier. I was in the first semester at the University of Michigan at the time. Freshmen couldn't play, so we just played some exhibition games.

In high school, I played in the Detroit Amateur Baseball Federation, the DABF. I played on some pretty good teams—played on Trumbull Chevrolet, played on a team called R. G. Moeller's. I played shortstop. When they signed me they had me working out at second base and when I got sent to the minors they made me into a third baseman.

*You first appeared in a major league game on September 22, 1953, and you struck out. Do you remember the pitcher?*

RB: It was Satchel Paige. He was with the St. Louis Browns. My first hit came in 1954. It was against a guy named Bob Chakales and it was a home run.

*How did the Tiger players receive you?*

RB: Very well. Guys like Pat Mullin, Steve Souchock, Johnny Pesky — they were real good to me. I was kind of a quiet kid — no popping off and that kind of stuff.

*The Tigers had several Bonus Babies along the way.*

RB: I think in '51 or '52 they'd ended up in last place. In '53 they were going for some kind of youth movement — trying to show the fans they were trying to build something.

*The team did well with its Bonus Babies. You were successful and Steve Boros and George Thomas were good ballplayers.*

RB: You better believe it. And you have [Al] Kaline. (Laughs)

*Your first manager was Fred Hutchinson. How did he accept you?*

RB: Very well. Fred was very, very protective — kind of a gruff individual on the surface, but very sensitive when it came down to a relationship with me.

**Reno Bertoia**

They were trying to get me to sign; I was working out with 'em for about a month and I had no intention of signing 'cause I wanted to go back to school. McHale came over and talked and I was working out with Detroit every game during their home stands. Hutchinson said if I signed with Detroit he'd buy me two suits, and he did. He was a fine individual.

*Did you receive helpful coaching?*

RB: Billy Hitchcock was a coach and Johnny Hopp was a coach. Guys like Pesky used to work with me a lot. Gerry Priddy, the guy who held up the Queen Mary, helped. The older guys that were on the way out, I guess they felt no threat, so they worked with me a lot. They were a lot of help.

*You continued to go to college.*

RB: Yeah. I lost my scholarship to the University of Michigan, but I went back to Assumption University here in Windsor [Ontario] and graduated from there in '58 — Bachelor of Arts. I've been teaching now for over 30 years. I teach history; I'm the Social Science head at our school.

*You scouted for a while.*

RB: Yeah — during the summer for a number of years, but I didn't find it too satisfactory. I think when I scouted I became more appreciative of my own talents because I didn't see too much out there.

*In 1956 you were sent to Charlotte.*

RB: In '56, I actually made the starting lineup without a year in the minor leagues as the second baseman and started out not too badly. I hit the ball fairly well but at somebody, then I started making a few errors, started pressing, and they said it would be best to send me down and get some experience.

I went to Charlotte and May to Labor Day, which is the season down there, I led the team in RBIs and I hit a respectable .289. Going into the last week of the season, I was hitting .290 something and went 0-for-5 or–6. That was my only year in the minor leagues. It was a good year.

In 1957 I didn't start the season. Ray Boone had been moved to first base and Jim Finigan, from the Athletics, started the season at third. They roomed us together; he was a real nice person. About two weeks into the season, something happened to his thumbs and I started to play and had a hell of a start. I was leading the league [in hitting] for a couple of weeks. I hurt my arm and got in the doghouse and I was in and out of the lineup after that. I think I ended up the season hitting .275.

Ray Boone was a class guy. We used to have him over to dinner at my parents' a lot. In fact, I used to bring Ray; [Earl] Torgeson, God bless his soul; Finigan; [Paul] Foytack — my mother used to be a real good cook.

With Detroit in '57 and '58 I'd start, do pretty well, then not well and sit down. Kind of a sputtering kind of thing.

*You were traded to Washington after the '59 season. How did you feel about that?*

RB: It was an opportunity, less pressure, playing away from home. I think that had some merit, although that year, again, I started well, [then] didn't do too well.

The year 1960 was my better year, which I thought was my most productive year as far as playing every day. They put [Harmon] Killebrew over at first, played me at third and I did pretty well. I hit .265 and, I thought, had a pretty good year.

The next year at Minnesota I put a lot of pressure on myself. In those days, if you had two good years you stayed for five and I couldn't get started. I sputtered and then they traded me to Kansas City and then I got traded back to Detroit and that was the beginning of the end.

*You left the majors at only 27.*

RB: They sent me out to Denver, then they sent me to Syracuse for the remainder of '62. I went to spring training with Detroit again in '63 and they sent me out to Syracuse and they had young kids coming up. They had the Don Werts and the Ray Oylers and those young kids and I wasn't playing every day.

They'd actually talked me into coming back and playing in the minor leagues. I said, "If I get a shot, fine." I went down there and they made me a coach. I think I hit .322 or something like that part time. Came August and nothing was happening. I called the ballclub and said, "If I'm not in the big leagues by September, I'm going home." And I went home. I was teaching in the wintertime every year so I had a job waiting for me. I had a family — a couple, of kids.

*Any regrets?*

RB: Not really. I think I was ready to retire. I was just not getting any better, that's all.

Some guys had great careers. I think most of us ballplayers struggle. It's not the rose-colored glasses thing that everybody sees. I'm very happy with my career — one of the few Canadians that played that long.

*Did the bonus rule hurt you?*

RB: I look at that year I went down to Triple-A ball — hadn't played a year of minor league ball, had played maybe 30 or 40 games in the big leagues — and did that well. Looking back, I think I would have been a better ballplayer if I had spent those first two years in the minors.

I think, emotionally, sitting on the bench as a kid and not playing and wondering whether you belong there, then being put into situations where you're not comfortable — that was tough on a young kid.

If they hadn't offered me that money, I'd have stayed in college. How life would have changed or whatever, I don't know. A lot of different things change because of certain decisions here and there. I'm pretty certain I wouldn't have signed a major league contract until I'd graduated from college.

If you had asked me this 20 or 30 years ago when I was still playing I would have made some kind of rationalization, but I think as time goes on you look back with a very objective eye. I think it was the stupidest rule that was ever made, although you've got guys like Kaline and [Sandy] Koufax — they're one in a million.

## Reno Peter Bertoia

Born January 8, 1935, St. Vito Udine, Italy
Ht. 5'11½" Wt. 185 Batted and Threw Right

| Year | Team, Lg. | G | AB | R | H | 2B | 3B | HR | RBI | BA |
|---|---|---|---|---|---|---|---|---|---|---|
| 1953 | Detroit, AL | 1 | 1 | 0 | 0 | 0 | 0 | 0 | 0 | .000 |
| 1954 | Detroit, AL | 54 | 37 | 13 | 6 | 2 | 0 | 1 | 2 | .162 |
| 1955 | Detroit, AL | 28 | 68 | 13 | 14 | 2 | 1 | 1 | 10 | .206 |
| 1956 | Detroit, AL | 22 | 66 | 7 | 12 | 2 | 0 | 1 | 5 | .182 |
|  | Charleston, AA | 125 | 446 | 70 | 129 | 26 | 7 | 12 | 67 | .289 |
| 1957 | Detroit, AL | 97 | 295 | 28 | 81 | 16 | 2 | 4 | 28 | .275 |
| 1958 | Detroit, AL | 86 | 240 | 28 | 56 | 6 | 0 | 6 | 27 | .233 |
| 1959 | Washington, AL | 90 | 308 | 33 | 73 | 10 | 0 | 8 | 29 | .237 |
| 1960 | Washington, AL | 121 | 460 | 44 | 122 | 17 | 7 | 4 | 45 | .265 |
| 1961 | Minnesota-Kansas City-Detroit, AL | 98 | 270 | 35 | 61 | 5 | 0 | 2 | 25 | .226 |
| 1962 | Denver, AA | 29 | 84 | 13 | 30 | 5 | 3 | 1 | 23 | .357 |
|  | Detroit, AL | 5 | 0 | 3 | 0 | 0 | 0 | 0 | 0 | .000 |
|  | Syracuse, IL | 55 | 173 | 13 | 39 | 3 | 1 | 3 | 26 | .225 |
| 1963 | Syracuse, IL | 52 | 121 | 18 | 39 | 5 | 1 | 3 | 17 | .322 |
| **Major League Totals** | | 612 | 1745 | 204 | 425 | 60 | 10 | 27 | 171 | .241 |

# 2 Tom Qualters

*Tom Qualters was one of the earliest Bonus Babies to sign, receiving $40,000 from the Phillies in 1953.*

BRENT KELLEY: *You struck out every batter you faced a couple of times in high school games.*

TOM QUALTERS: I struck out 21 in seven innings and 24 in eight innings. I think from my freshman year I averaged two-and-a-third strikeouts per inning.

*It's been said that you were pursued by 14 of the 16 teams.*

TQ: I really don't know that for a fact. I think I talked to just about everybody, but some of 'em knew they weren't financially in the running. And some of 'em dropped out and who knows at what point that happens.

The Phillies pursued me probably harder than anyone. There was a local scout, more like a birddog, and he probably got paid for how far a guy advances. I don't think he was on the payroll—Lefty somebody—and he was up in years in those days and just a fine gentleman.

The thing that was really weird in those days, and you don't know this until after you sign, I come to find out that a lot of those clubs—in those days we didn't have agents or anything—you walk in and you're talking to some pretty high-powered folks. All you want to do is play ball and your mother and dad are there and that's it. Come to find out that, from what I heard later on, I was the number one guy in the country. Whether it's bull or not, I don't know, but that's what the word was. Of course, I didn't know that. I couldn't care less. Seems like toward the end everybody started bailing out, so there must have been some word got out from somebody and it certainly wasn't me or my family 'cause we never even discussed numbers. Finally we took my oldest brother, who was three years older than I, to the airport and sent him off to Korea and we went to a hotel in Pittsburgh and sat down with the Phillie organization and we signed a contract.

## 2. Tom Qualters

When I got home we had two or three phone calls from teams that I thought had given up on me — said, "Whatever you do, don't sign," and all this kind of stuff.

From what I understand, there was a guy by the name of Bob [G.] Miller, lefthanded pitcher, lived up around the Detroit area, and there was a scout from Detroit came to me during a lot of my games — Italian fellow, can't think of his name — toward the end of my senior year and he said, "I guess we can't sign you." There was never, ever a dollar mentioned and he gave me a St. Sebastian medal — I'm Catholic and he was Catholic — the patron saint of athletes and warriors and all that. He said, "We can't sign you. We're no longer in the running."

Tom Qualters

I heard later — who knows if they're telling the truth or not — that there was a deal made that the Phillies were gonna go big bucks for one of us — me or Miller — and Detroit was gonna go big bucks for one of us. Supposedly they'd kinda made a deal. In fact, Bob Miller told me that. (Laughs)

*I guess today that would be collusion and there'd be a big fuss over it. Were the Phillies your choice?*

TQ: I really had no choice, but I did like the Phillies, which was really stupid on my part because the Phillies had great pitchers. But in my way of thinking at that point was they have some of the best pitchers — you know, Robin Roberts, Curt Simmons — and there was a whole lot of people in the major leagues and the minor leagues and in my mind that's the team I wanted to go to because I wanted to compete against those guys. I wasn't thinking about competing against the opposition. I had it in mind that I wanted to compete against those guys because they supposedly were probably one of the best pitching staffs anywhere that I was aware of. (Laughs)

*When you joined the team in '53, Steve O'Neill was your manager. A lot of players didn't care for him. He gave you one-third of an inning.*

TQ: I don't blame Steve O'Neill. I really don't blame him although I thought he was a horse's ass. I came into a ballclub; I had *no* business being in the major leagues. They had to take somebody off the roster and put him in the minor leagues to make room for me, so there was an immediate dislike for me by Steve O'Neill, the coaching staff, and every player on the team.

*Resentment from the players, too?*

TQ: Oh, there was no question. (Laughs) Resentment? Let me give you a good example, I joined the club in Cincinnati and I was six-foot tall and probably 200 pounds— 205, 207 — although my baseball cards say I weighed 190, but when I was a sophomore in high school I weighed 217. I show up and say hello and who I am and get a pretty damned cold reception. I go to the ballpark and introduce myself to the clubhouse guy; everybody's looking at me, but nobody's talking to me. First thing they do, the clubhouse guy — to this point I don't know his name, they called him "Unk" — he was there a hundred years, I guess. so he gives me a uniform and the uniform fitted me absolutely skin tight and just came right down to the bottom of my knees. In those days, everything was bloused out.

I said, "This uniform doesn't fit."

He said, "That's the only goddamned uniform we got. If you don't wanna wear the goddamned thing, you can leave."

So I figured, "Uh-oh, I'm in big shit now." I figured if they're gonna embarrass me, I'm gonna embarrass them 'cause I'll wear the son of a bitch. We're in Cincinnati and we had to go down through their dugout and out onto the field. Here comes this great Bonus Baby, and, of course, all major league ballplayers look for these guys. I just walked out on the field proud as I could be and just figured. "Screw y'all." It's hilarious. I figured, "What the hell; that's the way they play the game. That's the way we play the game." That was my first day in the major leagues.

And it really never got any better. I can remember I was there for that whole year and was never allowed to even get in and take batting practice with the pitchers. I was an outcast.

This is the old school. Later on in my life I understood what was going on, but when you're 18-years-old — I turned 18 in April and here I am in June and I'd never been away from home in my life — that's pretty ugly.

I walked into the hotel in Cincinnati and had never been in a hotel. I'd never been on a train. The longest trip I'd ever made I'd been down to Deep Creek, Maryland, which was about and hour-and-a-half from home, to go fishing. (Laughs) I don't think in those days I'd ever had a suit and we come to find out that everybody has to wear a coat and tie.

*Did any of the players try to help you?*

TQ: Yes. The very first day, and this is a very unlikely combination, when they put me in this tight uniform they had me work out. They had me throw on the sidelines. A lot of guys gathered around. In fact, Robin Roberts stood up there with a bat in his hand like he was a hitter to see what I had. Then we ran and did all this kind of stuff.

I came back in. You have to understand, I don't have *any* kind of equipment at all as far as the red-sleeved sweatshirt and all that. I don't have anything except what the clubhouse guy gave me, that one uniform. So I go in and my locker's right next to Earl Torgeson. That's a story in itself, outside baseball, his life in World War II. I'm sitting there and he's kinda breathing heavy and I'm not about to look at him and he's not looking at me. We're getting ready for the game to start. Finally, he looks over at me. He says, "Aren't you gonna change your shirt?"

I said, "I don't have a shirt."

He said, "What do you mean?"

So I told him that what I had was what he [Unk] gave me. He said he didn't have any.

He yells, "Hey, Unk! I need a sweatshirt." Suddenly there was a sweatshirt. Unk brought it over and gave it to Earl and while Unk was there, Earl handed it to me. I thought that took a lot of courage.

That didn't mean we were friends. (Laughs) Earl was one of those guys who knew what was right and what was wrong.

We came back to Philadelphia and they were gonna have this game between the Athletics and Phillies and I'm gonna pitch it. We came chugging in a train to Philadelphia and Jim Konstanty says to me, "Where you staying?"

"Geez, I don't know. I was gonna get a cab and have him take me to a hotel." I had no idea where I was at. I had never been there.

He said, "No, you come with me." And he took me to his home. On the way to the ballpark that night—I was gonna pitch against the Athletics—we stopped, got something to eat. I ordered a hamburger, French fries, and all this stuff, which a kid would do. After I sat there and ate it, he said to me, "Why would you order something like that before a ballgame?" I had no idea. I said, "I don't know. What are you supposed to eat?" (Laughs)

Robin Roberts and Curt Simmons were really good to me. These are top guys. They were very, very good to me. There was Granny Hamner, the second baseman; he was very, very good to me. Johnny Wyrostek, who didn't play every day, he was over the hill when I got there, but he was kind to me.

But for the most part, guys like Connie Ryan, who was on his way out, his whole day revolved around giving me a hard time. And there was a bunch of other guys, they weren't like Connie but they joined in.

The thing that really hurt me so bad was we'd be in a game getting beat 12-to-2 and they wouldn't even let me pitch. They're always talking about somebody being demoralized. How the hell could you be more demoralized than I was at that point? Let me go in there and get my head knocked off. I'd have went out there and let 'em take shots at me. But these guys there from the old school—he didn't come up through the ranks so he don't play.

So here I am for two years—a half year in '53, the whole year in '54, and then a half a year in '55—all I did was throw batting practice every day. I'd throw 45 minutes a day.

The only fun I had in life was every once in a while I had up a guy like Willie Jones, who *really* didn't like me. Willie "Puddin' Head" Jones. I'd saw the bat off in his hands. It got to the point it was a big game because the guys would sit behind the screen 'cause they *knew* I was gonna do it, but they weren't sure *when*.

I remember one day early in spring training. I got him up there and the guys were all standing behind the backstop and I unloaded one on him and he swung and the barrel of the bat and the ball hit the screen at the same time. (Laughs) He didn't like me and I didn't like him.

Connie Ryan, finally in my second year I think it was, I had enough of this stuff. I went over to him one day and I said, right in the clubhouse in front of everybody, "The next goddamned time you open your mouth and say something about me, I'm gonna knock you flat on your ass." I told it to him in front of everybody. (Laughs) He never said nothing. He got released and ended up with Cincinnati or somebody.

He was in spring training one year and he come to the plate and I threw at him four times. (Laughs) I didn't hit him, though.

*When O'Neill left, Terry Moore came in as manager. Was there a difference?*

TQ: Oh, a great difference. A *tremendous* difference.

I was throwing batting practice when Terry came in. I didn't even know it, nobody ever told me anything. I was too dumb to know, but when I threw the ball in a very relaxed motion the ball just moved all over the place. I'm throwing batting practice and the guys are having trouble hitting the ball.

Terry Moore says to somebody, "Who the hell's this guy?" (Laughs) This was in St. Louis and he and [Cardinal manager Eddie] Stanky had problems and we got into a hell of a brawl out there. Then Moore had a few rules and some of these rules leaked to the news media and the first thing you know, Terry Moore is gone. And Terry Moore was probably one of two *good* managers I ever played for. The other one was Al Lopez.

*The Phillies finished in the first division all three years you were there. Did you receive a World Series share?*

TQ: Yeah, I believe I did.

*You finally lived out your bonus and they sent you down.*

TQ: I went to Class B ball — Reidsville, North Carolina — and I played a half year there. Pretty much a starter.

There was one guy I have to comment on, a pitcher by the name of Karl Drews. Karl Drews probably disliked me as much as anybody that was ever there. I had a problem with control. I had great stuff and all that, like all kids do. Catcher by the name of Benny Bengough — greatest guy that ever lived, *super* guy — and I would throw to him *every* day. He'd give me the target out and I'd throw and I'd miss it. I can remember sitting down in bullpen sweating like hell, just totally disgusted with myself. Karl Drews — probably the first time he ever spoke to me — he said, "Where's the ball go when you just naturally throw it? Without thinking, where's it go?"

I said, "Well, it goes kinda low and inside to a righthanded hitter." He said, "Then don't ever try to hit any other spot but that. Once you can hit that spot with your eyes closed, *then* you try to hit some other spot." That was probably the best advice I'd ever had in my life. Nobody helped you!

*Did you have a pitching coach?*

TQ: If we did, I don't know who it was. No one ever told me anything about pitching.

*How much did not having any game competition for two years hurt you?*

TQ: I'm not sire. I'm not about to blame that. It's like a brain surgeon or an astronaut or anybody who has a long layoff — held out of his profession for three years — say, okay, you're gonna start even with everybody else.

There's no doubt in my mind, if I wouldn't have signed a contract where it forced me to go to the major leagues, I could have went to the minor leagues and I could get into competition and I could have pitched and probably within three years I would have been there.

Part of this is my fault. I left the major leagues knowing not a hell of a lot more than when I got there. Part of it's my fault because I probably didn't pay attention to the guys like Roberts, Warren Spahn, guys like that. I can't blame it all on somebody else. A lot of this blame has to go on me.

Maybe I wasn't smart enough, or mature enough — I don't know what it is—to understand that this is the big time and you better get your act together and you better learn every little thing, pay attention, keep your mouth shut and your ears open, and *learn*.

Probably ten years after this happened to me, I think players changed drastically and they did really try to help one another. But in that time I'd get in with the real old-timers and it was just a hard-nosed thing. If the hitter walked up to the plate and stared at you, you just knocked him down. That was the mentality we had then. I have no problem with that. (Laughs) But on the other hand, I didn't belong there, they *knew* I didn't belong and they wanted no part of me. Like I say, some of the guys, like Eddie Waitkus, were nice to me. He took me to his home and had me out for dinner at his home. He was just a nice guy, but he never ever said to me, "Hey, do this, do that, do this." Nobody ever said that.

Probably, in a quiet way, Curt Simmons and Robin Roberts tried to help me more than anyone. And Jim Konstanty, too. But they were so far above me in their level of thinking—as pro athletes—that maybe I just didn't comprehend.

*Who was sent down to make room for you?*

TQ: Jackie Mayo. I never met the guy, but he certainly would have been more of a benefit to the ballclub than I was.

*You made it back to the majors.*

TQ: To me, that was *the* big deal. I pretty much lost my fastball because of that two-and-a-half year period. It's damn near three years when you count it all up because I never had the opportunity to really throw. I don't know, some guys maybe can turn the ball loose in practice. I always figured I could, but the strange thing was, later in my career I could go out and throw 45 minutes of batting practice and throw as hard as I could throw and come out the next day and do it again, but I'd go and pitch one inning against hitters and the next day my nuts hurt. (Laughs)

I threw completely different in a game situation than what I did in batting practice. Believe me, I would go out there and I would try to throw the ball as hard and try to put myself in a game situation and I would do that and I'd come out there the next day and my arm felt like I never did anything. But let me pitch one inning and I'll guarantee you I knew it the next day.

*You must have had a great sense of satisfaction to get back.*

TQ: I think probably my greatest satisfaction was I came back and Bob [L.] Miller—Booger Miller, a righthanded pitcher, he's also from Detroit—broke his arm. I'm in Havana, Cuba, playing for Miami. This is my second year in Miami. I played half a year of [class] B ball and made the Triple-A ballclub the next year and here I am my second year in Miami and this is before the regular call-up time.

## 2. Tom Qualters

Booger Miller breaks his arm. I don't know how the hell he did it.

I spent two years down there and Satchel Paige was on the ballclub. Satchel Paige and I became about as close as two people can get. In fact, when I got the call and I said my goodbyes to everybody and the last guy I said goodbye to was Satchel Paige. Satchel gave me his glove. You know, a ballplayer would give you their *wife* before they'd give you their glove. (Laughs) We're only down there [in Havana] for a three- or four-day stand and so he'd have a glove I gave him mine.

This was an old, black glove, really an old-time glove. You put it on and you hold your hand straight out and the fingers fall off toward the floor. I used to kid him so bad about that glove that he thought that it was very important that he give me that. And I still have it. (Laughs)

I met the ballclub in Milwaukee. You have to understand, Clyde McCullough — catcher — was catching at Miami just before I went up and *everybody* thought I had one of or maybe the best curveball anywhere. Everybody knew about my curveball. They mentioned my name and everybody said, "Oh, yeah. Curveball."

Clyde McCullough made me realize I had a hell of a good fastball, maybe not great velocity — I was no Nolan Ryan — but I had a hell of a natural sinker.

We start a game and he may not call a curveball until the fifth inning 'cause everybody just beat it [the sinker] into the ground. He made me finally realize I had a pretty good fastball.

So I get called up. I go up there and I walked in the hotel and I run into Mayo Smith [Phillies manager] and in my opinion Mayo Smith is probably one of the greatest managers I've ever seen in a hotel lobby. On the field, he's got the intelligence of a cement block. You could print that. (Laughs) He was the Manager of the Year one year, I think. But you talk to anybody who ever played for him, they'll tell you the truth.

Anyhow, I'm carrying my bags and I walk in and he walks up to me and I say, "Hi, Mayo." I stick my hand and he don't even shake my hand. He sticks his finger in my chest and he says, "You're a curveball pitcher." I said, "What?" He says, "You're a curveball pitcher!"

So I get in a ballgame and I get somebody out and Henry Aaron's up there. All I can do is throw curveballs. I think I got him out, but I come off the mound and I was *so* frustrated. I was just absolutely frustrated. From Clyde McCullough to Mayo Smith, give me a break. Clyde was just an *outstanding* guy for young pitchers.

We finish out the year. I don't know if I got in any more games or what. To me, I hated being there so bad.

*You began '58 with the Phillies, but right after spring training they sold you to the White Sox. It was a new start in a new league. How was that?*

TQ: Great. I come to find, a guy by the name of Ray Berres had come to Richmond the previous year to look at a pitcher that the White Sox were trying to buy. I don't know his name. I come into the game and Berres sits there and watches me and he goes back, evidently, and tells [White Sox manager Al] Lopez or the powers that be, "Forget the other guy. We need to get Qualters." That's how the whole thing came about.

So I go to the White Sox. There's a complete different atmosphere. Al Lopez, you could not bullshit him. Like Mayo Smith, it got to the point where, if a guy hit a real soft dying quail over the infield or a dribbler between two infielders—one of those head-knockers and it just barely got through—he thought that was a bad pitch. If you threw the ball up there and somebody hit one of them screaming shots somewhere and somebody caught it, he thought it was a hell of a good pitch. That was his mentality.

Somebody'd get a hit and we'd finally get the inning over and he'd come right up in your face, "Where was that pitch!?" You'd say, "A low and away curveball." "Jesus Christ, you can't pitch him there! Pitch him high and tight!"

It got to the point where we'd come off the field and, like Stan Lopata, if the guy hit a low and away curveball, he'd [Smith] say, "Where was that pitch?" He'd [Lopata] say, "Oh, it was a high and tight fastball." "Jesus Christ, you can't pitch him there! You gotta throw him a low and away curveball!" That's the guy's mentality. On the field he was a complete idiot.

Al Lopez, I thought, was about as straight a guy as there ever was. He was not a friend; he wasn't one of these guys, "Let's go out and have a beer." You never seen him except at the ballpark. But Al Lopez would chew your ass out when you needed it.

I can remember going out on the mound and making a good pitch. Somebody would loop one over somebody's head, all this and that, and I would be so upset. Lopez never said a word.

Toward the end of the year we're playing Detroit and this kind of stuff happened to me all year. Somebody would hit one on the fist. Little things were just killing me and I was so frustrated. We had a pitcher on the team by the name of Ray Moore. Ray Moore was a coon hunter from Virginia and we fished together. If we could find chipmunks, we'd shoot at 'em. We're setting there and I get heated up and there's a pinch hitter so I know I'm going in. I sit down and get a towel and dry myself and I said to Ray, "I'm gonna go out there and throw the ball right down the pipe and see how hard these people can hit it." It's a late season game and doesn't mean a thing. I wouldn't even throw 'em a sinker. I'd turn the ball in my hand so I had that going-up rotation,

I go in the game. Earl Battey's catching. I don't know who the hitter is. I rear back and I throw the ball pecker high down the middle and this guy hits a bullet right at [Luis] Aparicio, a hot shot. Next guy comes up and Battey don't know what's going on and he calls a breaking ball and I shake him off. I rear back and throw a fastball right down the middle and this guy hits a shot right at Nellie Fox. Made Nellie's knees buckle.

Next guy is the catcher they had. I think his name was Wilson, Red Wilson. So Battey gives me a breaking ball sign and I shake him off. He's throwing fingers down there that I don't even have. I throw the fastball right down the middle. Red Wilson is shocked and he didn't even swing at it. (Laughs) The next pitch I do the *same* thing — right down the pipe — and he hits one back at me. When I finished up throwing, my glove was on my left side and he hit the ball right into my glove. If it'd been over six-eight inches, he'd have probably put a hole through me.

I walked off the field just laughing like an SOB. I thought, I threw four pitches, got three outs. The next day, I come to the ballpark and Earl Battey, his locker was right next to mine. Lopez walks over; he said, "You two guys get your uniforms on right now. I'll see you outside."

So we go outside and he told me, "Get hot." So I started warming up. He says, "Fastball low and away." He's telling me where to throw the ball and I'm throwing it there. "Breaking ball," and on and on. He had me throwing for 45 minutes! After it was all over, he turned to me and he looked me right in the eye. He got right up to may face and he said, "Look. The next time anybody ever hits the ball *that* hard on you, you're gone!"

So I didn't bullshit him one minute. (Laughs) Nobody on the ball field but me and he knew what was going on, I thought. But you didn't bullshit Al Lopez. He was one of the greatest.

After that year, we go to spring training the following year and he liked me. I'll tell you what he did. The very first time I pitched in a game, if I remember rightly, he brings me in the situation. We're playing in Chicago and 35-, 40,000 people are in the stadium. He brings me in the game against the Red Sox. Couple men on base, we're ahead by one run, I think. Ted Williams is the hitter. He was willing to risk the game to find out what the hell I was made of. I came in — I'll never forget this— and I get onto the mound. Sherm Lollar was catching. He [Lopez] gives me the ball and he looks at me, says, "How you gonna pitch this guy?," like he's Joe Six-pack.

I say, "Well, I'll try to miss low and away with the sinker. If he doesn't go for it, then I'm gonna go with breaking balls the rest of the way." He said, "Okay," turned around, and walked off the mound. He didn't tell me anything; he expected me to tell him. What I did, I'd learned the trick from an old pitcher I'd met my last year with the Phillies—Whitlow Wyatt—I went out there and everybody in the world knew about my curveball, so I did nothing during my warm-up except throw curveballs. Soon as Ted stepped in there, I threw the fastball and he jumped on it and popped it up. (Laughs)

I think what it did for Al Lopez was he felt I had the courage to face those situations, so the next year we're in spring training–'59, I guess—and we had rain, rain, rain. We're working out inside in some sort of quonset hut or something down in Tampa. We've been there about maybe two weeks and he finally came to me and he said, "You're gonna be the fifth starter this year. Get yourself in shape." Boy, that was great.

We had an outfielder, Don Mueller, used to be with the Giants. Don and I had been roommates the year before. We became very close friends. He knew of my interest in farming and fish and game and stuff like that.

So I'm gonna be the fifth starter and about a week or two before spring training breaks, they release Mueller. He was having problems; he had the gout. This really hurt me bad when he was leaving and he said—he lived out around St. Louis—"I have all the land, we have all the ponds, we can raise fish, we can raise beef, we can supply the restaurants. Raise corn, do everything. what we need is financing. Looks like you're gonna make some money. You keep playing ball and we'll go into partnership." That's what we basically figured on doing.

Turned out that before I left spring training I hurt my arm. Again, Ray Berres was the guy that got me to Chicago, but he was also the guy that tried to change my delivery that hurt my arm. I was too stupid at that point to say, "I made it here doing what I'm doing." He tried to change my delivery and there's no doubt in my mind—Ray was a great guy, a super, super guy—he was doing what he thought was right.

Al Lopez told me, "You stay here in Florida and work out with the minor league team and take as long as you want. When you're ready, give me a call and we'll bring you up."

I went out and I pitched. I beat Louisville, 1-to-nothing, 2-to-1, something like that, in the opening game in Louisville. Went to Indianapolis and beat somebody up there in a real close game, one or two runs. Shut 'em out in Knoxville. *Cold* weather, just bitter cold weather for both games.

Went to Charleston, West Virginia. Walker Cooper was the manager. Cruising along the first couple-three innings and all of a sudden my whole arm just died. And that was it.

The pain was in my shoulder, but I found out a couple years later the wing bone was rubbing on the tendons and every time I would throw they were kind of severing those tendons, but it was too late then.

## 2. Tom Qualters

The major leagues played 154 [games], we played 164, we did it in a month's less time, we did it with five less players. Ended up one time we got in a little bit of a jam an I volunteered and went in and that was that. Just plain stupidity. You just can't sit there and not contribute. At least, I couldn't.

I played 'til '61 or so. I could pitch Triple-A. I coached a half a year.

I quit. My wife had twin girls. I was playing at Dallas. I just said, "I'll see you later," and I went home. The guy wouldn't give me my release. I was home maybe about two or three weeks and he called me and he said, "Do you have a job?" And I said, "No." He said, "I'll pay you a thousand bucks. Go up to Williamsport and work for Andy Seminick."

I knew Andy and Andy was a good guy, a great guy. I went up there and was a coach for the rest of that year and then I tried it for Dick Schofield. We were in Dallas or Houston or some damn place and it just wouldn't work.

The guy that owned me, Mr. Johnson, owned the Indianapolis ballclub and then he owned the Dallas ballclub, never did give me my release. I was so young and these kids coming out of college — 23-, 24-years-old with no experience — he figured if my arm came around he was gonna make a bonanza. (Laughs)

When you've never done anything except play baseball and I'm interested in a job, the guys says, "What have you done for the last five, ten, whatever years?" You say you've played baseball, that really doesn't pull it for you for a hell of a lot of things.

A neighbor of mine who was a banker heard about a position with Atlantic Refining Company. I went down and interviewed for the position and here I come to find out they were *all* college graduates. That's the only people they hired, but the guy who was supposed to be doing the interviewing was sick and they had to bring a guy in from Philadelphia and he sure as hell didn't want to be in Pittsburgh and he happened to be a Phillies fan and he hired me. It turned out I'm pretty good with numbers and I did very well. In fact, I was one of the top three or four people in the company within a couple of years.

All I wanted to do in my life was work in conservation and I took the test and finally made it, so I left a job making $9,500 plus bonuses for a job in the Pennsylvania Fish Commission as a law enforcement officer for $4,227. Owned my own home, had to sell it. had a wife and five kids, had to move to Allegheny County in the Pittsburgh area to the north central part of the state at my own expense.

It was the greatest thing that ever happened to me. I could remember the first year or two up there two or three days before payday we were eating maybe cheese sandwiches or I'd know some farmer who'd allow me to go in and pick potatoes after the machines went through or somebody would bring us something.

My kids to this day prefer venison and most of these were road kills; a deer would get hit and I'd go out there and if they weren't too damaged I would skin 'em out and cut the chops and the backstraps and all that and the rest of it I'd give to the prison up there. I can remember Easter and Christmas and Thanksgiving and those great holidays when everybody was eating turkey or whatever, we were eating venison. (Laughs)

And to this day, with my son and son-in-laws we kill three to five deer a year and I can 'em and put 'em in jars and freeze 'em. We're still doing the same thing. I love it.

*You have the most career games appeared in without a win, loss, or save.*

TQ: I wondered about that. I was in games we were ahead and they'd take me out for a pinch hitter and then something would happen.

*The Bonus Baby rule failed. There were more guys like you than there were like Kaline and Koufax. What's your opinion of the rule?*

TQ: You have to understand, in those days the owners all belonged to the same country club. They were trying to do something.

For example, Danny Schell. Danny Schell was one of the really truly great pure hitters. He was an outfielder. Seems to me he hit over .300 in every league he ever played in.

They bring him up to the major leagues and he plays against left-handers for the Phillies. He hits .298 or something like that. Roy Hamey was the general manager, who I think is one of the great horse's asses in the world today. He sends Danny Schell a contract and says, "*If* you make the team, we'll pay you the minimum." I think the minimum at that point may have been 7,000 or 7–5.

Danny Schell was a fur trapper in Michigan. That's what he did all winter. In fact, the Chevy he drove to spring training that year he bought from selling furs.

He takes the contract, tears it up in little pieces, puts it in an envelope, and sends it back. Roy Hamey calls him up and says, "You'll never have the opportunity to embarrass me again." That boy *never* never got the opportunity to play in the major leagues again.

We were rooming together in spring training and we go over to Sarasota, or wherever the Braves were in those days, and he played. [Warren] Spahn was pitching. He hit three shots—three base hits. We come back that night, we're laying there in the bed, and I said "You had a pretty good day today, Danny."

He said, "Yeah."

I said, "That was pretty fast company you were facing."

"Oh, yeah?" he said. "Who was he?"

"That was Warren Spahn. That guy's probably gonna be in the Hall of Fame someday."

He said, "It don't make a difference to me. They all have to throw it over the plate and when they do, I'm gonna hit it." (Laughs) That was his hitting philosophy.

Another thing in those days. My second year in Miami, all the South American teams wanted me really bad. I called Roy Hamey from Miami and said, "I have an opportunity to go down and play winter ball. I could take my pick." We're talking 12-hundred bucks a month, everything paid. That was a hell of a lot more money than I was making then. I never really got tired or anything, so I said, "I'd like to go there and play. Is there any preference the Phillies have for an area or a manager?"

He went totally wild. He said, "I'll be goddamned; you're not going down there!" And he started screaming and swearing over the phone. Somebody had hurt their arm down there the year before and I wasn't allowed to go.

I get a letter that winter, telling me I can't ice skate, I can't do this and I can't do that. Can't ski. They owned you body and soul.

There's no doubt in my mind, everybody was in cahoots. *Every* major league ballclub, not just National League. All the owners were totally in cahoots.

When I hear people talk today about these ballplayers making so much money and that it's obscene — and I think it is, too — I just look back and just kinda chuckle to myself. I say, "You bastards. You got everything that you deserve."

It's unfortunate because at some point the bubble's gotta bust. You can take everybody that's out there right now, stop the whole thing for a year, then go back and say, "Okay, we're gonna pay everybody $30,000 a year." And the same guys are gonna be there. What else can they do? (Laughs)

And that's how stupid the owners are right now.

Right now, if you and I are competitors, you're pitching for one ballclub and I'm pitching for another and we're top dogs and you happen to sign a contract before I do, I'm gonna do any damned thing I possibly can to get more money than you got. It might be only ten dollars more, but it's more. and it's a psychological edge for me.

These guys, they're supposed to be businessmen?

## Thomas Francis Qualters

Born April 1, 1935, McKeesport, PA
Ht. 6' ½" Wt. 190 Batted and Threw Right

| Year | Team, Lg. | G | IP | W | L | Pct | SO | BB | H | ERA |
|---|---|---|---|---|---|---|---|---|---|---|
| 1953 | Philadelphia, NL | 1 | .1 | 0 | 0 | .000 | 0 | 1 | 4 | 162.0 |
| 1954 | Philadelphia, NL | | | Did not play | | | | | | |
| 1955 | Reidsville, CarL | 23 | 147 | 8 | 9 | .471 | 94 | 92 | 154 | 4.90 |
| 1956 | Miami, IL | 34 | 80 | 5 | 5 | .500 | 50 | 39 | 76 | 3.38 |
| 1957 | Miami, IL | 46 | 186 | 11 | 12 | .478 | 73 | 51 | 179 | 3.29 |
| | Philadelphia, NL | 6 | 7 | 0 | 0 | .000 | 6 | 1 | 12 | 7.71 |
| 1958 | Philadelphia, NL | 1 | 2 | 0 | 0 | .000 | 0 | 1 | 2 | 4.50 |
| | Chicago, AL | 26 | 43 | 0 | 0 | .000 | 14 | 20 | 45 | 4.19 |
| 1959 | Indianapolis, A | 36 | 148 | 7 | 11 | .389 | 53 | 49 | 155 | 3.34 |
| 1960 | Houston-Indianapolis, AA | 30 | 112 | 5 | 8 | .357 | 43 | 39 | 130 | 4.50 |
| | San Diego, PCL | 10 | 19 | 2 | 1 | .667 | 2 | 8 | 15 | 4.26 |
| 1961 | Indianapolis-Dallas-Ft. Worth, AA | 11 | 21 | 0 | 0 | .000 | 6 | 6 | 32 | 7.29 |
| | Williamsport, EL | 32 | 80 | 5 | 1 | .833 | 50 | 27 | 81 | 4.28 |
| 1962 | Dallas-Ft. Worth, AA | 5 | 20 | 0 | 4 | .000 | 15 | 14 | 32 | 10.80 |
| **Major Lg. Totals** | | 34 | 52 | 0 | 0 | .000 | 20 | 26 | 63 | 5.71 |

# 3 Mel Roach

*The Braves didn't sign the most Bonus Babies, but they had the highest average bonus paid. Mel Roach received $45,000 plus two years of college expenses from them in 1953.*

BRENT KELLEY: *How much was your bonus?*
MEL ROACH: I'm not sure it was ever publicized. It seems to me — let's see, two years of college were included. I think it was like $45,000.
*Who was the scout?*
MR: Oh, my gosh. He was a very, very dear friend, the head Braves scout in the eastern part of the country. Boy-oh-boy. He really was a great friend.
I was playing football at the University of Virginia at the time. I was playing three sports up there and he was badgering me from my high school days. I separated a shoulder playing football my second year at Virginia and he finally convinced me that injury problems can occur and I'd be throwing away this money, so he finally convinced me to sign. I really *cannot* remember his name to save my life. It'll come to me, though.
Gil English! His name was Gil English.
*Was college included in the $45,000?*
MR: Forty-five *plus* the education.
They allowed me to report late to Milwaukee and I stayed through the year and reported to school late, so they gave me a good deal as far as completing my education.
*How many other teams were after you?*
MR: Golly, I guess there were probably ten teams that I talked to or visited. Pittsburgh was probably the strongest one and I remember his name: Rex Bowen.
And then the White Sox [scout] was a guy named Harry Pasto and the Yankees were after me. I forget what his name was, but he was around *all* the time. I went to Cleveland and visited there. I would say in the neighborhood of ten teams.

*Were there other bonus offers?*

MR: Yeah. They were basically all on that basis.

I played on an American Legion that went to the national finals. I think I led the American Legion in hitting that year nationwide, or close to it, so that created a lot of interest, I think, at that time. I talked to a lot of folks all the way out to Omaha, Nebraska.

*Before the bonus rule took effect in 1953, they were talking to you under the rule that would allow you to be sent to a lower classification than the one that you signed under.*

MR: And early on, I was determined to go on and finish my college education and then look around to sign, but when I got hurt a couple times playing football it sort of changed my thinking. So, before, I really wasn't giving it much thought.

*How long did it take you to finish college after you signed?*

MR: In regulation: two years. I signed at the end of my second year and then finished in the next two years.

*What's your degree?*

MR: Economics.

Mel Roach

*Do you know your college record?*

MR: First year, I think I made all-state and led the state in hitting. Second year, same thing.

*You played very little for Milwaukee the first two years, then you went in the service.*

MR: As you might remember, to avoid the draft in those days you either took your chances or you went in the ROTC. I was in Naval ROTC, came out as an ensign, and spent one summer — Milwaukee had to let me go — on a two-week Navy cruise. Boy, they kidded me a lot about that, called me "Admiral Roach."

And then, at the end of school, I had to spend two years in the Navy as a result of the ROTC requirement.

## 3. Mel Roach

*How did you find the adjustment from college life to major league life?*

MR: It was no problem. I could see the problem with Joey Jay, though.

*He was only 18.*

MR: Yeah. He really had a difficult time coping with all of it. We had a couple of old-timers on the team who went back to the days of hazing and, you know, nailing your shoes to the floor and loading your glove up with tobacco juice, lighting your shoestrings— it went on and on. Walker Cooper, Sibby Sisti — they were old-timers and they made it tough.

Joey really had a tough time adjusting to that. I was somewhat older; in fact, I think I was the only college graduate on the team. My interest at that time was the stock market and I used to sort of help the guys doing some of their investing. I was in a different situation than Joey was.

*What kind of reception did you receive from your teammates? Was there a problem?*

MR: Somewhat. I guess I handled it better than most, but we had a group that really was great. Sibby Sisti sort of took me under his wing and he was my coach of record, I think, on the team. We knew we weren't going to play much so we went to the park early and took extra batting practice and a lot of fielding practice and I guess I spent more time on the field before the games than anybody and I think Sibby and those guys respected that. They liked the idea that I was working pretty hard at it.

But there were some that were pretty envious, I guess, and made a lot of cutting remarks and sort of ignored you.

*Were there any overt actions toward you?*

MR: No, other than what I thought at the time was pretty tough, like, you know, lighting your shoestrings. I came from a fairly poor background and to have a brand new glove filled with tobacco juice was sort of difficult, and to have brand new spikes nailed to the floor and those things.

It could be pretty funny because, in fact, they would do it to each other. Spahn and [Lou] Burdette were the two biggest cut-ups in the world. I mean, you'd be sitting on the bus going to the ballgame and reading a newspaper and they'd come up behind you and light the newspaper with a match. Putting lighted cigarettes in your belt loops— you know, we wore the old flannel trousers then — and the next thing you know you'd smell burning, but that happened to everybody. When they did it to you, you sort of felt like, "Well, I'm part of the team now."

*Do you know whose roster spot you took?*

MR: No, I really don't. I didn't even think about it at the time, but I'm sure somebody had to go down.

It was tough to some degree. I remember when I was on the team and

John DeMerit signed and came on and Hawk Taylor came on as bonus players. You knew that somebody had to go.

*Some teams seemed to accept the Bonus Babies better than others.*

MR: I think Milwaukee probably was as good as any, as good as we could expect.

*Your manager was Charlie Grimm. How was he toward you?*

MR: Charlie was fine, you know, ol' Jolly Cholly. I mean, nothing bothered him. He was always in a good mood and clapping his hands. We had *no* problems at all.

*Some of the managers were a little upset over losing a player for someone who might not contribute much.*

MR: I think I would be if I were a manager. But, at the time, we were not contenders and I think maybe if you were in contention and had to lose a couple of pretty good ballplayers it probably would be upsetting. But in '53 and '54, we were not contenders and it was a little bit easier, I think.

*You mentioned that Sibby Sisti helped coaching you. Overall, was the coaching you received helpful?*

MR: Yeah. I think Sibby was actually assigned by management to work with me. I noticed that, later on when I became a member of the team on my own, that very little coaching was done. I mean, it was assumed that when you got to the major leagues you knew what you were doing and that was it.

But I think because of my situation, they assigned Sibby to help me, so that was a little bit different, I think.

*You came back from the service in 1957 and got your first hit. Do you remember it?*

MR: Oh, yeah — a basehit to right filed against Pittsburgh, I think. I remember my first home run was hit off of the lefthander with the Phillies, Curt Simmons. My first at bat was against Robin Roberts. I struck out, I remember that. (Laughs)

In '57, they called me up because I think I wouldn't count against the roster because I was out of the military service. That was another small rule they had, so they called me up for the pennant drive, just in case a pinch hitter or pinch runner was needed.

*Red Schoendienst was hurt in '58 and you got a lot of playing time.*

MR: Yeah. I'd made the team as a utility player and then Red had broke his finger bunting one day and then I filled in for him and that was obviously the best year I had until I tore up a knee at second base. Daryl Spencer slid into me and tore my knee up and I guess I missed the next season.

## 3. Mel Roach

I was told by the doctor that I'd never play again, that the knee was in pretty bad shape, so I really had resigned myself that it was over. I came back home and worked on it and played a lot of handball and before I knew it, it came back pretty well. I missed almost the entire '59 season, as I remember

I came back in '60 and played a utility role. I remember Felix Mantilla and I, I think, were mentioned as the outstanding utility players in the league that year. After I hurt my knee, I never played like I did before. Felix, I guess, played everything. I played, I think, every position except maybe shortstop and centerfield and catcher.

*You went to the Cubs and then to the Phillies and they moved you to third base.*

MR: The Cubs was a disaster. They traded me for Frank Thomas and that's been known as one of the worst trades in baseball probably. You know, the Cubs had that Board of Coaches; they didn't have a manager and every two weeks, or whatever it was, they'd have a different manager on the field. I remember I roomed with Don Zimmer and Richie Ashburn and the three of us would take turns trying to buy beer for whoever we thought was gonna be the next manager so we'd get to play. It really was a joke.

For some reason, they [the Phillies] had Ed Bouchee playing first and I think they really wanted me to alternate with him, but I got over there and just never got to play.

About this time, my peer group from my graduating class were all getting ahead of me in business and I started thinking in terms of, well, I think I'll get a *real* job. And then the following year I went to spring training, as I remember, with Cleveland and trained in Arizona for the first time. I think I hit about ten home runs in spring training and one was a grand slam and all of a sudden everyone rediscovered the ability I had in hitting, but then they traded me to the Phillies because I think the general manager from Milwaukee had gone to Philadelphia. John Quinn. And he had always liked me, the way I played, and I think he traded for me so I went to Philadelphia and again played just in and out. We had a pretty sad team, really — it was a very poor team — and nothing happened there, so I just said to heck with it, that's it. I guess it was '62.

*The Phillies gave two players to get you, Ken Lehman, a pitcher, and Tony Curry, an outfielder.*

MR: John liked the way I played, but I got over there and we had Gene Mauch managing and Gene was more interested in playing golf than managing, in my own opinion, so it was another disaster.

*Did the bonus rule hurt as far as your advancement and ability to play major league ball, length of career, etc.?*

MR: Yes. Two years wasted.

*What is your opinion of the bonus rule?*

MR: You know, I see it happening in baseball now, the free agency and all the salaries that are being paid. I guess they have to put in rules to protect certain activities and I, myself, would say the bonus rule was a disaster as far as trying to, I guess, keep teams from putting out a lot of money.

*Would you sign for a bonus again?*

MR: Given the same circumstances I was in at the time, yes, I would have taken the money. That was a lot of money back in those days. I can remember going to my football coach and the athletic director at UVA and they both said, "How can we sit here and tell you not to take that kind of money, in spite of the fact that it'll hurt our program here?" I talked to a lot of good, trusty advisers and they all said, "Take it and enjoy it."

*Wayne Causey said the opportunity might never happen again if not taken when it was offered.*

MR: That's right. And I was going to college on a football scholarship; that's the only way I could afford to go, so I would have had to play two more years of football and that could've been the end right there.

*Any regrets?*

MR: No. The only regret I have, unfortunately, is having the knee injury. I was having a pretty good year that year. I remember the series against the Giants. They came in pretty close to us, maybe a game or two behind, and we beat 'em four in a row and I had a great series. I think I had two home runs and about 8-for-10 and there was no question that Daryl Spencer wanted me out of the lineup and he was a pretty hard-nosed player anyway. He prided himself on doing it. I saw him many times after that and he never apologized, never said a word about it, "How is the knee?" or whatever.

### Melvin Earl Roach

Born January 25, 1933, Richmond, VA
Ht. 6'1" Wt. 190 Batted and Threw Right

| Year | Team, Lg. | G | AB | R | H | 2B | 3B | HR | RBI | BA |
|---|---|---|---|---|---|---|---|---|---|---|
| 1953 | Milwaukee, NL | 5 | 2 | 1 | 0 | 0 | 0 | 0 | 0 | .000 |
| 1954 | Milwaukee, NL | 3 | 4 | 0 | 0 | 0 | 0 | 0 | 0 | .000 |
| 1955-56 | | | | Military Service | | | | | | |
| 1957 | Jacksonville, SAL | 70 | 254 | 30 | 79 | 15 | 1 | 6 | 33 | .311 |
| | Atlanta, SA | 37 | 147 | 22 | 43 | 3 | 2 | 1 | 20 | .293 |
| | Milwaukee, NL | 7 | 6 | 1 | 1 | 0 | 0 | 0 | 0 | .167 |
| 1958 | Wichita, AA | 20 | 76 | 12 | 20 | 7 | 1 | 1 | 10 | .263 |
| | Milwaukee, NL | 44 | 136 | 14 | 42 | 7 | 0 | 3 | 10 | .309 |
| 1959 | Milwaukee, NL | 19 | 31 | 1 | 3 | 0 | 0 | 0 | 0 | .097 |

### 3. Mel Roach

| Year | Team, Lg. | G | AB | R | H | 2B | 3B | HR | RBI | BA |
|---|---|---|---|---|---|---|---|---|---|---|
| 1960 | Milwaukee, NL | 48 | 140 | 12 | 42 | 12 | 0 | 3 | 18 | .300 |
| 1961 | Milwaukee-Chicago, NL | 36 | 75 | 4 | 11 | 2 | 0 | 1 | 7 | .147 |
| 1962 | Philadelphia, NL | 65 | 105 | 9 | 20 | 4 | 0 | 0 | 8 | .190 |
| Major Lg. Totals | | 227 | 499 | 42 | 119 | 15 | 0 | 7 | 43 | .238 |

# 4 Dick Schofield

*Dick Schofield was the first Bonus Baby signed by the Cardinals. They gave him $40,000 in 1953.*

BRENT KELLEY: *Who scouted you for the Cardinals?*

DICK SCHOFIELD: Walter Shannon and Joe — that's terrible. They've both passed away. I know his name as well as I know my own. Why would that not come to me?

*How many teams pursued you?*

DS: At the time, I think I could have signed with about 14 of 'em. There were 16 in those days. If I remember right, I never talked with Cincinnati. I can't remember who the other one was now.

*You were signed out of high school.*

DS: Back in those days, we didn't play many games in high school. We played maybe 15 games or something like that. We played mostly in the summertime. American Legion, stuff like that.

When I was about 17, we won the state Legion championship in Illinois. That's the last time a team from Springfield won it. We played in Indiana; we played Cincinnati and they won the whole thing. That's when the Nixon twins played on that team. They beat us, 1-to-0.

I don't remember how I did. The kid that pitched against us was a good pitcher. It seemed like he signed with Cincinnati, but I can't even remember how in the heck I did.

*You joined the Cardinals at 18 and were one of the first of the Bonus Babies required to spend two years on the major league roster. How were you received by the veteran ballplayers?*

DS: It's hard to compare, but I would say that I was treated *really* well. I could name a lot of names on that team that treated me really good. Solly Hemus, Peanuts Lowry, Harvey Haddix, Andy Anderson, even guys like Musial and Schoendienst — they treated me good, I thought. I'm sure they didn't want me there. Let's face it, you don't belong there, but I don't remember anybody giving me a real hard time at all.

*Whose roster spot did you take?*

DS: Vern Benson. He went on and got many years in the big leagues as a coach. He was fortunate in that he got a lot of good years on the pension plan, which makes that situation better.

*What about your manager, Eddie Stanky?*

DS: Stanky was *great* to me. He was absolutely great.

Joe Presko was another guy. Tom Poholsky. There was one guy that was a little tougher. That was Enos Slaughter. He was probably the toughest, but wasn't there very long. He was there in '53 and then in '54, at the start of the season, he was traded. He was probably a little hard-nosed, more than anybody else.

Dick Schofield

*Hard-nosed or actively hostile?*

DS: I don't think he was *actively* against me. I wouldn't even say *he* was. I wouldn't say that anybody disliked me for being there. I thought I was really treated good.

In fact, I would have to say I was treated as well then as I've been by a couple other teams I've played on in my life. I didn't think I was well-received [later by other teams], of course maybe I was in a little bit different frame of mind or something, too. I have nothing but good things to say about my experience.

*You hit two home runs at age 18. Do you remember them?*

DS: Yeah. The first I hit off of Frank Smith and the next one I hit off Jim Hearn. They stuck me in there and let me play a little bit and I think that's what I needed to do. If I could just have went ahead and played and do it my way, I think I'd have been better off, that's for sure.

*You were thrown out of a game before you ever played in one.*

DS: Right. That wasn't exactly my fault, though. That was Stanky's. He was just having a little trouble with the umpire and he just set me up.

The umpire come over and I had to throw a towel out on the field. The umpire came back; he said, "Who threw it?" and Stanky just told him I did it and he kicked me out. (Laughs) I got used a little bit there.

*After the first half of the '55 season, the Cardinals sent you to Omaha. That was their top farm club, so evidently you had shown them a little bit.*

DS: I went to Triple-A, right.

*You spent parts of two years there. When you came back, it was still a few years before you played regularly.*

DS: What hurt me the most was in '58 it looked like I was the shortstop. That's when they made a trade for Alvin Dark. They wanted to play him at third base and me at shortstop and Kenny Boyer in centerfield. That was probably gonna be the way it was, but Dark didn't want to play third base, so I was odd man out. That hurt me quite a bit. I was ready to play.

I was ready to play after the '56 season. It was harder to get a chance then than it is now. There wasn't too many places to play and there was no free agency and all that stuff, so you just kinda had to hang in there.

*You became a regular with Pittsburgh later.*

DS: I started playing in '63, '64, then I played with the Giants in '65 and basically with the Dodgers in '67.

I got hurt at the beginning of the '66 season and that's the year I went from the Giants to the Yankees to the Dodgers. I was hurt most of the whole year. That hurt me a *lot*. Near the end of the season I played everyday at third base when I got to the Dodgers.

*In 19 years in the majors, you played for a lot of managers. Who was the best?*

DS: I liked Danny Murtaugh and I liked Walter Alston. To be real honest with you, I never played for too many managers that I didn't like. I had pretty good experiences; I never had much trouble with managers. I used to always try to stay ready to play. Many times I didn't know where I was gonna play or when, so I tried to do the best I could to stay ready to play.

I think I only played for one guy I just didn't like. I didn't like him before he came, I didn't like him after I left.

I liked Dick Williams when I played for the Red Sox. He treated me very well. A lot of guys didn't like him. He was a little sarcastic at times, but he did right by me. I thought he was a good manager. I could see that every manager is not going to be liked by everybody, but I liked Dick Williams. I know a lot of guys that didn't.

The first year I was with the Red Sox, he played me a *lot*. He used me a lot. He got fired at the end of the season and the following year they didn't use me at *all*. It made no sense whatsoever. In that situation, here's a guy — Eddie Kasko was the manager and he was a good friend of mine — seems like he didn't want to show any favoritism towards me or something. I don't know. It just got to the point I just went down the tubes with the Red Sox. It was bad just because of never getting an opportunity, you know.

Like I say, most of the guys I played for I thought were decent people and decent managers. The only guy I couldn't stand was Harry Walker. He's terrible. He shouldn't ever be on a ballfield. I just didn't like the way he treated people and not only me. I just didn't like things he would say and do. He knew a lot of baseball. I don't think he lacked knowledge for the game. He knew *plenty* about baseball. I just didn't like the way he went about things sometimes. It was a personal thing, I guess. Basically, I don't think he liked me; it was one of those things where one guy doesn't want you and somebody else does, I guess.

*What is your opinion of the bonus rule?*

DS: Whoever decided on that, it was pretty stupid. It hurt me a *lot*. I needed to go out and play someplace. I think it hurt me real bad when I was young. Naturally, you don't get to develop like you should. It was a pretty silly rule to have and hopefully they'll never do anything similar to that anymore. (Laughs)

*There was a lot of talk about under-the-table payments. Were you aware of any of this?*

DS: I had a couple of teams that were willing to give me more money than I got. I guess that's what you call "under-the-table"; somebody else would have paid me or something like that. We just weren't too sure we'd ever get our money. I don't know how illegal it was or how much it was done, but I'm sure there was some done.

*Being offered a job in the major leagues, I guess it's awfully hard to think too straight.*

DS: I just kinda always wanted to play baseball and then all of a sudden the scouts start coming around and, especially in those days, $40,000 — I never heard of that kind of money. I didn't know anybody who had that kind of money. I probably didn't do the right thing, but, shucks, how would you ever know?

*If you were 18 again, would you do it the same way?*

DS: Yeah. If I was 18 again, I'd definitely sign to play baseball. Of course, you'd be drafted now and you know your worth up front almost 'cause if you're drafted high you're gonna get some money. It would make it a little bit easier and you wouldn't have to dicker with a lot of teams. Whoever drafted you, you sign with. Like I went through it with my own son. It was a little bit different.

*What do you think of your son's ballplaying?*

DS: It's something you dream about. It's pretty exciting, there's no doubt about that. I think he was as good a shortstop as anybody in baseball. I don't think anybody can play any better than him. Everything he does defensively he does so easy. There's other guys that are flashier, but they don't get the job done any better, I know that.

*I saw you both play and I'm not sure he's any better than you were.*

DS: It's hard to say. (Laughs) The infields are better now than they used to be. I don't think there's any doubt about that. All the conditions are better. But, shucks, the conditions were better when I played than the guys before. I think it's supposed to be that way.

*Do you get fan mail from people who saw you play, or is it mostly from kids?*

DS: Oh, you get both. Guys will write letters saying they were Pirate fans in the '60s and now they've got either children or grandchildren that they'd like to get something autographed for. You get something almost every day. I sign 'em and send 'em back. I don't see no problem in doing that.

In defense of the players today who don't sign, I just think there are *so* many more people who collect baseball cards. I'll get a letter and there'll be ten of 'em in there, 15 of 'em sometime, and they'll want you to sign all of 'em and send 'em back. People kinda overdo it. a lot of people are in it for money nowadays, too. It's a big business now.

*You'd sign a bonus contract today?*

DS: Oh, yeah. I wouldn't have no choice, so I would do it.

*Do you have any regrets from your career?*

DS: I don't think so. I guess, unless you're a superstar, you'd always liked to have had a couple of things work out just a little bit better. There's a lot of teams I could've been playing for instead of sitting on the bench, I know that, in my early years. There's teams I could have played on and really helped myself out long before I got a chance. I just think the sooner you get a chance, the better chance you have to be a good player. You don't develop any bad habits.

## John Richard "Ducky" Schofield

### Born January 7, 1935, Springfield, IL
### Ht. 5'9" Wt. 163 Batted Both, Threw Right

| Year | Team, Lg. | G | AB | R | H | 2B | 3B | HR | RBI | BA |
|---|---|---|---|---|---|---|---|---|---|---|
| 1953 | St. Louis, NL | 33 | 39 | 9 | 7 | 0 | 0 | 2 | 4 | .179 |
| 1954 | St. Louis, NL | 43 | 7 | 17 | 1 | 0 | 1 | 0 | 1 | .143 |

| Year | Team, Lg. | G | AB | R | H | 2B | 3B | HR | RBI | BA |
|---|---|---|---|---|---|---|---|---|---|---|
| 1955 | St. Louis, NL | 12 | 4 | 3 | 0 | 0 | 0 | 0 | 0 | .000 |
|  | Omaha, AA | 107 | 366 | 56 | 100 | 14 | 4 | 6 | 38 | .273 |
| 1956 | Omaha, AA | 108 | 396 | 60 | 117 | 18 | 8 | 11 | 57 | .295 |
|  | St. Louis, NL | 16 | 30 | 3 | 3 | 2 | 0 | 0 | 1 | .100 |
| 1957 | St. Louis, NL | 65 | 56 | 10 | 9 | 0 | 0 | 0 | 1 | .161 |
| 1958 | St. Louis-Pittsburgh, NL | 65 | 135 | 20 | 27 | 4 | 1 | 1 | 10 | .200 |
| 1959 | Pittsburgh, NL | 81 | 145 | 21 | 34 | 10 | 1 | 1 | 9 | .234 |
| 1960 | Pittsburgh, NL | 65 | 102 | 8 | 34 | 4 | 1 | 0 | 10 | .333 |
| 1961 | Pittsburgh, NL | 60 | 78 | 16 | 15 | 2 | 1 | 0 | 2 | .182 |
| 1962 | Pittsburgh, NL | 54 | 104 | 19 | 30 | 3 | 0 | 2 | 10 | .288 |
| 1963 | Pittsburgh, NL | 138 | 541 | 54 | 133 | 18 | 2 | 3 | 32 | .246 |
| 1964 | Pittsburgh, NL | 121 | 398 | 50 | 98 | 22 | 5 | 3 | 36 | .246 |
| 1965 | Pittsburgh-San Francisco, NL | 132 | 488 | 52 | 102 | 15 | 1 | 2 | 25 | .209 |
| 1966 | New York, AL | 25 | 58 | 5 | 9 | 2 | 0 | 0 | 2 | .151 |
|  | San Francisco-Los Angeles, NL | 31 | 86 | 14 | 19 | 0 | 0 | 0 | 4 | .221 |
| 1967 | Los Angeles, NL | 84 | 232 | 23 | 50 | 10 | 1 | 2 | 15 | .216 |
| 1968 | St. Louis, NL | 68 | 127 | 14 | 28 | 7 | 1 | 1 | 8 | .220 |
| 1969 | Boston, AL | 94 | 226 | 30 | 58 | 9 | 3 | 2 | 20 | .257 |
| 1970 | Boston, AL | 76 | 139 | 16 | 26 | 1 | 2 | 1 | 14 | .187 |
| 1971 | Tulsa, AA | 18 | 43 | 8 | 8 | 0 | 1 | 0 | 3 | .186 |
|  | Milwaukee, AL | 23 | 28 | 2 | 3 | 2 | 0 | 0 | 1 | .107 |
|  | St. Louis, NL | 34 | 60 | 7 | 13 | 2 | 0 | 1 | 6 | .217 |
| **Major Lg. Totals** |  | 1821 | 3083 | 394 | 699 | 113 | 20 | 21 | 211 | .227 |

**World Series Record**

| Year | Team, Lg. | G | AB | R | H | 2B | 3B | HR | RBI | BA |
|---|---|---|---|---|---|---|---|---|---|---|
| 1960 | Pittsburgh, NL | 3 | 3 | 0 | 1 | 0 | 0 | 0 | 0 | .333 |
| 1968 | St. Louis, NL | 2 | 0 | 0 | 0 | 0 | 0 | 0 | 0 | .000 |
| **Totals** |  | **5** | **3** | **0** | **1** | **0** | **0** | **0** | **0** | **.333** |

# 1954

Only six bonuses were paid in 1954 and two of the players turned out to be bargains. The Senators gave $30,000 to Harmon Killebrew, a strong young man from Idaho, and Baltimore signed Billy O'Dell for $24,000. The always broke St. Louis Browns had moved to Baltimore after the 1953 season, and with fresh money the team eventually signed the most Bonus Babies (nine) of any team.

# 5 Paul Giel

*The New York Giants signed All-American football player Paul Giel in 1954 for $60,000.*

BRENT KELLEY: *You were one of the top college football players in the country.*

PAUL GIEL: I was a unanimous All-American two years in a row–'52 and '53. That means AP, UP, *Look* magazine, *Collier's* magazine, the NEA — all of that.

*You weren't a big man for football.*

PG: About 5'10½", around 180.

*The Chicago Bears drafted you.*

PG: They drafted me in the ninth round. George Halas [Bears' owner and coach] had talked to me when I was finishing up my college career and wanted to know my interest factor in pro football as opposed to baseball. I said, "I'll be honest with you. If I get a chance to go to professional baseball and if the contract is right, I'm leaning toward baseball." He said, "We'd draft you higher, but we just can't take a chance on a much higher choice if you're leaning towards baseball."

*Were you tempted at all to play football?*

PG: I was tempted because I loved the game obviously. I thought that, while I might not make it as a halfback because of my size and I wasn't very fast off the single wing, I had a strong enough arm and a good enough arm that I could be developed into a pretty good quarterback. At that time, they were starting to experiment a little bit with the shotgun. We had some of the spread formation in college. I thought I was a fairly decent scrambler and runner so that if I had to, I could run with the ball and throw.

*But the New York Giants offered you $60,000 to play baseball.*

PG: Yeah, roughly $60,000, when you included the bonus plus the salary.

*That's hard to turn down.*

PG: Yes. (Laughs)

And baseball was do much further ahead at that time as far as the bonus, the ability to go to the minor leagues if you didn't make it right away and at least work your way back, or try to; whereas in football, if you didn't get hurt physically and you couldn't cut it, you were really out. There was no place to go.

*That's the story of the other top college back of your time, Johnny Lattner.*

PG: Yes. Johnny Lattner beat me out for the Heisman trophy [in '53].

*Just barely, if I recall correctly.*

PG: At the time, they used the expression, "... in one of the slimmest votes in the history of the Heisman."

*He probably had a higher profile, being at Notre Dame.*

PG: I don't know about that. I had a great career and a lot of wonderful memories.

I got to meet Johnny Lattner as a member of these All-American teams and we got to be good friends. We haven't seen each other since '75 when we went back for one of these Hall of Fame dinners at New York.

But I didn't envy him. He was a very fine athlete and a good person.

*He wasn't a big man, either.*

PG: He's a little taller than I am. He's probably closer to six feet tall, I'd say. About 190.

He played one year with the Pittsburgh Steelers, had a pretty good rookie year, and then he went in the service and he got hurt playing service ball. He never really recovered from that.

The scouting report on the guy was that he wasn't fast enough to get around the bend, average passer and average punter and he did all three things for them [the Steelers] and if he wasn't rookie of the year he was right up there.

*In your first major league game*

Paul Giel

*after signing with the Giants, you faced the Pirates. It was a situation that never happened before or since: you pitched to another Big 10 All-American football player and a Heisman trophy winner, Vic Janowicz, and you struck him out.*

PG: That's right. That was the first *league* game that I'd pitched in; I had one exhibition game. Yeah, I struck him out. I thought I struck out the side.

*Right. In your first inning you struck out the side and he was one of them.*

PG: I think one of the O'Brien twins was in there and I can't remember who the other one was. It seems to me it was the first baseman for Pittsburgh, but I couldn't be sure.

*An impressive start.*

PG: (Laughs) I should have quit right there.

I had just come in to finish. Bob Friend, I think, won that game for Pittsburgh and they beat us pretty soundly that day. The game was over when I came in in the top of the ninth, but I got a little experience.

*The next year you were very effective.*

PG: Yes, I had a pretty good year. I think I was 4 and 4 or something like that, with about a 3-point-2 or so earned run average in about 80-some innings pitched and I had pretty good confidence in myself.

Then I went in the service for two years and when I came back they were the San Francisco Giants. I kind of struggled so the Giants sent me down to Phoenix and I won about three games there. They called me back and I made it the rest of the way through the '58 season, but I was always the tenth man on a ten-man staff, really. Kind of hanging on, never had quite enough.

*You pitched extremely well in that short stay in Phoenix.*

PG: Yes. I had a great team, too. We had Joey Amalfitano, an old roommate of mine, and we had Leon Wagner and Willie McCovey and Tommy Haller. I'm trying to think of the shortstop we had — played with the Giants for a while.

*Was it Eddie Bressoud?*

PG: I don't think so. [Jose] Valdevielso, I think.

*It may have been a good team, but you were effective nonetheless. [5 games, 3–0, 2.77]*

PG: As I look back, probably I should have stayed with that team the entire year. But to get called back to the majors is quite a thrill, so I did finish out the rest of the '58 season [with San Francisco] and then in '59 I went, on the cut-down date, to the Pittsburgh Pirates.

Then I finished '59 at Columbus and went to spring training in '60 with the Pirates and I was on a Salt Lake City contract. I started the year with Pittsburgh and after the All-Star break in July they brought back a guy by the name of George Witt, who'd had a sore arm, and they cut me and sent me to Salt Lake City.

Then I finished out the season there and was gonna get out of baseball and Calvin Griffith called me. He said they [the Twins] had bought my contract from Pittsburgh.

I thought, "Well, I'll give it one more try in my own backyard," and then in June of '61 they traded me to Kansas City along with Reno Bertoia for Bill Tuttle. I went there for one day, pitched against the old Washington team, and thought I had pretty good stuff and they batted me around quite hard. I decided, "That's it," and I retired from baseball.

If they had the thing that clocks your fastball, I'm sure that I would have been, *at best,* in the low to mid 80s. Whatever the reason, I never could develop a good overhand curveball and I had a mediocre slider and I'd try to throw change-ups now and then, but sooner or later you have to come in with that mediocre fastball and I just did not have enough for the majors. I was always hanging on, I was trying hard, then finally at the end I really lost a lot of confidence in myself. I thought, "If you're not going out to the mound in relief with confidence, [instead of] just *hoping* to get 'em out, then you've got a problem."

I wasn't being fair and honest to myself, nor was I being fair to the ballclub, and so, after one day with Kansas City, I quit.

*Do you think the bonus rule hurt you? Do you think you could have accomplished more with minor league seasoning?*

PG: I would have to think so. Maybe if I'd been in the minor leagues I would have been able to work on the slider and the curve and the change-up a little bit more because, when you're in relief in the major leagues, you haven't got time to experiment. You've gotta go with whatever you've got at that time.

There were some games I went out and had good stuff, but day-in and day-out I just didn't have enough. I think I'm competitive, so I don't think it was because I didn't try or I gave up. I'm not the only guy that's happened to. That's why players get cut.

I saw Sandy Koufax when he came up. When I was with the Giants, we went over to Ebbets Field one day. Here's this kid, but honest to God, he could throw *bullets!* That was in '55.

When I was with the Giants out in San Francisco a little bit in '59 before they sent me to Pittsburgh, I remember the Giants saying when Sandy Koufax was pitching, even in 1959, "Stay close. Sooner or later he'll walk the park and you'll beat him." He didn't really find himself 'til the early '60s, even with what he had going. I'd *love* to have that kind of stuff. But don't tell me you can learn a fastball.

## 5. Paul Giel

*Where did you go when you left Kansas City?*

PG: I went back to graduate school at the University of Minnesota until the Minnesota Vikings had their inception and I joined them in public relations for a couple of years.

From the Vikings, I went to WCCO radio, a big CBS affiliate here that did the Vikings and the Twins and the Gophers, as their sports director. I did some on-air work — sports shows, the color on the Vikings and the Gopher football. I was there for eight years before I left to go to the University of Minnesota as the men's athletic director.

I left the university in July of '88 and went with the Minnesota North Stars for a year in sales. Then, since October 1 of '90, I was the Vice-President for Public Affairs for the Minnesota Heart Institute Foundation.

I had bypass surgery in December of '83 and then in '85 I had to have an angioplasty done. These are the people that took care of me and so I have a great interest factor in finishing out my career as a professional fund-raiser for a very worthy organization.

*You're still well-remembered around the country, but in Minnesota I imagine you're still a very big name.*

PG: I've been very fortunate. I was inducted into the Minnesota Sports Hall of fame, along with Herb Brooks, whom I hired as my coach at Minnesota; and a guy by the name of Pud Lund, who was an All-American back in '34 on Bernie Bierman's great team; John Kundla, who had the old Minneapolis Lakers when they won six NBA titles and he coached at the university; and a wonderful woman skier by the name of Cindy Nelson. That was a nice honor.

*What were your biggest thrills in both football and baseball?*

PG: I think my biggest thrill in football was in my senior year in '53. I was captain of the Gopher football team and Michigan came in here rated number one in the country. I think they were 4-and-0; we were maybe 2-and-2. We had been defeated by Michigan in '51 and '52 *at* Ann Arbor pretty soundly. I wanted very *badly* to beat Michigan and we beat 'em, 22-to-nothing.

I had a big individual day. I think I had 284 total yards. At that time, I set a record that held up for quite a few years of handling the ball, either running or passing, some 53 times in that game. We played the single wing where the tailback does most of the handling of the ball. That was my number one thrill in football.

I can't say exactly in college baseball what my biggest thrill was. It might have been my sophomore year. I got off to a bad start in pre-season and I was just about ready to hang it up, thinking maybe football's my sport. Then we got into the Big 10 [schedule] and I won five straight games and led the conference in ERA with a two-point-something and only averaged about 1.1 walks a game. Coming from almost quitting to winning every one of my games meant a lot to me.

As a professional, I didn't win that many games, but I got my first win in relief in Wrigley Field against the Cubs when I was with the New York Giants. I pitched three innings and shut them out over that period of time. That was where I saw my first pro baseball game when I was a kid. Just to be in the major leagues and finally win a game was a great thrill. I think I won 11 in my total career. 11-and-9 or something like that.

*You had two teammates, one with the Giants and one with the Pirates, who were two of the greatest players of the last half of the twentieth century: Mays and Clemente. How do you compare them?*

PG: Obviously they were both great ones. I didn't spend as much time with Roberto Clemente as I did with Willie. I was with Willie in '54 when he came out of the service and had his fabulous year, and then '55 and most of '58, whereas I wasn't with the Pirates all that long.

I would say Willie was a little smoother doing his thing than Roberto. Roberto, when he was running, for example, he *ran* hard, thundering. Willie was a little smoother running. Both had great arms and could hit for power. I'd maybe give the edge to Willie.

*Do you still have your silver football?*

PG: I've got *two* silver footballs. That was a nice thrill for me. Up until Archie Griffin, I was the only player in the history of the Big 10 to win the Big 10 MVP two years in a row. That's the *Chicago Tribune* award. Then Archie Griffin came along years later and he won it twice, along with his two Heisman trophies.

*If you went back, would you do it the same way again?*

PG: Yes. I say that without hesitation. As a kid growing up in Minnesota, I loved baseball and football and the Gophers were my team.

I have *no* regrets. I got a degree, I had a lot of nice things happen to me, nice opportunities when I was out of professional baseball even though I didn't make it very big certainly. (Laughs)

I've had a very interesting career. Almost 17 years at the University of Minnesota, with all the ups and downs and the visibility and the problems in athletics—it was quite an experience for me.

## Paul Robert Giel

Born September 29, 1932, Winona, MN
Died May 24, 2002, Minneapolis, MN
Ht. 5'11" Wt. 185 Batted and Threw Right

| Year | Team, Lg. | G | IP | W | L | Pct | SO | BB | H | ERA |
|---|---|---|---|---|---|---|---|---|---|---|
| 1954 | New York, NL | 6 | 4 | 0 | 0 | .000 | 4 | 2 | 8 | 8.32 |
| 1955 | New York, NL | 34 | 82 | 4 | 4 | .500 | 47 | 50 | 70 | 3.39 |
| 1956-57 | Military Service | | | | | | | | | |
| 1958 | San Francisco, NL | 29 | 92 | 4 | 5 | .444 | 55 | 55 | 89 | 4.70 |
|  | Phoenix, PCL | 5 | 39 | 3 | 0 | 1.000 | 19 | 15 | 32 | 2.77 |
| 1959 | Columbus, IL | 22 | 91 | 5 | 5 | .500 | 47 | 43 | 114 | 4.75 |
|  | Pittsburgh, NL | 4 | 8 | 0 | 0 | .000 | 3 | 6 | 17 | 4.03 |
| 1960 | Pittsburgh, NL | 16 | 33 | 2 | 0 | 1.000 | 21 | 15 | 35 | 5.73 |
|  | Salt Lake City, PCL | 14 | 53 | 0 | 3 | .000 | 33 | 19 | 55 | 4.08 |
| 1961 | Minnesota-Kansas City, AL | 18 | 21 | 1 | 0 | 1.000 | 15 | 20 | 30 | 12.00 |
| Major Lg. Totals | | 102 | 240 | 11 | 9 | .550 | 145 | 148 | 249 | 5.39 |

# 6 Harmon Killebrew

*The Washington Senators gave Harmon Killebrew $30,000 in 1954 to sign. He was the team's first bonus player. He was named American League Most Valuable Player for 1969 and led the league in home runs six times and runs batted in three times. He was an 11-time All-Star.*

BRENT KELLEY: *Did any other team offer you a bonus?*
HARMON KILLEBREW: No. in fact, the club I talked the most to was the Boston Red Sox. They had a scout up in the northwest by the name of Earl Johnson, who was an old lefthanded pitcher with the Red Sox for a while. He used to come down to my hometown and — I don't know what the rules were in those days — he took me out to dinner and we played golf together and I saw a lot of him. He made me promise that if I received an offer from a club that I liked that I'd call him first before I signed with 'em. So when I got the offer from Washington, I called him and I said, "I've got this offer from Washington. What about the Red Sox?" He said, "Well, I don't think the Red Sox can match that. You better go ahead and sign with 'em." I saw him a lot after that and we laughed about it.

I'd never seen Fenway Park or Griffith Stadium. I thought with Washington I had a chance to play right away because they weren't winning very much and the thing I didn't realize was they had Eddie Yost then and he was a fixture at third base. It took a trade of Yost to the Tigers before I even got an opportunity to play.

It was 408 feet down the leftfield line. I'd never seen a major league park before I signed with Washington. I joined 'em in Chicago in Comiskey Park and then we went to Connie Mack Stadium in Philadelphia before we got to Washington. When we got in Washington I took batting practice there. They had Johnny Schmitz throw to me and I didn't know who Johnny Schmitz was. What did I know; I'd hardly been out of Idaho. He was throwing *everything* at me — curveball, sinkers, sliders, everything — and I was hitting 'em up there in those seats and I didn't know any better.

(Laughs) Then I found out that was one of the biggest ballparks in the world.

*It was a par five down the line in Griffith Stadium.*

HK: (Laughs) Yeah, and in Fenway Park it was a chip shot. I finally got to Fenway Park and I saw that park and I said, "Oh, my gosh! I signed with the wrong club!" (Laughs)

*Do you know whose roster spot you took when you joined the Senators?*

HK: They sent Jim Lemon to the minor leagues. They sent him to Charlotte. The odd thing about it is Jim could've been real bitter about the thing, but we became *really* good friends. Jim's been one of my best friends.

**Harmon Killebrew**

*How did the veteran ballplayers receive you?*

HK: Exceptionally good. They were really great to me, maybe because I was so young and they were a bunch of older veteran players on that ballclub. They all tried to help me. My first roommate was Johnny Pesky; he was a great guy.

*What about your managers, first Bucky Harris, then Charlie Dressen?*

HK: I wish I could have played with Bucky Harris when I was a regular player because he was a sweetheart. He let me go home early at the end of the year so I could enroll in college. He was a very nice man.

Dressen was a different sort. (Laughs) I don't know what to say about Charlie. When he came over to our ballclub we had finished just out of the first division and some of his firm comments were, "I can steal you enough games to put us well up in the first division." I'll never forget that, and we finished dead last under Dressen. I didn't really dislike him that much; he was all right.

*You were pretty green, just coming out of high school. Did you receive good coaching in Washington?*

HK: I think I did. [Cookie] Lavagetto was the coach under Dressen, later became the manager. Cookie was a much better coach than he was a manager. Cookie taught me a lot about playing third base and I'm so thankful that he was there and I got that kind of experience.

*Did the veteran players help?*

HK: Not so much. They were nice to me and all, but I can't think of anything anyone bent over backwards to tell me about. Yost was always a great guy.

*He was there every day. That was almost the one position in the major leagues a young player couldn't take.*

HK: That's exactly right.

*Do you feel the bonus rule hurt you?*

HK: To me, I don't really think it did that much damage. Maybe I got a chance to play quicker, I don't know. It was a rule that didn't help the player or the club, but as far as hurting me, I don't know. I was so young and I still was able to go to the minor leagues and get the experience that I needed and that's the only way you can get it is by playing every day. I could have just as well got it with the Washington club because they weren't going anywhere, but because Eddie was there I think that was the main reason I went to the minor leagues.

I had some good years there in the minor leagues, but like I was saying, I learned things playing every day that you can't learn by just sitting on the bench watching. You've gotta be in there and learning those things playing every day. They can talk to you and in practice you can do all kinds of things, but unless you're in a competition and getting that experience you aren't really learning. That's the only way you can get it.

Harmon Killebrew (courtesy Heath Kelley)

You need to be under fire. You need to go through the experience of the game situation — what to do in certain situations; that's the only way you can get it.

*Would you sign for a bonus again in the same situation?*

HK: I think I'd probably do it the same way. The thing I would do, I'd make sure I got my college education. I thought I would go back and get it. I did after the first year and then that was the end of it. I never got back again. I think it's important to get that education.

*In those days, if you wanted to eat in the off-season, you had to work.*

HK: That's right. That's what I had to do. I had to work in the wintertime. Today, these guys have an opportunity to work out year-round, where they're not working. That's a decided advantage, also.

*You played your first major league game on June 23, 1954. Do you remember it?*

HK: I sure do. I pinch hit twice before I actually played in a game. My first pitcher that I faced was a guy by the name of Sid Hudson and I hit a ground ball to second base. And then I pinch hit against Mel Parnell and I did the same thing — I hit a ground ball to shortstop.

And then I played in my first game. I played against the Philadelphia Athletics in Connie Mack Stadium, went 3-for-4, played second base. I got two singles and a double, drove in two runs. The pitchers were Sonny Dixon and Alex Kellner.

*Do you remember your first home run?*

HK: Oh, yeah. That was the next year. I hit it off Billy Hoeft in old Griffith Stadium, probably one of the longest home runs I ever hit in that ballpark.

Frank House was the catcher — Pig House — and he said, "Kid, we're gonna throw you a fastball." I didn't know whether he was telling me the truth or lying to me or what, but, sure enough, here comes the fastball and I hit it 476 feet. When I ran around the bases, came in at home plate, and touched home, he said, "Kid, that's the last time we'll ever tell you what's coming." (Laughs)

*You were only 17 when you joined the Senators. How was the adjustment?*

HK: I think the biggest adjustment for me is I was from a small town. I'd never been out of the state of Idaho hardly and to go to the nation's capital at that age was a traumatic experience for me. (Laughs) There were all kinds of people at the ballpark there or other places — the president, the vice president, congressmen, senators, members of the cabinet. That was a big experience.

*Was there help?*

HK: My first roommate was Johnny Pesky. Johnny helped me. There were other people. I was introduced to an older gentleman that I lived with in Washington who was a great help to me. He, at that time, worked for the Pullman Company; his name was Russ Tuckey. Russ was a big help; he was an older fellow; he'd been a professional basketball player, he'd been business manager for the Ice Follies, and he'd been in politics. He'd done a lot of things, so he was a big help to me. But, overall, it wasn't a bad experience. I was too young to be scared, perhaps.

*Your first year as an everyday player for the Senators was 1959.*

HK: That was my first year as a regular and the interesting thing there was we got [Reno] Bertoia for Yost from the Tigers and they thought Bertoia was gonna play third base. I had a good spring training and I opened up at third and I hit a home run Opening Day and I just kept going and I hit one on the last day of the season and tied with [Rocky] Colavito for the home run championship.

That really was my rookie year basically, and, of course, that would have been a record, but it wasn't considered a rookie year because I'd been up for years prior.

*You had a great career. What stands out the most?*

HK: It's hard when you play that long to pick out one thing. It's everybody's dream, I guess, to play in the World Series; that was a big thrill. But that year I dislocated my elbow in a play at first base in August. Russ Snyder of the Orioles ran into me at first base as I stretched out for a ball. I was leading the league in home runs and RBIs at the time, then I was out until the last ten games on the season. I played at third base those ten games and then in the World Series at third base. To play in the World Series was great, only it was a little tougher for me because I had just come off an injury.

All-Star games were always big thrills, but I got a real serious injury in that '68 All-Star game in Houston. I ruptured a muscle in my leg and I was out the rest of the year and the doctor even thought I was through playing, but I worked hard that winter and came back and had my best year the next year.

*Regrets?*

HK: I never thought too much about statistics until I quit playing and then started broadcasting. They make such a big deal out of stats today and we never did. I knew how many home runs I hit and how many runs I'd driven in and that's about it.

Batting average is the thing they made a big deal of. I think I would've probably tried to hit for a higher average because that's the thing they always mention. I was always a high average hitter when I was a kid and in the minor leagues and when I was in the major leagues I didn't worry about it; I was just trying to drive in runs, really. That was a thing that I regret.

The other thing that always has bugged me is when I came up as a young player I was catalogued as a bad defensive player and I really *worked* at being a good defensive player over the years, but that label always stuck with me, even from being 17 all through my career. I don't know how I could have changed it. I could have refused to go to several different positions, too. I agreed to go from third to first and back and forth and then I played leftfield for three years. I could've refused to do those things and just say, "No, I'm gonna stick to one position," and that would've been a lot easier, too. But I always thought that if you could help the ballclub any way you could, than that's what you did.

*What do you consider your best position?*

HK: Gee, I don't know. Either first or third. I played about as much at first, I guess, as third. I enjoyed playing first base more than third because there was a lot more action over there. Even though I got a couple of real serious injuries at first, I still liked playing that position.

Outside of Brooks [Robinson], I don't think anybody played any better at third than I did at that time. Well, they had [Clete] Boyer in the league, too. We had [Graig] Nettles on our ballclub and I was playing third and they got rid of Nettles because they didn't think he could play third base. (Laughs)

I don't know. I came up so young that I really didn't know a lot about playing the position and it just took me a while to learn all the nuances that you have to learn. Like you said, baseball's a mental game and you have to *think* before each play to know what you're gonna do before the play develops and, not only that, if the ball's hit to you and you boot it, then what you're gonna do after that. So there's a lot of things people don't realize about baseball. I have to laugh at people who say, "Oh, I think baseball's a simple game and I really enjoy football because of all the action." Football is a simple game. In baseball, you've got nine different things defensively and then you've got the hitter and the umpire all involved and it's a very complicated game.

## Harmon Clayton Killebrew

Born June 29, 1936, Payette, ID
Ht. 5'11" Wt. 210 Batted and Threw Right

| Year | Team, Lg. | G | AB | R | H | 2B | 3B | HR | RBI | BA |
|---|---|---|---|---|---|---|---|---|---|---|
| 1954 | Washington, AL | 9 | 13 | 1 | 4 | 1 | 0 | 0 | 3 | .308 |
| 1955 | Washington, AL | 38 | 80 | 12 | 16 | 1 | 0 | 4 | 7 | .200 |

| Year | Team, Lg. | G | AB | R | H | 2B | 3B | HR | RBI | BA |
|---|---|---|---|---|---|---|---|---|---|---|
| 1956 | Washington, AL | 44 | 99 | 10 | 22 | 2 | 0 | 5 | 13 | .222 |
|  | Charlotte, SAL | 70 | 249 | 61 | 81 | 16 | 7 | 15 | 63 | .325 |
| 1957 | Chattanooga, SA | 142 | 519 | 90 | 145 | 30 | 7 | 29 | 101 | .279 |
|  | Washington, AL | 9 | 31 | 4 | 9 | 2 | 0 | 2 | 5 | .290 |
| 1958 | Washington, AL | 13 | 31 | 2 | 6 | 0 | 0 | 0 | 2 | .194 |
|  | Indianapolis, AA | 38 | 121 | 14 | 26 | 5 | 1 | 2 | 10 | .215 |
|  | Chattanooga, SA | 86 | 299 | 58 | 92 | 12 | 1 | 17 | 54 | .308 |
| 1959 | Washington, AL | 153 | 546 | 98 | 132 | 20 | 2 | 42 | 105 | .242 |
| 1960 | Washington, AL | 124 | 442 | 84 | 122 | 19 | 1 | 31 | 80 | .276 |
| 1961 | Minnesota, AL | 150 | 541 | 94 | 156 | 20 | 2 | 46 | 122 | .288 |
| 1962 | Minnesota, AL | 155 | 552 | 85 | 134 | 21 | 1 | 48 | 126 | .243 |
| 1963 | Minnesota, AL | 142 | 515 | 88 | 133 | 18 | 0 | 45 | 96 | .258 |
| 1964 | Minnesota, AL | 153 | 577 | 95 | 156 | 11 | 1 | 49 | 111 | .270 |
| 1965 | Minnesota, AL | 113 | 401 | 78 | 108 | 16 | 1 | 25 | 75 | .269 |
| 1966 | Minnesota, AL | 162 | 559 | 89 | 160 | 27 | 1 | 39 | 110 | .281 |
| 1967 | Minnesota, AL | 163 | 547 | 105 | 147 | 24 | 1 | 44 | 113 | .269 |
| 1968 | Minnesota, AL | 100 | 295 | 40 | 62 | 7 | 2 | 17 | 40 | .210 |
| 1969 | Minnesota, AL | 162 | 555 | 106 | 153 | 20 | 2 | 49 | 140 | .276 |
| 1970 | Minnesota, AL | 157 | 527 | 96 | 143 | 20 | 1 | 41 | 113 | .271 |
| 1971 | Minnesota, AL | 147 | 500 | 61 | 127 | 19 | 1 | 28 | 119 | .254 |
| 1972 | Minnesota, AL | 139 | 433 | 53 | 100 | 13 | 2 | 26 | 74 | .231 |
| 1973 | Minnesota, AL | 69 | 248 | 29 | 60 | 9 | 1 | 5 | 32 | .242 |
| 1974 | Minnesota, AL | 122 | 333 | 28 | 74 | 7 | 0 | 13 | 54 | .222 |
| 1975 | Kansas City, AL | 106 | 312 | 35 | 62 | 13 | 0 | 14 | 44 | .199 |
| Major Lg. totals | | 2435 | 8147 | 1263 | 2086 | 290 | 24 | 573 | 1584 | .256 |
| **League Championship series** | | | | | | | | | | |
| 1969 | Minnesota, AL | 3 | 8 | 2 | 1 | 1 | 0 | 0 | 0 | .125 |
| 1970 | Minnesota, AL | 3 | 11 | 2 | 3 | 0 | 0 | 2 | 4 | .273 |
|  | Totals | 6 | 19 | 4 | 4 | 1 | 0 | 2 | 4 | .211 |
| **World Series** | | | | | | | | | | |
| 1965 | Minnesota, AL | 7 | 21 | 2 | 6 | 0 | 0 | 1 | 2 | .286 |

# 1955

More (22) Bonus Babies were signed in 1955 than in any other year.

The Brooklyn Dodgers made their only venture into the bonus waters by signing a wild young lefthander named Sandy Koufax for $24,000. Eventually he proved to be worth it.

Lindy McDaniel (Cardinals, $50,000) turned out to be a steal. Other solid major leaguers signed in 1955 were Clete Boyer (Kansas City A's, $30,000, Yankees' money), Wayne Causey (Baltimore, $32,000), and Jim Pagliaroni (Boston Red Sox, $85,000).

The Orioles also signed Bruce Swango for $36,000, but his control was so bad that he never appeared in a game and was released before his two years were up.

# 7 Jim Brady

*Jim Brady signed in 1955, the third year of the bonus rule.*

BRENT KELLEY: *The Tigers signed you at age 19. How much was your bonus?*
JIM BRADY: Thirty-seven-five.
*Out of high school?*
JB: After one year at Notre Dame.
*Did you play ball there?*
JB: No, they had j.v. then. Freshman ineligibility rule. Made sense, too.
*Were you pursued by teams other than the Tigers?*
JB: I really thought I was going to sign with the Red Sox. They were the number one team that was after me. In fact, I spent a week in Boston after I finished my high school senior year and was offered $65,000 by Tom Yawkey. My father, however, who was an Irish immigrant, said, "No. You've got a full scholarship to Notre Dame and your Notre Dame education is worth more than $65,000." So he wouldn't give me permission to sign.
*Academic scholarship?*
JB: It was a baseball scholarship.
*Why did he change his mind a year later?*
JB: I guess I was a pain in the neck. I kept bothering him all year because I really wanted to play pro ball. What we ended up doing was I almost had to promise him in blood that I would go back to Notre Dame in the off-season to pursue my education, which I would have done anyway.
*How long did it take you to finish?*
JB: Six years.
*Then you went on to get a Master's and a Ph.D.?*
JB: Yeah.

*Who scouted you?*

JB: For the Tigers, a fellow named Rabbit Jacobson, from Elizabeth, New Jersey. The Red Sox scout was a fellow named Bill McCarren and he was from Jersey City. He's probably long deceased. He was up in age then.

*The high school schedules were short then. Where did you play summer ball?*

JB: I played semipro in the summertime. That was back when companies had teams. I played for a team called the Cloverdale Dairy team. It was very good baseball.

If you were successful you'd end up in Wichita at the NBC [National Baseball Congress]. You were playing against, in a lot of cases, some former minor league players, once in a while a former major league player.

I played against Don Newcombe and Whitey Ford during the Korean War. They were at Fort Dix and we played Fort Dix. I was a 16-year-old kid and I was in awe. Also the O'Brien twins—Eddie and Johnny O'Brien—great basketball players, played with the Pirates a little bit.

I played in that league three years.

*How many teams scouted you?*

JB: I never counted 'em.

I had played for a guy—basically a milkman—Howard Wimpy, a black fellow, who really taught me just about everything I knew about pitching back then. He was the coach of Cloverdale Dairy. In fact, he coached Johnny Kucks, who played with the Yankees, and Dick Brodowski, Leo Kiely, Jim Hannan all played at one time or another for Howard Wimpy.

*You were president of Jacksonville University.*

JB: I love the school. It's a great school. Private school, 500 students. Beautiful campus on the St. John's River and very strong pre-med, science programs.

*You've come a long way from the Bonus Baby days. Very few of you guys have progressed to your level.*

**Jim Brady (courtesy Detroit Tigers)**

JB: I don't know. I always wanted to be another Dizzy Dean and now I am one. (Laughs)

*You joined the Tigers in mid 1955 and didn't pitch.*

JB: They signed me with a bad arm. I went out there for a tryout and I think I threw every day. I threw batting practice, threw on the side, and then on Friday, the last day of the week, I didn't expect to throw and then somebody said Muddy Ruel, who was the general manager, hadn't seen me throw,

I started throwing on the side by the dugout and all of a sudden the old arm just made a weird sound and I just destroyed the tendon in the elbow.

I was really crushed. They took me to the hospital and said it's not deadly, it'll come along with rest, so they signed me anyway. It ended up that I couldn't throw that entire year. It came back over the winter. We weren't into weight training back then. The trainer said to go out and bowl, do a lot of bowling. So I did. It started to come around, so in '56 if I iced it for two days afterwards it was fine.

*You pitched in '56, but in '57, when you were still on the roster for half the season, they didn't use you. You were sent to the minors in mid-season.*

JB: They pretty well knew before the winter that I needed experience and it was really an extremely poor rule. It was poor on the player, poor on the team, and certainly with pitchers there's a lot to learn and you really need to serve your apprenticeship.

I went to Augusta in the Sally League. I did terribly probably the first three weeks. I didn't know where the plate was and I was throwing balls up against the screen, 'cause I had that long layoff and I really had to relearn pitching. Then toward the end of the season — the last month — I started coming around and doing well.

The following year I played somewhat at Double-A and then back at Augusta again. I had one more year in Knoxville. I showed up late; I missed spring training to finish school and I think I was only there about a month before they released me.

I went back to school and went on for a Master's and went in the Army — the Berlin crisis — and played baseball in the Army. We had a great team — ten major leaguers, all 30 professional players— at Fort Lewis in Washington. We had [Tony] Kubek, George Thomas, a whole bunch of guys.

*Did you consider a comeback?*

JB: I tried to catch on. I gave it one shot. Jack McKeon was with Kansas City back then. I wrote him a letter and there wasn't any interest.

I really think I could have continued pitching. I still had very good stuff, but the whole thing, and I've told my kids, that if you're going to go into pitching there's a lot to learn and you really have to work your way up. I would have done that except for the bonus rule. It was a terrible rule.

*How was the reception by your teammates when you joined the Tigers?*
JB: Mixed.

*Were some of the veterans pretty antagonistic?*
JB: Not overtly, but it was there. You could detect it. there was some jealousy, I'm sure, and fellows saying, "Look, life's not fair. Here's this young kid, never played pro ball at all, coming in with all this money." You could understand that.

I knew what I was walking into. It was a little bit hostile, but I think that's where I recognized the importance of a sense of humor and disarming people with humor.

They used to refer to Jim Small and me as the "James Boys." 'cause we held the club up. (Laughs)

*Did any of the players go out of their way to be helpful?*
JB: Not in a professional way, in terms of pointing out some tips on pitching. I think in terms of little things, you know, how to tip or how to dress and that type of thing, but on-the-field professionalism, where somebody would come up and say, "Look, you've really got to start pitching to spots, you ought to consider holding the ball across the seams as opposed to with the seams"—nobody came forth to help you in that regard.

I was pretty disappointed in the *quality* of instruction. I learned more from Wimpy than I ever learned from anybody with Detroit.

There was a lot of politics in the game in terms of who got coaching jobs. It wasn't based on what you know and that's probably why the New York Yankees were so strong because they operated in a professional manner and if you coached for 'em, you were expected to produce and *teach* youngsters as well as oldsters. The Yankees were the exception, I think, to the rule.

Most of the other teams, their coaches were politically appointed. [They were] big names, usually, in the yesteryears and as a favor to them or because they had nothing else to do, the teams put 'em on as first base coach or third base coach. Very few were picked or appointed in a professional manner, saying this guy really knows his stuff, he knows the skills, he can teach young people. That's changed today, I'm happy to say. There's much less of that today.

*What about the adjustment from home and school to a professional baseball team?*
JB: It's a tremendous shift in mind-set for a high school kid. As I grew up, my dad was a longshoreman in Hoboken; he loaded and unloaded

ships. Both my parents were immigrants; we lived in a tenement, so it was quite a change. It was for most of the guys that signed back then.

*Very few of the Bonus Babies were older than 20. A few had been to college; maybe that helped.*

JB: It was a horrendously ill-conceived rule. I don't see how anybody could have stayed up any hours at night and thought up a bonus rule, because if you thought about it you would have said, "This is counterproductive. It's going to hurt the ballclub, 'cause you're using up spots on the roster, and it's going to hurt the young player, because he's not getting any experience anywhere; he's just sitting there."

*There was a great deal of talk, then and now, about under-the-table payments and cheating on the bonuses. Some boys were actually signed for more than the $4,000 but it wasn't reported as such. Were you aware of it at the time?*

JB: I didn't hear much about it. I heard rumors about it. I didn't have any proof of it, but I did hear about it. I didn't pay too much attention to it.

*Bucky Harris was your first manager. He liked young players.*

JB: We have Bowie Kuhn on our Board of Trustees at J. U. and I was out with him one time and we were talking about Bucky. Bucky was really a grand old manager. A fine gentleman. Really showed a lot of respect for the kids that were signed.

His son was also a fine young man. General manager in the Senators' organization. Stanley.

You'd be interested to know that John McHale is on the Board of Trustees, too. John's a great guy.

*Jack Tighe was your manager while you were there in '57.*

JB: Jack was a fellow Jerseyite. We had a good relationship. Jack was bullpen coach and, to be candid, I never had an opportunity to learn anything from Jack or, in our case, Schoolboy Rowe, who was the pitching coach. Nice man, but you had to learn from the minor leagues on up. Nobody was really going out of their way to teach you or grab you on the side and say, "Here's how you throw the curveball" or "Here's how you grip a ball if you want to throw a sinker." There was none of that. That goes for spring training as well. The expectation was you learned by doing and then they did not let you do. You had to sit on the bench, so you weren't going to learn anything.

If they had good teachers, that would have helped a little bit. If you had a coach or coaches who would, in the bullpen, work with you, say, "Here's a grip on a change of pace; why don't you work on it," and that type of thing, where you were learning, even if it was on the sidelines. It would have been a help. But it's still no substitute for the actual getting in there and throwing in a ballgame against hitters. [But] it would have been much better than nothing.

I notice that coaches are today much more coaches than then. It was political; you hired a guy because — well, he may have had problems. He may have had a drinking problem, you felt sorry for him and he had been a great player, so you made him a coach — gave him a job as coach. Never works out, not at all.

*In retrospect, could anybody have foreseen the disaster of the bonus rule before it happened?*

JB: If I were placed in the same situation again, with no changes, I probably would have made the same mistake.

I loved the game, I still love the game, I think it's a *wonderful* game. But if I were aware of the fact that I was not going to get an opportunity to have excellent coaching and teaching, even though I wasn't going to play very much, or I wasn't going to get the opportunity of playing at *all*, let's say, I would have stayed in school. If I had *known* that, but I didn't know that.

*What happened to your scholarship when you signed?*

JB: I surrendered that and I had to pay my way the rest of the way.

*Did your bonus take care of that?*

JB: Yes. I made sure that it did.

It was an opportunity. In any endeavor you're always a little frustrated because you just want the opportunity to succeed *or* to fail and if you're not given the opportunity — a *good* opportunity — then you're always frustrated and say, "Gee whiz, I never was in a position to say whether I could have been very good or not." Two years of sitting on the bench really hurt. It destroyed me.

I'm just grateful. I thank God for just that opportunity—just wearing a major league uniform. And I met a lot of great people and friends and I have a lot of fond memories. It opened a lot of doors for me, even though I didn't play that much.

## James Joseph Brady

Born May 2, 1936, Jersey City, NJ
Ht. 6'2" Wt. 185 Batted and Threw Left

| Year | Team, Lg. | G | IP | W | L | PCT | SO | BB | H | ERA |
| --- | --- | --- | --- | --- | --- | --- | --- | --- | --- | --- |
| 1956 | Detroit, AL | 6 | 6 | 0 | 0 | — | 3 | 11 | 15 | 28.42 |
| 1957 | Augusta, SAL | 17 | 102 | 6 | 5 | .545 | 90 | 72 | 65 | 3.00 |
| 1958 | Lancaster, EL | 10 | 53 | 3 | 3 | .500 | 49 | 33 | 50 | 3.57 |

## 7. Jim Brady

| Year | Team, Lg. | G | IP | W | L | PCT | SO | BB | H | ERA |
|---|---|---|---|---|---|---|---|---|---|---|
| | Thomsville, Ga-Fl | 10 | | 1 | 3 | .250 | | | | |
| | Kokomo. MWL | 10 | 37 | 1 | 3 | .250 | 22 | 24 | 47 | 6.57 |
| | Augusta, SAL | 11 | 30 | 0 | 2 | .000 | 25 | 33 | 19 | 4.80 |
| | Birmingham, SA | 3 | | 1 | 1 | .500 | | | | |
| 1959 | Panama City, Al-Fl | 13 | 31 | 0 | 2 | .000 | 36 | 24 | 29 | 6.97 |
| 1960 | Durham, CarL | 25 | 101 | 5 | 7 | .417 | 114 | 76 | 91 | 3.48 |
| | Victoria, TxL | 1 | | 0 | 0 | — | | | | |
| 1961 | Knoxville, SAL | 8 | | 0 | 0 | — | | | | |

# 8 Tom Carroll

*Tom Carroll was signed by the Yankees in 1955 for a reported $62,000 bonus.*

BRENT KELLEY: *Was $62,000 your actual bonus?*

TOM CARROLL: It's been so long I have to think about that. I think it was $50 over three years.

*Including your major league salary?*

TC: No. Salary was on top of that. When I was doing well, it was [reported as] $50,000; when I was doing not so well, it was $40,000. (Laughs) It had a slightly floating aspect to it.

*You were one of only two Bonus Babies signed by the Yankees, but there was talk then of the Yankees paying money to boys under the table and then sending them to the minor leagues. Were you aware of that?*

TC: I was not aware of it and I doubt it very much. I was offered under-the-table deals by at least one other club, not the Yankees. It was the Phillies, actually.

*The Phillies were active in pursuing, but they really didn't sign many. The Red Sox were also very active in pursuit; did they show interest in you?*

TC: Yes. In fact, they were the earliest team that offered me a bonus.

*Apparently Lou Boudreau, the Red Sox manager, did not want Bonus Babies and for that reason the team signed very few.*

TC: I played most of my sandlot ball on Long Island and I thought they were *very* active in scouting. A Red Sox scout was the first scout to talk to me when I was about 14 or 15. Over the years, there were several others that took looks at me. I don't think Boudreau was managing the Red Sox when I signed.

*Most of the Bonus Babies I've spoken with said the Red Sox were in the hunt.*

TC: Oh, they were very much in the hunt with me. In fact, I would say they and the Tigers were the most active in pursuit.

*Who were the scouts?*

TC: I can't remember the Red Sox scouts. Joe Labate was the scout with the Phillies and I met everybody there from the director of scouting to the general manager.

*Why did you not sign with the Phillies?*

TC: The deal they offered was they would give me a scholarship to the college of my choice and they would sign me to a minor league contract and make up the difference between a certain set bonus with a bonus under the table. I was a very straight arrow (laughs) and I did not like it at all — the whole proposal. And I had, in effect, the college of my choice through other scouts and other organizations.

**Tom Carroll**

Frankly, in those days, kids 17-years-old were very different from today when kids coming out of college at 21 — they've got a college education, they're mature, and they're very dollar-oriented. They've got lots of professional and semiprofessional advice and they make a very cold and calculating decision on where they're gonna get to play first and all this. I signed with the Yankees because I was a Yankee fan. I signed with the Yankees for less money than I would have gotten from the Cubs or from the Tigers and I think from the Red Sox.

There's no question in my mind that it cost me. The Tigers had four or five bonus players playing. I could barely get in a game as a pinch runner with the Yankees. I wasn't even played my first year in games that were either laughers or completely out of reach.

I'm not saying that I was gonna take anybody's job or share time with anybody, but it's roughly equivalent to a college coach these days playing his second- or third-string quarterback when the score is 45-nothing one way or the other. The other teams, it seemed to me, *did* that kind of stuff and Stengel didn't do it. I pinch ran, I don't know, maybe 15 times the first season, did not get up [to bat] until we clinched the pennant in Boston on a Saturday. The last day of the season was a double header against the Red Sox, so I played the double header and went 1-for-3 in each game. (Laughs) So I was a .300 hitter for the year, which comprised one Sunday afternoon. (Laughs)

I didn't play considerably more the next year in '56, but I'm sure it was the furthest thing from Stengel's mind. But the attitude was quite different in Detroit. People like Reno Bertoia were not ready yet — Kaline was ready — and several other people were not ready and they got to play regularly. That was just out of the question with the Yankees.

*The difference in ability between the Tigers veterans and the Bonus Babies was not as great as the difference between the Yankees veterans and the Bonus Babies.*

TC: I'm not talking about starting or anything; I'm talking about going in in the eighth inning, which happened a little the next year. You know, going in and playing one inning in the field for somebody who was pinch hit for or something like that.

*How many teams were after you?*

TC: Fourteen of the 16 teams. The Yankees were the fourteenth. They weren't very good, they were incredibly overrated in their scouting and this goes back to the point I was making earlier that *many, many* kids signed with them because of the pinstripes and Joe DiMaggio and Babe Ruth and Miller Huggins and the whole aura, the whole mystique of the Yankees.

Actually, the way I got signed by the Yankees says a lot about the scouting first of all. I played all my baseball within a 40-minute drive of Yankee Stadium. In fact, much of it much closer than that. I was contacted when I was 15-years-old by about three or four different scouts: Giants, Dodgers, Red Sox, and Phillies. And the Indians.

By the time I was 16, I'd been contacted by a whole bunch of scouts. By the time I was 17 and I was a senior in high school, they were flying me out to Detroit and flying me here and bringing me down to Reading to work out with the Indians farm team. I'd been playing semipro ball over in Jersey for a Dodger birddog scout for two years.

The Giants scout started arranging scholarships to college and I had all kinds of offers to go to various colleges throughout the country. They were athletic scholarships arranged by professional scouts. My baseball scholarship to Notre Dame was arranged by the Giants scout.

I had a *very* close relationship with the Dodgers and when I was 16 I played on a Dodger "scout" team with a lot of kids who had graduated from high school and gone to college. The Dodgers got a good look at

## 8. Tom Carroll

these players. I met [Al] Campanis and dozens of Dodgers scouts. I worked out at the Polo Grounds and I worked out at Ebbets Field all the time.

I was only 17 when I graduated from high school and I went out to Notre Dame on a baseball scholarship and still had never heard from the Yankees and was really perplexed and puzzled about this. Everybody else was lusting after me, but I guess I just wasn't good enough for the Yankees. (Laughs)

I had a godfather who was an old semipro pitcher. He pitched for the fire department in New York. He had a friend in the ticket office in Yankee Stadium. My godfather was aware of all of the scouts coming around. He asked his friend, "What's going on? Everybody seems to be interested in my godson but the Yankees don't seem to be interested at all."

Apparently, based on this, shortly after I went to Notre Dame, I got a little postcard in the mail. I'll never forget it; it was called an "Application for Tryout." (Laughs) I thought it was pretty funny because you had all these other guys fawning over you and chasing you and entertaining you. I used to get paid in New Jersey for playing semipro ball, which was a big thing for a 15-year-old kid.

There was like a three-day tryout and it was timed during college Easter vacation. I went to the tryout at Yankee Stadium and they really liked me all of a sudden. I had already signed to play in a semipro league that summer in Halifax, Nova Scotia, and Paul Krichell, the famous Yankee scout, called me over and introduced me to a guy by the name of Bob Decker, a birddog who was managing the Halifax Cardinals.

Krichell kind of just insisted that I go up to this league, which I was going to anyway, with this Halifax team rather than the other team. (Laughs) You got paid up there in those days in Canadian dollars — 300 and change Canadian dollars a month.

I liked Decker and I was flattered at last that the Yankees were expressing some interest and I went up there that summer — the summer of '54 — and had a good year up there and all kinds of teams were interested in signing me. The Yankees were *very* interested in me, but they were begging and pleading with me to hold off a year 'cause they had [Frank] Leja. He'd been on the team one year and was coming back for his second year and they didn't want to carry two bonus players.

The major league owners at their meeting in July at the All-Star game in the summer of '54 had passed a rule — you know, they used to make up the rules as they went along and they would cheat on the rules that they had made (laughs) — they were constantly recycling these rules, revoking old ones and putting in new ones. One that they put in in '54 — they were just starting to sign people out of college — and apparently, after signing a couple of players who were half-way through college, they received some criticism. They put in a rule so that they would have roughly the equivalent of what the NFL had: not signing a college player once he'd started his sophomore year 'til his class graduated.

That was what I was facing. I was a second-semester freshman that fall. I had started school in January. I was faced with having to sign or waiting until I graduated from college.

That fall I made up my mind I was going to sign. The Tigers, the Cubs, Red Sox, and the Yankees were all very interested. The Yankees, while they dithered about it, they eventually came through when they saw that I was going to sign. I signed with them for less money than I would have gotten from the Tigers.

I only played freshman ball at Notre Dame. It wasn't much of a schedule.

*Where did you go to high school?*

TC: I went to a catholic high school in Brooklyn. My junior year we won the city championship—catholic city championship. We played four different prep teams in Ebbets Field.

*Were you always an infielder?*

TC: Yes. I was a shortstop.

*You continued at Notre Dame and received your degree.*

TC: Yes. It took me from January of '54 to the end of 1961, even though I did it in seven semesters. I played winter ball one year and I was in the Army another year. After my first two semesters, which were the second semester of one school year and the first semester of the next school year, I only went in the fall. So I went two semesters consecutively and then I went back three fall semesters, then I was out of school while I played winter ball in Maracaibo. When I came back—I had five semesters—I stayed for the whole school year.

I have an undergraduate degree in history with about 15 hours of graduate work, so I've got a history major and a minor in International Relations.

*On leaving baseball, you went in the diplomatic service.*

TC: Yeah. I was actually in the intelligence community. I retired at the end of 1987. Most of it was overseas and two of my four children were born overseas.

*Do you know whose roster spot you took when you joined the Yankees?*

TC: I went to spring training that year. You never take anybody's particular roster spot. There are 40 people on a major league roster and 25 after cut-down date. Since people are retiring and people are coming up and going down, there's not *a* spot that I took. Somebody was not with the Yankees that year that *would* have been if I wasn't there.

## 8. Tom Carroll

I signed immediately after that fall semester, which in those days was over around the third week of January. They had the big press conference for me and they had [Phil] Rizzuto there. I was supposedly signed to replace him. (Laughs) Thirty-five years later he's still there. He was cut half-way through that season; he was released. Very nice man.

*What kind of reception did you receive from your teammates?*

TC: I received a relatively very good reception. There was a certain amount of good-natured kidding. Most of the infielders—Rizzuto, [Jerry] Coleman, [Billy] Martin, [Gil] McDougald, [Joe] Collins—were very friendly and outgoing and helpful.

I would say I got a frosty reception from Hank Bauer, a big, tough Marine, you know, and got to the majors very late and here's a kid coming in and getting big money and getting it on a silver platter.

I got a good reception from Mickey Mantle; he was very nice to me. I was roommates with Tom Sturdivant and we were good friends.

[Enos] Slaughter wasn't there. He came over much later, in '56, I think. I was semi-established then. He didn't give me any trouble.

Yogi [Berra] was in his own little world and I'd say Andy Carey was in his own little world, too.

Rizzuto was very helpful — taking me places and showing me things.

*You were a city boy. Did you find the adjustment difficult?*

TC: Yeah, I was a city boy. I had followed the Yankees very closely. I think most bonus players feel like hostages, you know. I had decided when I was in third grade that I was gonna be a major league baseball player. I started to read *The Sporting News* from the third grade on and I had been working toward it sort of way down the pike. And all of a sudden — Bam!— I'm there! There's something wrong here. I never had that great year at [Class] C ball and two years in A and Triple-A, so there was that aspect to it. I was kind of always a little bit old for my age, I'd say, and the adjustment from that point of view wasn't tough. In fact, I was kind of amazed at how childlike some of the older ballplayers were. (Laughs) They were pretty childlike.

As a for instance, I remember one time we were over in Miami during spring training. I think it was '56. Sturdivant was my regular roommate and we checked into a hotel in Miami. We were playing the Orioles; they trained in Miami in those days. We'd come over by bus and we checked in at the hotel in downtown Miami and Sturdivant and I went out to dinner. We were out for a couple hours looking around and we came back. We weren't aware of it, but Martin and Mantle, who were roommates, were in the adjoining room. The way hotels were set up, there were usually adjoining rooms.

They had found our door unlocked and Sturdivant and Mantle were good friends. They were both Oklahomans.

We had a very big room and they had gotten in there and they must have spent an hour-and-a-half of very hard physical labor. As a joke, they had taken all the furniture — the beds, the pictures, all the furnishings — and they'd stacked them up in one big pile in the middle of the room. (Laughs) This thing must've taken them hours to do. It raises certain questions about the maturity. (Laughs)

*The Yankees had a reputation for having coaches who coached. Were they helpful?*

TC: The two principal coaches were [Frank] Crosetti, who was the third base coach, and [Bill] Dickey, who was the first base coach and the catchers' coach. They were both very serious, professional, full-time coaches. Dickey was a fairly quiet guy and Crosetti was sort of a holler guy. *Very* nice man; he was very helpful to me.

As a matter of fact, I have a story to tell you. I live in Miami Beach because it's close to my office. We have a house that backs up to one of the golf courses here, at a country club. I'm a social member. I was over on the driving range hitting balls; it was kind of a grey, rainy day and there was only one other guy on the driving range. I'm hitting balls and an older man comes along with a yellow sweater on who I immediately recognized as my only hero, other than my father: a man by the name of Joe DiMaggio. He comes up and he starts hitting. He was my boyhood hero; he finished playing a couple of years before I got there. I never actually talked to him; I saw him around occasionally.

He was hitting balls for a fairly long time there and not badly, either, for a 72-year-old gentleman, so I went over and talked to him. He didn't really remember me, but I told him when I played.

I asked him about Crosetti and he said that he saw him occasionally; he was living out in Stockton. They were actually teammates.

Then there was the famous — or infamous — Jim Turner, who was the pitching coach and the power behind the throne; the *eminence grise,* you know. He thought he was the unofficial manager. He was a very pushy guy, kind of intruded into a lot of areas. He was *soundly* disliked by the pitchers, people like Whitey Ford, and by Mantle. But he was a very serious, very professional coach,

There were no old drinking buddies of the manager, who was one of the better drinkers there or in *any* league at the time. (Laughs)

*Many of the Bonus Babies report that they received very little coaching, especially the pitchers.*

TC: I don't know. I think that's being probably quite inaccurate. There were a *lot* of good pitching coaches around and several after Turner, like Johnny Sain.

There was a very nice man. I saw him a while back and he's in terrific shape. He's a real gentleman and he was a *great* pitcher and he really knows his craft. I'm amazed by him; he looks very little changed from the way I remember him years ago.

*Casey Stengel had a reputation of not paying attention to the players who couldn't help him.*

TC: Casey was a very complex man. He was very different from his newspaper image. This guy was a master of pubic relations before it became popular. He manipulated the press. (Laughs) The good-natured, amiable clown image that he had — he was a much darker image than that and a much more intelligent figure.

He was an alcoholic; he used to drink the writers into the ground. He had an incredible memory for everything but names. Really, his Stengelese was a fact.

But he liked me. He liked holler guys and I was kind of a holler guy. And he liked the idea that I had kind of a work ethic. Didn't like Leja. Frank was sort of just sitting there biding his time. He liked the type of ballplayer that Billy Martin was — the kind of guy that would scratch and fight and holler and kick and always thinking, always chattering, not the most talented guy in the world. So he liked me more than he should have and was always very kind in print to me and never gave me a problem. He probably kind of ignored me, but I didn't get any harassment.

I saw him be fairly cruel to a lot of up-and-coming players who were being sent back to the minors only because the Yankees were so overstocked with talent.

He had a tremendous ego. He used to refer to the team by the personal pronoun. He was a great teacher and a lousy game manager, often falling asleep on the bench. Turner used to make (a) the decision on the pitching rotation, and (b) largely the decisions on Yankee pitchers. That is the most basic power that managers have.

The older players there when I joined the club — Rizzuto and Bauer and people like this, particularly Bauer, who was one of the people affected — always felt that they would have won the pennant by bigger margins in the early '50s than they did if the platoon system hadn't been in effect. I don't know that that was so, but that was their sort of consensus.

He was one of the guys, of course, that really brought platooning in in a big way. The difference was you replaced Hank Bauer with Gene Woodling or Irv Noren. You can put a guy up from the other side of the plate who is also a .300 hitter. You get a lot smarter a lot faster.

*You played more your second year and you hit the ball: .350 after two years. Did you go in the service then?*

TC: No. I played at Richmond the next year.

*How long did you play altogether?*

TC: I played two full years in the minors: '57 and '58. I was in the Army that winter ['58-'59] and got to spring training late. George Weiss threatened to fine me if I wasn't in shape, you know, after coming off of national service if I wanted to discuss my contract or anything.

I had played a lot in spring training before; in fact, the two before that, and I didn't play at all, virtually. They started making cuts and I'd had a pretty good year in Triple-A and Double-A and back to Triple-A. it was obvious I was not gonna be on the Yankees roster, was not gonna play, and was not gonna make the team. I was thinking, which Triple-A team am I going to?

I figured I'd be one of the first cuts and I wasn't. Then the second, third, and fourth cuts were made and I still wasn't. Bob Turley, the player representative, said, "You know, I don't think they can cut you this year." These vagaries of baseball, nobody knew what waivers and options and that sort of thing were available. You're supposed to be able to be optioned out three times. I'd been in the majors two years under the bonus rule and then I'd been optioned in '57 to Richmond and optioned in '58 to Denver, so I figured, being able to count to three, I could be optioned a third time that year, but Turley suggested to me that he believed I couldn't be optioned without getting waivers on me because a year in the majors counts as an option.

By that rationale, as I had had two years, I couldn't get there from here. (Laughs) If a year in the majors counted as an option, I could have been optioned only in '57 and not '58. Or in '59. If it didn't count, then I could be optioned.

But, anyway, that apparently was the case. I came north with the club and the season opened and we played the Red Sox in the opening series. Then that Sunday, which was about the third day of the season, I was running before the game out in the outfield. Stengel called me in and told me I'd been traded to Kansas City.

*How did you feel about that?*

TC: Mild shock, never having been traded before. (Laughs) I wasn't as shocked by that as I was shocked by not being sent to a minor league team much earlier in spring training.

*The options, etc., must be difficult. General managers are still screwing up on it.*

TC: It's not very difficult if you can count to three. The point is that these rules are constantly violated and evaded, at least they were in the old days. They kept changing the rules and this tight little club they'd made up of owners, it was a cartel. (Laughs) They made their own rules and then they'd cheat on them. It would be like playing a game of poker and deciding, because some guy had four-flushed, that four-flushes were okay now. (Laughs) Then they go a couple of more rounds and decide that three-flushes were okay. They did a lot of that.

When my original major league contract ran out, they offered me a cut — I was still on a major league contract — that was more than 25 percent of what my major league salary was and I gently pointed this out to them in negotiations. I had been reading *The Sporting News* since I was nine-years-old and had been aware of that provision. Lee MacPhail, who was the farm director at the time and later president of the American League, he was a gentleman, a very courtly type. He allowed that because that was so, would that be acceptable to me? (Laughs) Afterwards I was trying to figure out was this a flim-flam? (Laughs)

It was just outrageous, the stuff that went on in the old days. The meager amount of money that the established stars on the Yankees made in those days was a joke. The pendulum swung from one extreme to another.

Those guys like [Bill] Skowron, who were tearing up the league, they were making $20-to-$25,000. And they were telling all these guys like [John] Blanchard, who were just tearing the cover off the ball in the high minors, "Go back out and hit .300 again." (Laughs)

One of my friends, a guy by the name of Zeke Bella, was up for a cup of coffee with the Yankees, one time when he had hit about .370 at Binghamton and played at Kansas City and never hit less than .300 and Stengel was sending him out again. Stengel said, "Go down and hit .300 and we'll see you later." He said, "I hit .300!" (Laughs)

*What happened to you when you joined Kansas City?*

TC: I sat on the bench there behind Joe DeMaestri. I sat there on the bench for about half a season and they had trouble getting me waived out. When they finally got waivers on me, they sent me to Charleston in the American Association. I was down there about two weeks and I got beaned by Steve Ridzik and put in the hospital.

I was in the hospital three-four days. It knocked out several teeth. I guess I was out of action about two weeks and then I went out to Portland in the Pacific Coast League and played the rest of the year out there. That was '59.

Then in '60 I played in the American Association at Dallas a half a season and the second half at Houston. I got married that winter, so I was married that year. I still had two semesters to go to get my degree and I went back to college and completed the fall semester and I got a contract for Double-A from Kansas City. I had played eight weeks in the Southern League in '58 and made the All-Star team in the Southern League and I got recalled back to Denver, Triple-A, where I had started the year.

I thought that was a very bad sign. Instead of going sideways, I was going down. So I decided to stay in school the spring semester and get my degree. They came back and said do that, but I'd been in college since I was 18-years-old.

I started applying to government agencies. I decided to take the government up on its kind offer, so when I graduated I went to work and that was the end of my baseball career.

*What is your opinion of the bonus rule?*

TC: The bonus rule was ridiculous. It was ridiculous for everybody — for the teams, for the ballplayers it kept out of the majors, for the bonus players themselves.

I'm convinced I would have had a much better chance of being a major leaguer if I had been able to start in the minor leagues. I think I could have started very high; I didn't have a bad year in Richmond in Triple-A in 1957 after sitting on the bench in New York for two years. If I had been able to start off in [class] A ball or something like that, I think I would have probably had a full-length career.

*So the bonus rule hurt you?*

TC: Oh, yeah, I think it did. I think not playing for that period of time, two years, was very harmful at that age and at that stage of development.

I learned a lot. In some ways, it wasn't *all* a lost cause. I know Jerry Coleman was kind enough to tell me in '56 in spring training — I'd played quite a bit in spring training and gotten a couple of key basehits — he'd never seen anybody that had improved from on year to the next as much as I had. I don't know if that was even true, but it was nice of him to say it. (Laughs)

I'm the third youngest player to have ever appeared in a World Series game. I was 19 three weeks before and when you go out there, you know everybody in the country is watching you. It was a big deal. It was the Dodger series and I went in to pinch run and you're scared to death! You're afraid you're gonna screw up and it's stressful, to say the least. You're wondering whether you're really adequately prepared to be there.

*What kind of advice were you given before you signed?*

TC: It was kind of interesting. I didn't get a lot of advice. My father really wasn't a terrifically well-situated individual. Guidance counselors and people that I talked to, it was kind of amazing, maybe I talked to two or three people in that category. I already had lots and lots of college scholarships and I had already decided that I wanted to go to Notre Dame. That was a nice piece of change in itself, a full scholarship, but it was chicken feed compared to what it costs now.

What was interesting to me — $30,000, $40,000 was a *lot* of money in those days — those two or three people I talked to and put weight to what they said, were *unanimous* that I ought to go to college. I signed because of that rule about signing college players, not because I wanted to grab the money.

My plan had been to go to college and play college ball, play semipro ball in the summer, and sign at the end of my junior year. I was young when I went to college —17— and I had it all figured out that by the time I was 21 it was too late to start to do an apprenticeship in the minors. I figured that it was around 19 or somewhere between 19 and 20 would be best. But as I said, this rule changed that. I didn't want to be in a position where I would not be able to sign because of that rule. It was passed and in effect, but it was a dead letter within the year.

## Thomas Edward Carroll

Born September 17, 1936, Jamaica, NY
Ht. 6'3" Wt. 186 Batted and Threw Right

| Year | Team, Lg. | G | AB | R | H | 2B | 3B | HR | RBI | BA |
|---|---|---|---|---|---|---|---|---|---|---|
| 1955 | New York, AL | 14 | 6 | 3 | 2 | 0 | 0 | 0 | 0 | .333 |
| 1956 | New York, AL | 36 | 17 | 11 | 6 | 0 | 0 | 0 | 0 | .353 |
| 1957 | Richmond, IL | 137 | 474 | 51 | 101 | 16 | 6 | 13 | 63 | .213 |
| 1958 | Denver, AA | 57 | 204 | 29 | 59 | 7 | 6 | 3 | 17 | .289 |
|  | New Orleans, SA | 72 | 252 | 31 | 70 | 8 | 6 | 4 | 29 | .278 |
| 1959 | Charleston, AA | 20 | 64 | 8 | 18 | 4 | 0 | 0 | 14 | .281 |
|  | Kansas City, AL | 14 | 7 | 1 | 1 | 0 | 0 | 0 | 1 | .143 |
|  | Portland, PCL | 19 | 32 | 4 | 5 | 1 | 1 | 0 | 0 | .156 |
| 1960 | Dallas/Ft. Worth– Houston, TxL | 115 | 323 | 42 | 81 | 16 | 3 | 7 | 33 | .251 |
| Major Lg. Totals | | 64 | 30 | 15 | 9 | 0 | 0 | 0 | 1 | .300 |

# 9 Wayne Causey

*Wayne Causey received a $32,000 bonus from the Orioles in 1955.*

BRENT KELLEY: *How many teams were after you?*
WAYNE CAUSEY: I can't remember how many. Detroit, the night after I graduated from high school, flew me up there to work me out a couple of days. Baltimore, for some reason, felt like I had been offered a bonus by Detroit, but the only thing they offered me was the minimum that they could pay me without getting into a bonus situation, and a Triple-A contract.

And the Phillies were willing to meet or do better than anything that I was offered, whether it be a bonus or whatever. But at that time, I thought I was a third baseman — that's what I was signed as— and Puddin' Head Jones was going great guns with the Phillies and Baltimore looked like they were trying to get a bunch of young guns in line to try to build. I just thought that I was better off getting into that organization than signing with the Phillies at that time. But I feel like the Phillies would have probably given me more than what Baltimore gave me if I would have just told 'em what I was being offered.

There were four of us that signed out of the same high school. There were three boys ahead of me that were seniors when I was a junior and they ended up going to college on scholarships. In fact, two of 'em went to Alabama and that's where I was going if I hadn't signed. One of 'em went to LSU, but they all ended up signing pro contracts after a couple years in college. One of 'em made it to the big leagues and the other two played Triple-A ball.

The one that made it was a pitcher by the name of Art Swanson; signed with Pittsburgh. He went to LSU a couple of years and went ahead and signed a bonus contract.

*Did you play American Legion ball in the summers?*
WC: I played American Legion ball starting when I was about 13, a

real early age. Between my junior and senior years in high school I actually played semipro ball in a league with college guys and some old-timers around here that had been in the league for a lot of years.

There was Jim Davenport. He played shortstop for us. Mississippi State had some guys over here, and Ole Miss, too, so I was really in a pretty fast semipro league between my junior and senior years in high school.

There was a league down here called the Big 8 League and back then you just didn't have TV and air conditioning and people getting out of the house at night would go to the ballpark. We had nice crowds.

*You attended college in the off-seasons. Did you use your bonus money?*

WC: Yeah, that, and I worked. I worked at a job for a half a day and I'd

**Wayne Causey**

go to school for a half a day. My dad managed a warehouse there in Monroe and I'd have morning classes, then get there about 1:00 and I'd work four hours a day there and study at night. It took me nine years to get through there.

*Degree?*

WC: Accounting.

I was a plant manager for Ball Corporation in their glass container division and I really have not used that degree. It helped me get a job there back in '74 when I started, but I kinda got into the manufacturing part of it and I was plant manager there since '84.

It's been good to me, but it's one of those jobs where you go on vacation you leave your number and you call back and make sure everything's okay. It's a 24-hour operation seven days a week and pretty demanding.

*When you joined the Orioles, you had more playing time than any of the Bonus Babies just out of high school.*

WC: The Orioles had a lot of guys [Bonus Babies] there and [Paul] Richards wanted to give me an opportunity to get my feet wet. No doubt about it, I was over my head.

[Bruce] Swango, he never could find home plate with a pitch. He was there when I got there. I think he had just signed. I don't know whether they released him and the Yankees signed him, trying to make an outfielder out of him, or what but I'm not sure they kept him there the full two years. He had a heck of an arm, but he just never could find the plate, not even in batting practice.

What was that little town he was from — Welch, Oklahoma? I took my son to a baseball camp in Missouri back in about '74 or '75 and there was a guy there at that camp who had a son there and was from Oklahoma. His son was gonna pitch a ballgame over in Oklahoma one night and asked me did I want to drive over there to the game with him. We drove over there and I'll be John Brown if I didn't run up on Bruce Swango out there. I believe it was at Welch, working at a plant or something out there.

He didn't have the pitcher's body; he was strongly built, 5' 11" probably, an old country boy, I guess, but extremely strong and stocky. He had a heck of an arm. I used to sacrifice my body a lot hitting off of him. (Laughs)

*What about the others?*

WC: [Tommy] Gastall got killed. Of course, [Bob] Nelson, he looked like, from what I remember, he had more tools than anybody — big ol' strong boy, had a good swing — but just never did put it together. He played a little bit before his two years were up, but just never did make it back up.

*What was the reception by the veterans on the Orioles when you joined the team?*

WC: I flew up there into Detroit and I caught a cab from the airport right to the ballpark. At the baggage claim I ran into one of the coaches, Al Vincent, who had been out scouting, so I rode in the cab with him. He carried my luggage and everything. Of course, I was scared to death, being 18-years-old and didn't know anybody.

But I can remember, they were really nice to me. I don't remember anybody giving me a hard time. You expect to get some harassment, but

**Wayne Causey**
**(courtesy Wayne Causey)**

they treated me fine. Hoot Evers was my first roommate. They couldn't have put me with a nicer guy.

In fact, the second night there we caught a train from Detroit to Chicago. We got in about seven in the morning and, of course, everybody got cabs to the hotel and ate breakfast. Well, I went around the corner and found a breakfast for 50 cents. When I got back to the room, there was a 'Do Not Disturb' sign on the door and I didn't go in there. I went down to the lobby and I stayed down there, sitting in the lobby, 'til about two o'clock. Hoot came down and said, "Where in the world have you been?" I said, "Well, I came in, went up to the room, and there's a 'Do Not Disturb' sign on the door and I wasn't going in there!" "That was for the maid so we could rest up!" "Well, I wasn't going in there." (Laughs) He was a real nice fellow.

*One day you were in high school, living at home; the next day, you were a major league ballplayer traveling the country. Did you have a problem with the adjustment?*

WC: It was definitely a learning experience for me because I had never been anywhere.

There were some guys coming in there like Swango and Nelson and [Jim] Pyburn — he was an old country boy from over there in Alabama but he was out of college — and we had a room in a house right out there by the ballpark in Baltimore. There were a couple of families that really took us under their wings.

There were a lot of things that I had to learn to do — all the tipping and so forth. You just kinda grew up fast in those situations. My eyes were wide open — bug-eyed — with what I was going through as far as being up there, traveling with those guys and getting into some games. It was quite an experience.

I went to South America and played winter ball and I came home and made up my mind I wasn't going to spring training — that would be my first spring training — without my girlfriend. When I came home from winter ball, we set a wedding date in February, We kinda grew up fast. She says she wouldn't go back through it again. (Laughs) She used to make some trips across country with our kids, driving by herself — things there's no way you'd let your wife do the way things are now.

*Did you receive coaching when you joined the Orioles?*

WC: They were into this youngster program and I just kinda lived on every word that they told me, how I should do and what I should do. I felt that Al Vincent and Harry Brecheen and Luman Harris knew what they were talking about. And [Paul] Richards, of course. I thought that I was well coached. I had no idea of what kind of coaching to expect. I know it's changed a lot as far as what they think these guys oughta be doing. Heck, they've got weight rooms and everything else now. When we came through there, we never touched a weight; they thought we'd get all tied up.

At home, they would have us come out to the ballpark in the morning at ten for special instructions—hitting and fielding. They were trying to force-feed us and I felt like they were good teachers. I can't ever recall thinking that I wasn't getting the proper instruction that I needed.

I remember when they sent me to San Antonio, Joe Schultz was my manager down there and I was probably 0-for-40 and he could have called up there and told them to send me down to [Class] B ball, that I was over my head in that Double-A league. And then all of a sudden—he stayed with me—I started hitting a little bit and ended up hitting about .247 after a horrendous start.

'Course, in the minor leagues, all they had was a manager then and there wasn't that much instruction. There was a pitcher that was the first base coach and third base coach; the manager kinda did it all. When I got to Vancouver, Charlie Metro managed and Spider Jorgenson was there as a player-coach. I can't recall having a pitching coach in the minor leagues.

The main thing was to *play*. The more you played, the more you learned, the more confidence you got. That's where you really advanced or matured—just having a chance to play every day. They can tell you and show you this and show you that, but until you go out and play every day you don't know what you can do. I don't have any problems with the way Baltimore handled me. They gave me a chance and I've always appreciated that.

*Paul Richards loved young players. What did you think of him?*

WC: I was 18 years old. I was scared of the man, I guarantee you! When he said something, I jumped! (Laughs) I felt like the man was God. After looking back at the nucleus that we had, I'm sure he did an excellent job with what he had to work with.

I remember I missed a pop fly in Baltimore one night. It was kinda foggy and the pop-up went up and, heck, I called it. I missed that ball ten feet! He called me in the office after the game and said, "Son let me tell you something. If you call that ball, you better catch it. I might have to take some of that money back away from you." (Laughs) I should have let [Willie] Miranda have it for sure, but I just took charge of it. I never saw the thing 'til it was about 15 feet from the ground coming down.

I ended up my career with Richards in Atlanta. He was in Atlanta and I was with California in '68 and he bought my contract. I started out with him and I finished my career with him.

At the end of '68, when I announced my retirement to become the ticket director for the Royals, he called [Cedric] Tallis up and told him he felt like they should get a ballplayer for me, that I was still on the roster and they had talked me into retirement. I had already made up my mind. That gave me ten years in the big leagues and the kids were in school and I had had enough of it. And he wanted a ballplayer from the Royals because they had hired me as ticket director. (Laughs) Of course, Tallis didn't end up doing anything.

*The Orioles traded you to Kansas City. What did you think of that?*

WC: Oh, I was tickled to death. I was in the minor leagues and to get a chance to go to the big leagues was great. I was right in middle of finals when they called me and told me that I had been traded to Kansas City. If I hadn't gotten up there, I know I'd have just stayed in school 'til I'd gotten out and that'd been it for me.

*You had two years—'63 and '64—when no shortstop in the American League outperformed you.*

WC: Yeah. I had a couple of pretty good years there.

In '61, when they got me from Baltimore, I went to spring training with 'em and I don't think I got in but one game the whole spring. That was the year that [Dick] Howser had had such a good year at Shreveport in the Texas League and he had the shortstop's job and they had Andy Carey at third. Joe Gordon was the manager. When we opened the season, I think they released Carey and got Reno Bertoia and he was playing third. About the first week in June, they fired Gordon and Hank Bauer became manager. He called me in the office one night and told me, "You're my third baseman 'til you show me you can't handle it." From June until the end of the year, I think I knocked in 48 runs, had eight homers, hit .261.

Then the next year I hurt my shoulder early diving for a ball and [Ed] Charles got in there — that was '62 — and I couldn't get back in the lineup. Howser broke his thumb in Chicago in about August, I guess, and I played short the rest of the season.

In '63 I didn't have a job 'cause Charles had had a heck of a year and Howser had shortstop back, so I went to spring training as a utility infielder. That was the year when Howser hurt himself. He tore a rib cage muscle about the first week of the season. He wasn't hitting and went out for some extra hitting in that cold weather and tore a cartilage and, heck, I got in there and I was hitting so good that whenever he got where he could play, they couldn't afford to take me out of the lineup. Charles was going great guns at third, so they traded Howser to Cleveland. I had about three years there of playing shortstop that really were my best years.

One year there, [Luis] Aparicio was the All-Star shortstop and something happened that he couldn't go. I felt like they would invite me and they took [Jim] Fregosi, I think.

*A lot of people have condemned the bonus rule, but some good players came out of it. How do you feel about it?*

WC: I feel that it definitely hurt me as far as how quick I was able to develop. I really think that that was the drawback to it. You had to go up there and you had to more or less sit. Practice is about all most of us got.

A lot of people probably felt that, if you were a bonus player, you were gonna be given a lot more opportunities. They'd stay with you longer than if you received $4,000 and a Triple-A salary or something.

To me, then, the bonus rule was great. If they felt you were deserving of a bonus, you got some money in your pocket and you got to go to the big leagues for two years, and at that time that was pretty good money — a $32,000 bonus. The bonuses that these boys are getting now are just a drop in the bucket of what they can make. The bonus isn't the big thing now; it's what they can make after. Heck, they get 3- and 400,000 dollar raises for just being on the roster. (Laughs)

I had two years at .280-.281 and I got like a $5,000 raise. Now, you do something like that — get 170 hits two years in a row — man, you can get a 500–600,000 dollar raise.

But I felt like the bonus rule gave me an opportunity and also gave me some money to put in the bank. If they hadn't offered me a bonus, I would have probably gone on to college. I might have been making a mistake, too, because a lot of those that passed up that $10,000, or whatever it was, went to college wanting to get more and they reached a plateau and didn't get any better and they never had another opportunity to go into pro ball. If they hadn't offered me a bonus, I might have made a mistake and gone on to college and never developed enough to get a chance to play after that. I don't know what would have happened to me if they hadn't offered me that bonus.

*So, in retrospect, it was in your best interests that you signed when you did?*

WC: Oh, yeah! If I had it to do over again, I'd do the same thing.

### James Wayne Causey

Born December 26. 1936, Ruston, LA
Ht. 5'10½" Wt. 175 Batted Left, Threw Right

| Year | Team, Lg. | G | AB | R | H | 2B | 3B | HR | RBI | BA |
|---|---|---|---|---|---|---|---|---|---|---|
| 1955 | Baltimore, AL | 68 | 175 | 14 | 34 | 2 | 1 | 1 | 9 | .194 |
| 1956 | Baltimore, AL | 53 | 88 | 7 | 15 | 0 | 1 | 1 | 4 | .170 |

| | | | | | | | | | | |
|---|---|---|---|---|---|---|---|---|---|---|
| 1957 | Baltimore, AL | 14 | 10 | 2 | 2 | 0 | 0 | 0 | 1 | .200 |
| | San Antonio, TxL | 79 | 267 | 25 | 66 | 9 | 4 | 1 | 22 | .247 |
| 1958 | Louisville, AA | 127 | 448 | 51 | 109 | 20 | 6 | 4 | 35 | .243 |
| 1959 | Vancouver, PCL | 91 | 231 | 21 | 56 | 6 | 2 | 1 | 18 | .242 |
| 1960 | Vancouver, PCL | 143 | 430 | 62 | 130 | 24 | 10 | 5 | 38 | .265 |
| 1961 | Kansas City, AL | 104 | 312 | 37 | 86 | 14 | 1 | 8 | 49 | .276 |
| 1962 | Kansas City, AL | 117 | 305 | 40 | 77 | 14 | 1 | 4 | 38 | .252 |
| 1963 | Kansas City, AL | 139 | 554 | 72 | 155 | 32 | 4 | 8 | 44 | .280 |
| 1964 | Kansas City, AL | 157 | 604 | 82 | 170 | 31 | 4 | 8 | 49 | .281 |
| 1965 | Kansas City, AL | 144 | 513 | 48 | 134 | 17 | 8 | 3 | 34 | .261 |
| 1966 | Kansas City-Chicago, AL | 106 | 243 | 24 | 58 | 8 | 2 | 0 | 18 | .239 |
| 1967 | Chicago, AL | 124 | 292 | 21 | 66 | 10 | 3 | 1 | 28 | .226 |
| 1968 | Chicago-California, AL | 63 | 111 | 8 | 18 | 2 | 0 | 0 | 7 | .162 |
| | Atlanta, NL | 16 | 37 | 2 | 4 | 0 | 1 | 1 | 4 | .108 |
| **Major Lg. Totals** | | 1105 | 3244 | 357 | 819 | 130 | 26 | 35 | 285 | .252 |

# 10 Jim Derrington

*Jim Derrington was signed by the Chicago White Sox at the age of 16 in 1956 for a bonus of $78,000.*

BRENT KELLEY: *You signed for a bonus of $78,000. What was it announced as?*
JIM DERRINGTON: Fifty.
*I've found very few who actually received the amount announced.*
JD: Yeah. I think that's the way it was done.
*Who scouted and signed you?*
JD: Hollis Thurston scouted me. I was actually signed by [Charles] Comiskey, though. They flew me to Chicago; I didn't sign here. Comiskey signed me himself. Thurston was the scout in southern California.
*Do you know how many teams were after you?*
JD: Not really. Three or four that I know of.
*Did you receive other offers?*
JD: Oh, yeah. The White Sox basically said they'd beat any offer I got from the start. It didn't really matter; they wanted to sign me.
*Do you know whose roster spot you took when you joined the team?*
JD: I really didn't take one 'cause when I went there it was in September and the roster was expanded, so it really wasn't a one-for-one replacement.
*What was the reception you received from the veteran players?*
JD: I would say the majority was fine. I got a lot of razzing, you know, kidding about the amount of money because at that time it was more than most of them were making. Other than maybe a couple isolated cases, there weren't any hard feelings or anything.
*Were the veterans helpful?*
JD: Yeah, I would say so. Definitely, on the overall.
*Was the adjustment difficult?*
JD: No, not really. I was only 16, but my uncle had played in the major

leagues and had played about ten years in the Pacific Coast League and my dad had played a couple years of professional ball. It wasn't foreign to me.

*Who was your uncle?*

JD: His name was Herm Reich. He played a year or so with the Cubs and Cleveland, played in the Coast League for a lot of years.

*Were you well coached?*

JD: I really didn't have any coaching at all, as far as pitching. I didn't do that much pitching. I got a lot of coaching playing first base and the outfield from my uncle and from my dad. As far as pitching, my dad tried to keep me as far away from it as possible because you hurt your arm, you're out of there. Other than straight baseball knowledge from those two people that knew something about it, I really didn't have much coaching as far as the pitching end of it.

Jim Derrington

*Was there any coaching when you joined the White Sox?*

JD: Not near as much as I would have expected.

*Did they expect you to do it yourself at that point?*

JD: Yeah. You had the pitching coach, *per se.* I think I learned more about pitching itself from other pitchers there than I did as far as straight coaching. It was very limited.

*Was there anyone in particular who went out of his way to help you?*

JD: Yeah. Dick Donovan did. He was a very private person, but I happened to wind up rooming with him. He was a very straight-laced, diehard Irish catholic from New England and maybe that's why they put me with him — keep me in line. I found him to be a very straight person, very honest, very *dedicated;* took him about ten years to get to the big leagues. He knew a lot about pitching and he knew a lot about the game itself. I guess I was fortunate in a way to room with him 'cause he didn't go out of his way to relate anything to a lot of people, but he talked with me quite a bit and he liked me a lot. I was Irish catholic, too; he kinda liked that, too. (Laughs)

*He had the reputation of being a tough man.*

JD: Oh, *absolutely!* (Laughs) He was tough on the mound, too. He was nasty. Nobody was gonna take his job: "Took me a long time to get here and ain't nobody takin' it away. No hitter walkin' up there takin' it away." (Laughs)

*Your first manager, Marty Marion, had a reputation of not liking young players. Your second manager, Al Lopez, did.*

JD: I was only there the end of 1956, so I couldn't really comment on Marion at all. With Lopez, I spent '57 there and spring trainings. As I look back, not very communicable at all. I mean I didn't talk with him hardly at all.

But as I look back now, he *really* gave me a lot of opportunity. We were in a pennant race all of '57 there and we damn near could have won the thing and he brought me in a lot of games—I think about 15 games or so in relief—and I started five games. Being 17-years-old in a pennant race, I look back and as I see things happen now, he used me a hell of a lot under the circumstances. So as far as being given a chance to throw and everything, he did a lot. As far as communication with him, there was almost none.

*You were one of the more used Bonus Baby pitchers.*

JD: Yeah, I know. That's why when I look back I see it now. At the time, I thought I wasn't getting any chance at all. (Laughs) As I look at it, yeah, I really did.

*Were you voted a World Series share?*

JD: Right.

*Do you remember your first start?*

JD: I was really actually more nervous pitching. I really hadn't pitched all that much. In fact, I got a base hit the first time up. [Note: He was the youngest ever to get a hit in the American League.] After the first inning or so, it wasn't too bad. I kinda settled down after that and I think I threw two, three, or four innings there and shut 'em out. It was really hell the first inning or two; I was all over the damn place with it. I'd played a lot of ball against professionals and everything and it wasn't really as much as who I was against; it was just being *in* professional ball.

In fact, that was one of the reasons Comiskey, when I signed, wanted to meet me first because of my age and whether he thought I was able to handle just living day-to-day under the circumstances—big cities and stuff like that—and whether I would be able to go out on the field and even play against major league ballplayers at 16-years-old. He said, "I've gotta meet this kid before anybody signs him anyway."

I'd always been around ballplayers. I really knew a lot about the game itself and how players acted. It wasn't that much of a cultural shock or having to look up to people I'd read about all my life, as I'm sure a lot of kids had it happen to 'em. All of a sudden it's "Good god! These are major league players!" Well, I knew major league players; it was not that much of a factor.

*Control probably did you in: six walks in six innings.*

JD: Yeah. The first two innings I was all over the place, probably four of 'em in the first two innings.

*Who was it against?*

JD: Kansas City.

*The bonus rule was rescinded after the 1957 season. Where did you go?*

JD: I went to Indianapolis for about the first two or three weeks and I got a little sick there. I started opening night in Denver in the snow, for Christ's sake, and I was out a week or so and then they sent me to Colorado Springs in the Western League, an A league, and I finished the season there.

After Colorado Springs, in '59 I went to Charleston in the Sally League, made the all-star team, and I was top four or five in everything: ERA, strikeouts, innings pitched, everything. The end of the year, just before the season was over, I got notification I got sold to Sacramento in the Pacific Coast League and I was thrilled to death because at that time that was a Brave farm team. They had no pitching at all! Man, I was thrilled to death! I finished the season in Sacramento, which was only a couple of weeks.

But then, during the winter I got notification I was sold from Sacramento to San Diego. San Diego happened to be the Triple-A farm club of the White Sox, so I was right back where I started from.

*How long did you play from that point?*

JD: I went to spring training in 1960 with San Diego and after the '59 year I'd had, which was *real* good, I was supposed to be the opening day pitcher and I was throwing as good or better then I ever had and that's when I hurt my arm in spring training.

I still could hit real well. In fact, opening day for San Diego I was playing rightfield and I played there for about two weeks or so until the season opened at Charleston. They sent me back to Charleston; I played all year as a first baseman and outfielder. That was in '60.

That winter I found out that if I was gonna be back in the big leagues in any way, shape, or form, it would be as a pitcher, so that winter I worked hard and was ready for spring training, went to spring training, and they sent me to Mobile in the Southern Association, which was a Mets farm club. That was the top farm club of the Mets their first year. It was their first farm club and they needed ballplayers, so I got sent there.

I was thrilled to death about that, but I was there about a month and they sent me to Lincoln, Nebraska, which was a White Sox farm club. (Laughs) I finished the year out there and I got through there and I knew then that my arm felt okay — it felt fine — but I just couldn't throw. And the doctors told me that when I'd hurt it. I asked at the time what was the situation. They just gave me a bunch of cortisone and the doctor said, "Well, you'll be able to throw again, but you'll never be able to throw like you did before."

And that's exactly what happened. I went back to pitching and I could throw and I got 'em out. I was at Class B Midwest League and I got 'em out there, but I just didn't have it. I figured, "Well, I'll give it one more winter," and then I went back to spring training in '62 and just didn't have it and they gave me my release.

*Do you think the inactivity as a result of the bonus rule had any effect on you, do you think this was part of your problem, or do you think the arm was going to be hurt anyway?*

JD: Geez, that's a hard one to answer. Who's to say? That's almost impossible.

*What is your overall opinion of the bonus rule?*

JD: Personally, I had no problem with it at all because I had played against professional players and had a couple of rocky starts, but the 15 or so relief appearances I had I think my ERA was under two. I had no problem; I felt like I could pitch there. I thought it was fine. I would have liked to have pitched more. By saying that, I guess I'm saying I shouldn't have been there because they really couldn't afford to use me as much as I'd like to have thrown.

*In 1957, the White Sox had two 17-year-old pitchers on the roster at the same time. I believe that's the only time that ever happened. You were one and the other was Stover McIlwain. Do you remember him?*

JD: Oh, he was a very, very good friend of mine. *Very* good friend. I lived with him in the minor leagues at Charleston.

I think he was a lot better than he thought he was. He fought himself a lot. I think he was always trying to do more than he needed to do; he was good enough as it was. He had a lot more mental problems pitching than he did physically. He had good stuff. I played with him all through the minor leagues, off and on. He came up for a couple of weeks there at the end of '57.

## Charles James Derrington

Born November 29, 1939, Compton, CA
Ht. 6'3" Wt. 190 Batted and Threw Left

PITCHING RECORD

| Year | Team. Lg. | G | IP | W | L | Pct | SO | BB | H | ERA |
|---|---|---|---|---|---|---|---|---|---|---|
| 1956 | Chicago, AL | 1 | 6 | 0 | 1 | .000 | 3 | 6 | 9 | 7.50 |
| 1957 | Chicago, AL | 20 | 37 | 0 | 1 | .000 | 14 | 23 | 29 | 4.86 |
| 1958 | Indianapolis, AA | 4 | | 0 | 1 | .000 | | | | |
| | Colorado Springs, WL | 31 | 139 | 10 | 8 | .556 | 125 | 97 | 180 | 7.06 |
| 1959 | Charleston, SAL | 40 | 176 | 10 | 8 | .556 | 134 | 108 | 173 | 3.68 |
| | Sacramento, PCL | | | 0 | 0 | .000 | | | | 0.00 |
| 1960 | San Diego, PCL | | | 0 | 0 | .000 | | | | 0.00 |
| | Charleston, SAL | 2 | | 0 | 1 | .000 | | | | |
| 1961 | Mobile, SA | 5 | | 0 | 0 | .000 | | | | 0.00 |
| | Lincoln, III | 25 | 109 | 7 | 5 | .583 | 102 | 76 | 102 | 3.47 |
| Major Lg. Totals | | 21 | 43 | 0 | 2 | .000 | 17 | 35 | 38 | 5.23 |

BATTING RECORD

| Year | Team, Lg. | G | AB | R | H | 2B | 3B | HR | RBI | BA |
|---|---|---|---|---|---|---|---|---|---|---|
| 1956 | Chicago, AL | 1 | 2 | 0 | 1 | 0 | 0 | 0 | 0 | .500 |
| 1957 | Chicago, AL | 20 | 4 | 0 | 0 | 0 | 0 | 0 | 0 | .000 |
| 1960 | Charleston, SAL | 84 | 264 | 36 | 59 | 8 | 3 | 2 | 39 | .226 |
| 1961 | Lincoln, III | 40 | 57 | 6 | 10 | 1 | 0 | 2 | 6 | .175 |
| Major Lg. Totals | | 21 | 6 | 0 | 1 | 0 | 0 | 0 | 0 | .167 |

# 11 Don Kaiser

*Don Kaiser was the first Bonus Baby signed by the Cubs. They gave him $15,000 in 1955.*

BRENT KELLEY: *In several cases, the actual amount of the bonus and the amount announced were different.*

DON KAISER: In my case, they were a lot different. The papers stated $50,000 and I got 15 — one-five. (Laughs) I asked a sports writer here in Ada, "What in the world's wrong with you? Why didn't you print the right figure?" He said, "Well, it's just more interesting for people to read." I guess he was right. My dad got 5,000 of it 'cause I was underage; I was 20-years-old. It was quite a bit of money back then and we were farm people and lived out in the country.

*Who scouted you for the Cubs?*

DK: Roy "Hardrock" Johnson for the Cubs. I had several of 'em from different clubs. I nearly got 60,000 from Boston. Wog Rice was the Boston scout and he followed me all through high school; he even furnished me with a car when I was dating my wife, who I'm married to now, 40-some-odd years. He went through his whole office and it all passed except Lou Boudreau was their manager then and he didn't want another bonus ballplayer as long as he was managing the ballclub. It fell through because of him — for $60,000.

My dad was sheriff here for 16 years and then he retired and went into the tag office business — tag agency. That particular day after graduation from high school, there were several scouts interested in me and we set a date for everybody to come up there and the highest bidder I was gonna go to. Wog Rice, from Boston, even though he knew that he couldn't get me, was gonna come up there and up the bid and get me more money, but nobody but him showed up. (Laughs)

*How many scouts wanted you?*

DK: I'm not sure. I wanna say just practically all of 'em; there were several of 'em. That's the reason we set a certain date for everybody to come in and bid.

*You were 49-and-1 in high school.*

DK: Yes, sir. Seven no-hitters and two perfect games.

*You began college.*

DK: That's right. I was on a basketball scholarship in my home town. It's East Central State University now; back then it was East Central State Teachers' College. I played one semester and I had told my coach I was trying to sign a professional baseball contract. He said that was okay; "It would be nice to have you as long as we can have you anyway." (Laughs) I did sign in February of '55.

*Did you go back to college after you signed?*

Don Kaiser

DK: Yeah. I got a total of 73 hours in. I was in law enforcement and I retired from there. I was sheriff here.

*Did you receive needed coaching with the Cubs?*

DK: Bob Rush was the number one starter, and Warren Hacker and Paul Minner. Sam Jones stands out more than anybody. Dutch Leonard was my pitching coach, but I learned more about pitching from Sad Sam Jones than anybody. I feel like I could have spent a lot more than three years in the major leagues if I had the proper coaching. I hate to say it about Dutch Leonard, but he did not help me *one bit*. But Sam would. He'd try to get out there and watch what I was doing and when he wasn't pitching would get out in the outfield and I'd go through a few things he saw I was doing wrong. Sad Sam was a very close friend. He was great.

Dutch, all he wanted to do was please the crowd — autograph baseballs and what have you. I don't know how he stayed up there myself as a pitching coach because he did not help me *one bit*. He was around a long time.

When I was out there pitching, in a little groove from what I'm normally pitching, well, he wouldn't try to correct me. He wouldn't do *nothing*. Not a thing. He wouldn't say between innings, "You're doing this and that." Or after a game on the following day, he wouldn't get out there and work with me. He never did.

You need help. You're out there working so hard on trying to get that batter out, you may get into a different groove, not trying to but it so happens you do. It's so easy to do.

I'd love to get back into baseball. I'd *love* to, as a scout or a coach or whatever. I look at 'em and I envy 'em now. Even though I've been in law enforcement all these years and sheriff and I'm retiring at the age of 57 and I've still got some time left and I think that I could help somebody.

*When you joined the Cubs, what kind of reception did you receive from your teammates?*

DK: Kinda negative. It was kind of a negative reaction because I was the first bonus ballplayer that they had. I wasn't treated bad or anything, but just not overwhelmingly great, just kind of another ballplayer.

*Stan Hack and Bob Scheffing were your managers.*

DK: Stab Hack was great.

Bob Scheffing won the Pacific Coast League out in Los Angeles in '56 and he brought his ballclub up there in '57. (Laughs) Bob Speake, Jim Bolger, and several others. Of course, he had a good ballclub in L.A. and they helped the Cubs a lot, but he did bring a lot of his ballplayers with him.

I had Clyde McCullough as a coach, and also Walker Cooper — the old veterans. I'd get out there and warm up in spring training in my first year–'55 — and I'd throw a curveball and I'd say, "Here comes a drop, like we called it in high school." (Laughs) He'd come out there and say, "You're in the biggies now. A curveball's a curveball." (Laughs) I never will forget that.

*Did you find the adjustment from farm boy to major league player tough?*

DK: I did. I sure did. I had to ask some of the other ballplayers, "How much do I tip?" and this and that. I had to ask what to do when we went somewhere, especially on a road trip. After the first round, you get to know what you need to do.

*Were the players helpful?*

DK: Yeah, they were. They were real helpful to me.

*Coming from a farm, you were probably more lost than a kid from the city.*

DK: Oh, was I ever! I never will forget the first time, right before the season opened at Wrigley Field, I was staying in a hotel about seven blocks from the ballpark. I walked to the ballpark for practice and after practice I came out of the ballpark and I turned the opposite way from the hotel. I bet I walked a country mile. (Laughs) I hailed a taxi cab and asked him to take me to the Sheraton Plaza Hotel and he said, "Yes, sir. You're quite a ways from it." (Laughs) I made a mistake by telling some of the other guys in the clubhouse the next day and I realized the sportswriters were swarming everywhere and the headline in the *Chicago Tribune*, I think, the following day said, "Bonus Baby Gets Lost in City." (Laughs)

*In '56, your second year, you pitched a lot and well.*

DK: June the sixteenth or eighteenth, 1956, I got my first start against the Dodgers. They won the [World] Championship the year before. It was in Wrigley Field and Stan Hack said, "I knew you were gonna start the night before, but I didn't want to tell you because I was afraid you wouldn't have a good night's sleep," which I probably wouldn't have. About 20 minutes before game time, he gave me the ball and said, "You're in there today, son." Bob Rush was scheduled to pitch, but he came up with a sore arm or something. I didn't have time to get scared, so I went out there and warmed up and I threw a two-hitter against the Dodgers, 8-to-1. And I got to start every four or five days after that.

*Later, you threw a shutout.*

DK: It seems like it was 7-to-nothing against the New York Giants or Pittsburgh Pirates, I'm not sure which.

*You weren't on a real good team. The Cubs in those days didn't have a whole lot of talent.*

DK: It was a second division ballclub. Ernie Banks stood out, and Gene Baker was the second baseman; of course, he was just an average ballplayer. Dee Fondy at first base, Randy Jackson at third.

*Your ERA was 3.59, considerably better than either the team's or the league's. You seemed to be on your way at that point.*

DK: I pitched better ball against first division ballclubs than against the second division and why, to this day, I can never figure it out.

I had two Games of the Week, on Saturdays when Dizzy Dean and his crew did the Game of the Week on Saturdays. I had one in Ebbets Field against Don Newcombe; that was when I first met Dizzy Dean in '56. Of course, Ebbets Field was a real small ballpark in itself. He beat me, 3-to-2, but I pitched the whole game.

I'll never forget the first time I batted. I batted lefthanded and I just closed my eyes and swung at one and hit a line shot to Duke Snider in centerfield in the farthest part of the ballpark. I backed him up and I didn't hold the bat tight and, I'm telling you, it rung!

I don't know what it was, but I just pitched better ball against first division ballclubs. I guess I faced Willie Mays 25–30 times and he got two hits off of me. One of 'em was a single, one of 'em was a home run. It's hard to tell you this, but the single was hit harder than the home run.

When you're playing in the Polo Grounds, down each line was about 240, you know. I knocked him down this one particular game and I came back with a sidearm curveball and he just reached across the plate and hit an opposite field home run, a 240 feet job. (Laughs)

*What happened in '57.*

DK: Bob Scheffing brought his people in and then you had Dick Drott and Moe Drabowsky and I kinda got out of the rotation. Then I just wasn't sharp. I might pitch every five, maybe seven days and I just wasn't sharp at all. When I did pitch, they'd knock me out pretty fast and then it'd be that much longer before I'd start another one.

That got me sent down to the minors for six weeks and I came back up at the end of the season. I went to Portland, Oregon, for six weeks and I think I had a 7-and-5 or 6-and-5 record out there. Then I was sold to the Milwaukee Braves in the winter of '58.

*How long did you play in the minors?*

DK: I played four more years. I went to the minors in '58. I spent some time with Milwaukee, but they had three 20-game winners in Triple-A at Wichita, Kansas: Joey Jay, Juan Pizarro, and Carlton Willey, so I knew where I was going then.

I spent '58 in Wichita, '59 I went to Double-A ball in Atlanta, Georgia, and I was traded to the Detroit Tigers in the winter of '59. I spent '60 with the Denver Bears and then I went to Birmingham, Alabama—Double-A ball—in '61 and I was released in spring of '62 from Hawaii, an independent ballclub at that time. And that was it.

*What is your honest opinion of the bonus rule?*

DK: I think it was bad back then. We were out to get as much money as we possibly can, but I think that minor league experience would have really helped a lot.

*You can say that the bonus rule was damaging to you?*

DK: Yes. Kaline and Koufax are exceptions.

*If you realized that you were not going to get the coaching, would you do this again?*

DK: No. I would go ahead and go to college and play college ball. Of course, if I had done that then, they would have knocked out the bonus rule by the time I got out of college. Who knows, you know? I would have had that college experience, too.

*You evidently had a world of talent, from what I've read and heard.*

DK: I had a free ride in college, if I just took it, kind of foresee the future, I guess you might say. We had a good four years in high school in baseball and basketball. Out of four years in baseball, we won three state championships and in my final year we won the state basketball championship, also.

Between my junior and senior years, I played semipro ball in Oklahoma with what we called the Duncan Cementers and we went to the national tournament. I had the honor of playing against Billy Martin when he was in the service with the Wichita Bombers back then. We didn't win, but I made honorable mention for All-American in that tournament.

My dad played sandlot ball around here for years and he was the sheriff here from '33 to '49. He always wanted me to follow his footsteps once I got out of baseball. We had an American Legion here and he used to transport our team in a pickup with benches in the back of it. That's the way we traveled. He always followed me real close. I followed his dream before he died and became sheriff here, but I've had it as far as law enforcement. I've had my share of it. There's a lot of headaches and you've just gotta handle criminals with kid gloves anymore 'cause they're gonna sue you. I'd much rather be back in baseball.

## Clyde Donald Kaiser

Born February 3, 1935, Byng, OK
Ht. 6'5" Wt. 195 Batted and Threw Right

| Year | Team, Lg. | G | IP | W | L | Pct | SO | BB | H | ERA |
|---|---|---|---|---|---|---|---|---|---|---|
| 1955 | Chicago, NL | 11 | 18 | 0 | 0 | .000 | 11 | 5 | 20 | 5.40 |
| 1956 | Chicago, NL | 27 | 150 | 4 | 9 | .308 | 74 | 52 | 144 | 3.59 |
| 1957 | Chicago, NL | 20 | 72 | 2 | 6 | .250 | 23 | 28 | 91 | 5.00 |
|  | Portland, PCL | 12 | 73 | 6 | 5 | .545 | 27 | 20 | 74 | 2.72 |
| 1958 | Wichita, AA | 10 | 34 | 2 | 2 | .500 | 9 | 5 | 44 | 6.09 |
|  | Atlanta, SA | 12 | 55 | 3 | 2 | .600 | 14 | 19 | 67 | 4.25 |
| 1959 | Louisville, AA | 33 | 123 | 10 | 3 | .769 | 47 | 51 | 122 | 3.37 |
| 1960 | Denver, AA | 35 | 142 | 7 | 10 | .412 | 106 | 51 | 174 | 5.72 |
| 1961 | Birmingham, SA | 23 | 95 | 4 | 6 | .400 | 35 | 24 | 96 | 5.19 |
| **Major Lg. Totals** |  | 58 | 241 | 6 | 15 | .286 | 108 | 85 | 155 | 4.15 |

# 12 Lindy McDaniel

*Lindy McDaniel signed with the St. Louis Cardinals in 1955 for $50,000, Among Bonus Baby pitchers, only Sandy Koufax has more career wins. He was an All-Star in 1960.*

BRENT KELLEY: Who scouted you for the Cardinals?
LINDY MCDANIEL: Fred Hahn was the Cardinals' scout that scouted me. When I signed, I signed in St. Louis and Joe Mathes was the head of the scouting system for the Cardinals and Mr. Meyer, vice-president of the club, and Bing Devine, was the general manager at the time. I think Harry Walker was the manager of the big league ballclub.
*You attended college for a while before signing.*
LM: I went to college one year. Oklahoma University. I was on the freshman team. We played basketball and also baseball; I was on a double scholarship.
After I signed, I went to college for two more semesters. I didn't finish college.
*When did you join the Cardinals?*
LM: I signed in August and I didn't join the club until September the first, when they expanded the roster, so that I wouldn't knock anyone off.
*Were your new teammates receptive to you?*
LM: I think so. I didn't come in as a smart-aleck, for one thing, and we had some older players, like Murry Dickson and Walker Cooper, and some of the older players kind of took me under their wing, in a way, to help me in adjustments and things like that, so I didn't feel that kind of pressure at all. In fact, when I started games, I think Walker Cooper did a lot of the catching and he was just like a father, kind of, to me.
*Who was your first roommate?*
LM: Willard Schmidt, I believe.
*Harry Walker was your manager your first year and Fred Hutchinson the second year. How were they toward you?*

## 12. Lindy McDaniel

LM: I only played for Walker that one month and Hutchinson took over the next year. Walker was very helpful when I tried out in St. Louis. Everything went really well in the workout and throwing batting practice. I did have a lot of poise and had a lot of experience to be an amateur, so I had a very mature arm for age 19.

I threw batting practice two days in a row and they could hardly get a solid hit. When we negotiated, that all played for me and Walker was extremely in my corner so far as wanting the Cardinals to sign me. He's the one that had to talk to Mr. [August] Busch to convince him, because initially he turned it down totally. When he found out what I wanted, then he turned it down. Bing Devine was the one that was talking to him

Lindy McDaniel

and then Harry Walker got on the phone with him. He was in his railroad car somewhere in the country — I don't know where — and they had to contact him by phone. When Walker got through talking with him, then he said yes.

*How was Hutchinson?*

LM: He was a very good man to play for and he was protective, I think, of the younger players and he was like a father image to the players, to the younger players especially, and brought them along slowly and was concerned about not putting too much pressure upon them too quick and this type of thing.

I was kind of worked in gradually. I was used as a long relief pitcher and a spot starter at times. I won my first four games and then I lost six in a row, and then I won my last three.

*How was the coaching you received?*

LM: I thought I had good coaching, especially Howie Pollet was good. Bill Posedel was good with young pitchers.

In my case, I was rather unorthodox, but it was more just some of the basic mechanics and things that I'd not been taught that well and smoothing out some of the rough spots. They didn't try to change your motion altogether or anything like that. I didn't have that kind of pressure on me.

*How was the adjustment from the country to the big city?*

LM: I think it is a culture shock to be thrown into a situation like this that you're pretty much on your own. I went to a small [high] school; of course, I went to Oklahoma University and that's a pretty big jump from a real small school to a very large university.

I had a strong sense of who I was, so that was helpful. I was not naïve in the sense that I would all at once go wild or change my values or anything like that.

How to adjust to a new situation — I guess my way of adjusting was more in isolation and developing friends outside the ballclub, people outside the ballclub that would help me, whereas if I'd gone at an older age I could have mixed a lot more freely and kept my identity, but when I was that young that's a very hard thing to do.

If I'd have approached it at age 30 or 35, then my approach would have been different. I would have been able to get a lot closer to the players.

*Do you recall your first game?*

LM: My first game was in Chicago the first day I joined the club. I came in in relief and pitched two innings. Walker Cooper hit a home run off of me, I remember. I think I gave up one run in two innings. I think he hit the home run in the bottom of the eighth.

Home plate looked like it was a long way off. I guess it was just the excitement of being in the big leagues and all this and you're out there the first time and it looks like it's about a hundred feet away.

I had a lot of raw ability and I could throw hard and everything, but you've got all that adjustment. Walker Cooper said that all he wanted to do, because I did have a very live fastball, was just to bat and get out of there and not get hurt. I gave him too good a pitch to hit.

*You spent about a month in the minor leagues.*

LM: In '58 I went down one month. I was having a terrible adjustment because my normal way of pitching was about three-quarters overhand and a lot of side motion, a lot of twist in my body, and a long stride, and a natural sinker. In '58, I started losing my natural stuff on the ball so that the sinking fastball was not sinking as well and hitters were waiting on it a lot more and I had to bring it up in the strike zone and I was getting hurt bad with it.

What I did, I had to adjust totally to a new way of pitching: straight overhand, which was short-stride, a different way of getting the power that I wanted and everything, so I made a total adjustment at the big league level, which is very hard to do, but I was forced to do that.

In '59, when I made the adjustment to straight overhand pitching — that was in May when I went to the bullpen. The next three months I actually picked up enough wins and saves that assured me of the Fireman Award if they had had it at that time.

Then in '60 was when I came up with the forkball in addition to the speed I had, so that's when I had it all together. At that time, when I made the adjustment to straight overhand, I was very natural in a way that I was in a pattern and I didn't have to think about it very much.

In another way, it wasn't natural because it was not the way that I was trained to pitch from a kid on up, so then in '61 I started having mechanical problems because what seemed to be natural all at once was falling out of place, then I had a terrible adjustment. That didn't happen until '61.

*Did you ever have arm trouble?*

LM: Not really, not any serious arm trouble. I did in 1963 in spring training hurt my elbow and I pulled some muscles in my elbow. I probably overextended trying to make the ballclub, trying to impress the Cubs, and I'd come off the two off-years with the Cardinals and I hurt my arm in spring training.

From that time, for many years, I had to take whirlpool treatments on my elbow to make sure that I could straighten out my arm good and everything. In fact, in 1963 I took whirlpool treatments before every ballgame and I led the league and got the Fireman Award.

Once I got through with that, in later years I never had any trouble like that at all, never had to use whirlpool treatments or anything like that. My velocity stayed pretty well good, pretty well constant.

I had to make a real severe adjustment in '69 when they lowered the mound and that was rather devastating to my particular delivery until I adjusted out. Then I found out I didn't need the high kick, I didn't need a lot of these other things that were extra motion that didn't really contribute to my control or speed. Once I made that adjustment with the Yankees, I was real good.

*Going back, you were traded to the Cubs after being with the Cardinals for eight years. How did you feel about that?*

LM: At that time, I was mentally tired because I had come off of two mediocre years with the Cardinals. Basically I would have liked to stay with the Cardinals, but the only way I could stay with the Cardinals was to make some severe changes in my delivery that they felt like I had to make to be successful. It was basically going back down to three-quarters overhand pitching and other things I didn't think would work because I'd been through that anyway. I knew I'd lost the natural sink on my fastball and I had to make it with control and speed and I didn't think that would work, but I didn't have the answers of what would work and I couldn't put the process together with the Cardinals. I started getting a *lot* of pressure from the Cardinals and from the manager [Johnny Keane] and I think the pressure really built up to the point that I was willing to be traded. To me, it was the lesser of two evils at that point.

*Did you get help in Chicago or did you straighten yourself out?*

LM: That's quite a story. I found out after I was traded to the Chicago Cubs that one reason I was traded was that Fred Martin, their pitching coach, believed that he could convert me into pitching the way he used to pitch. That was three-quarters overhand and curl my leg and throw the sinking fastball and this type of thing. Their idea was, they got me in order to convert me and in my own heart I didn't think that would work.

They worked on me from the first day of spring training and I said, "Oh, no. I'm in trouble." I had a lot of pressure on me there, so that's when I hurt my arm. I was really trying to overextend it without having my timing and my coordination correct.

So what happened, after three weeks of whirlpool and everything, I started coming out of it. I went into a beautiful delivery and coordination that I can't really explain, but my old stuff was back and my old fastball was back and my control was back and my delivery was back. When they put me in the games, I was successful.

I asked them, "Give me three weeks and if I don't satisfy you in three weeks the way I'm throwing, then I'll do whatever you tell me to do. I'll go ahead and throw your way."

They agreed to allow me that and that took some immediate pressure off. Then that's when I hurt my arm, after that. That delayed it further, and then by the time I came back I was on the beam.

That's a little bit hard to explain. I think part of it, I was trying too hard with the Cardinals and I was overdoing things in trying to find the answers. I didn't have any film of myself pitching in 1960, which would have been the pattern. Even today, I have no film of my pitching at any time. We've tried to find it through the archives of baseball and everything, but we haven't been able to.

If the Cardinals had had it in 1960, when I was really on the beam, I could have used that as a pattern. See, my problem was that I was so unorthodox that I couldn't look at another pitcher and say, "Well, this is what I should do." I would have to look at what I was doing when I was successful. 'Course, they have that being done all the time today.

*Your brother, Von, also received a $50,000 bonus. Did your brother, Kerry, receive a bonus, too?*

LM: Yes, he did. He received what we had received plus $30,000 more and that went to Dad. That was something we *all* felt should be done and Kerry Don was in agreement because we paved the way for him. Everyone was happy with that kind of arrangement.

*How far did Kerry get?*

LM: He played two years. It was kind of unusual circumstances, but he had back trouble and he did not continue to develop and continue to get better. Some of it goes back to his physical problems and some of it may go back to high school, where he was overused, I think. He pitched one game — he was a junior, first game of the year — and they pitched him 14 innings. It was cold weather; my dad had to go out and take him out of the game himself. My dad felt from that point on, as we look back, that he never had the same zip on the fastball and that type of thing.

That may have been a factor, I don't know. It's really hard to go back and try to figure it out. You're in a very competitive sport and just because you don't make it doesn't mean that you did something wrong necessarily.

*You are one of the shining successes of the bonus rule, but for everyone like you, there were several who got nowhere. What is your opinion of the bonus rule?*

LM: I think it's very hard to predict what anyone will do at the big league level, just based upon talent — how hard he can throw or how fast he can throw — because there's just a lot more to it. I don't think any one really knows, untried. There's such a leap from high school or college to pro ball and even a leap from the minors to the majors.

Today, what they're doing, I guess, is putting the clock on everyone — the pitchers — to see how hard he throws. It's just a big gamble.

You have Sandy Koufax and he threw very hard, but he couldn't control the ball. So then you have a lot of pitchers that can throw hard but they can't control the ball, but will they be another Sandy Koufax? Well, they don't all develop that control later.

I think character has a lot to do with it. I think what's inside the person, in addition to his ability. When I signed with the Cardinals, the first thing Bing Devine did was take me to another room and talk to me personally about whether that was my goal — to sign for $50,000 — or whether

I really wanted to be a ballplayer, whether or not my heart was in really succeeding as a ballplayer. I think that's a lot of it, because you can overcome all kinds of problems if inside you want to and you're highly competitive and you have the heart to do it. You don't know what's inside that person.

*The bonus rule was kind of a crapshoot.*

LM: Yeah, I think so. I think it was just hit or miss.

In my situation, I was a pitcher and it worked because I had a very strong amateur background, I had quite a bit of maturity for my age, but I had to go through adjustments at the big league level and I was very fortunate to survive.

You have an Al Kaline that was a very natural hitter, a very good hitter. I would think it would be more difficult for a hitter to make the adjustment than a pitcher 'cause a pitcher initiates all action; if he has a good catcher and he can hit the target, and he's got a good catcher to quarterback him, then he can succeed because he initiates all action. However, a hitter has to react to the pitcher and so he has to *learn* he's not gonna hit a great curveball unless he's seen 'em.

*Would you sign a bonus contract again?*

LM: I looked at a bonus contract at that time to assure that I would get an opportunity, whereas if you don't have the bonus contract you don't know that you'll get the same opportunity. I've always felt like I must prove myself, but in order to prove yourself you have to get the chance to do that.

Probably under those circumstances, I would do the same thing today as I felt like it would give me a better chance to have an opportunity. I have been in situations I always felt in baseball I wasn't looking for, necessarily, a level playing field. I always felt like I needed to be the best at what I did and *make* them take me. I was going to be good enough that it wasn't gonna be a choice.

That was always my thinking, really. It got me in trouble a few times because I think I got abused a few times with that thinking, but, anyway, that's basically my thinking. I don't want anything handed to me, but I want the opportunity.

I've been with organizations that I did not get the opportunity. I did not get the opportunity with the San Francisco Giants. Things occurred there where I was not given a good situation at all. Then I was traded to the Yankees in which it was a total reverse of that, where they really stood behind me and they gave me a *real* good shot to do what I could do, so I was able to succeed.

'Course, I'm looking at relief pitching. A relief pitcher is only as successful — he can't be any more successful — than the people that manage him feel like he is, because a relief pitcher is dependent totally almost on the manager's opinion of him in *how* he is used. There has to be that support, otherwise this can be very devastating. Ralph Houk in New York had confidence in me, felt I could really do the job.

*So you feel the bonus rule helped you.*

LM: Yes, I think it helped me. I don't know that I would have gotten the same opportunity without it. To say whether or not it was good overall — I believe in the free enterprise system — some people today feel if a ballplayer makes a million dollars or two or three million dollars, how terrible it is and here's teachers not making very much compared to ballplayers, but I don't think that's the fault of the ballplayer. I think it's part of the system and it's also part of the value system that we have in this country where people are willing to pay the ticket prices and watch the TV and all this. Without that, it wouldn't work.

You probably have a lot of greed that's going on, too. I don't like at all the idea of players not honoring their contracts or anything that's going on like this. I think if you say you're going to do something, that's what you should do. If you sign your name to it, then certainly you should.

Ballclubs allow that to happen and owners allow that to happen. Whether the money is there or not, I don't know. That's something that only the owners know. They're getting long-term contracts and commitments way into the future and is the money going to be there? I don't know. I would hope that it would be financially sound in what they're doing,

I think it becomes an ego trip or whatever. They [the owners] want another trophy for their mantelpiece and they're willing to pay a high price for that, but if it's not economically sound so far as the revenues are coming into baseball and everything, I don't think it's healthy for the sport.

### Lyndall Dale McDaniel

Born December 13, 1935, Hollis, OK
Ht. 6'3" Wt. 195 Batted and Threw Right

| Year | Team, Lg. | G | IP | W | L | Pct | SO | BB | H | ERA |
|---|---|---|---|---|---|---|---|---|---|---|
| 1955 | St. Louis, NL | 4 | 19 | 0 | 0 | .000 | 7 | 7 | 22 | 4.74 |
| 1956 | St. Louis, NL | 39 | 116 | 7 | 6 | .538 | 59 | 42 | 121 | 3.41 |
| 1957 | St. Louis, NL | 30 | 191 | 15 | 9 | .625 | 75 | 53 | 196 | 3.49 |
| 1958 | St. Louis, NL | 26 | 109 | 5 | 7 | .417 | 42 | 31 | 139 | 5.78 |
|  | Omaha, AA | 6 | 42 | 4 | 1 | .800 | 18 | 6 | 44 | 3.64 |
| 1959 | St. Louis, NL | 62 | 132 | 14 | 12 | .538 | 86 | 41 | 144 | 3.82 |
| 1960 | St. Louis, NL | 65 | 116 | 12 | 4 | .750 | 105 | 24 | 85 | 2.09 |
| 1961 | St. Louis, NL | 55 | 94 | 10 | 6 | .625 | 65 | 31 | 117 | 4.88 |
| 1962 | St. Louis, NL | 55 | 107 | 3 | 19 | .231 | 74 | 29 | 96 | 4.12 |

| Year | Team, Lg. | G | IP | W | L | Pct | SO | BB | H | ERA |
|---|---|---|---|---|---|---|---|---|---|---|
| 1963 | Chicago, NL | 57 | 88 | 13 | 7 | .650 | 75 | 27 | 82 | 2.86 |
| 1964 | Chicago, NL | 63 | 95 | 1 | 7 | .125 | 71 | 23 | 104 | 3.88 |
| 1965 | Chicago, NL | 71 | 129 | 5 | 6 | .455 | 92 | 47 | 115 | 2.56 |
| 1966 | San Francisco, NL | 64 | 122 | 10 | 5 | .667 | 93 | 35 | 103 | 2.66 |
| 1967 | San Francisco, NL | 41 | 73 | 2 | 6 | .250 | 48 | 24 | 69 | 3.72 |
| 1968 | San Francisco, NL | 12 | 19 | 0 | 0 | .000 | 9 | 5 | 30 | 7.45 |
|  | New York, AL | 24 | 51 | 4 | 1 | .800 | 43 | 12 | 30 | 1.75 |
| 1969 | New York, AL | 51 | 84 | 5 | 6 | .455 | 60 | 23 | 84 | 3.44 |
| 1970 | New York, AL | 62 | 112 | 9 | 5 | .643 | 81 | 23 | 88 | 2.01 |
| 1971 | New York, AL | 44 | 72 | 5 | 10 | .333 | 39 | 24 | 82 | 5.01 |
| 1972 | New York, AL | 37 | 68 | 3 | 1 | .750 | 47 | 25 | 54 | 2.25 |
| 1973 | New York, AL | 47 | 160 | 12 | 6 | .667 | 03 | 49 | 148 | 2.86 |
| 1974 | Kansas City, AL | 38 | 107 | 3 | 1 | .750 | 42 | 24 | 109 | 3.45 |
| 1975 | Kansas City, AL | 49 | 78 | 5 | 1 | .833 | 40 | 24 | 81 | 2.89 |
| Major Lg. Totals | | 987 | 2139 | 141 | 119 | .542 | 1361 | 623 | 2099 | 3.45 |

# 13 Jim Pagliaroni

*The Boston Red Sox signed Jim Pagliaroni in 1955 for a bonus of $85,000, the third highest figure under the bonus rule.*

BRENT KELLEY: *Your bonus was announced as $70,000, but it was actually $85,000.*

JIM PAGLIARONI: That's correct.

*The Red Sox were very active in scouting in the 1950s and were after many of the Bonus Babies, but signed only two, you and Billy Consolo.*

JP: First of all, there was a $4,000 cap at that time. Anything over that required that a player had to spend two years on the roster, so it really was a penalty against ownership and the players active roster to carry somebody that didn't have the talent to play in the big leagues that may be 17-, 18-, or 19-years-old. I think that was really one of the reasons in those times, economically, that if somebody was gonna sign for a very heavy bonus, he was going to be something substantial. They had to then put the player on the roster and could not send him out to the minor leagues for seasoning. He had to actually be on the bench for two full seasons.

*Who scouted you for the Red Sox?*

JP: Joe Stephenson. His son [Jerry] ended up being a pitcher in the big leagues for a little while. [Joe] Stephenson was a major league catcher, but his chief claim to fame came as a scout. [He signed such players as Fred Lynn, Dwight Evans, Rick Burleson, and Bill Lee.]

*How many teams were after you?*

JP: In the final, there was three: Milwaukee, the Dodgers, and Boston.

*Did they all offer a bonus?*

JP: Yeah. Boston said they didn't care what was offered, they would top it. And they did.

*Where did you go to high school?*

JP: Woodrow Wilson High School in Long Beach, California. I'm in their Hall of Fame, or whatever they call it. I was named all CIF [California Interscholastic Federation] Player of the Year in '55 when I graduated.

*Did you attend college?*

JP: No. I came right out at 17, had a Red Sox uniform on two days after I graduated and I was standing in the Red Sox clubhouse.

*Was the adjustment from high school to the major leagues difficult?*

JP: Oh, absolutely. I was 17-years-old. One of the key reasons I signed with the Red Sox was that as a kid all the way up I followed Ted Williams. He was my hero and there he was. June 16th or 17th I was on the bench and he was the first guy that came up and shook my hand. My lifetime hero.

I stayed with the club from June through the end of the year and went to spring training the following year — in '56 — and then Joe Cronin, who was the general manager, called me in and said, "You've still got a year and three-quarters left to do on your two years." At that time, the military still faced us. There was no six-month program; there was a two-year program. "Before you get drafted, why don't you volunteer *now* because you can go into the service for two years, get out with an early three-month discharge, and you get your service out of the way, and we have to pay you your salary plus your bonus checks while you're in the service *plus* the two years you're in the service count toward your pension."

Jim Pagliaroni

So I did. I think in March or so of '56 I went in the service. I really killed three birds with one stone: I got my bonus checks, which I had spread out for five years; I got my two year salary while I was in the service; got my service out of the way; and, also, he said, when I got out of the service, by that time that bonus rule was ineffective so I could come out and go right to the minor leagues. Instead of staying two years on the bench and still having my military in the way, it really worked out well. When I came out in, I think, March of '58 I went right to spring training and then I went to the minor leagues.

*The end of the bonus rule was beneficial to you and several others.*

JP: Oh, sure! One of the things that hurt Billy Consolo was that he had to sit on the bench for two years.

*Did you play ball in the service?*

JP: Oh, yes. I was stationed in Germany and we played something like 85 ballgames.

*What was your reception on the Red Sox like?*

JP: At that time, there was a pretty fierce competition. Even though I was a very amiable person — very outgoing — there was still a great deal of animosity. You could feel a lot of the tension, hear some of the crisp comments. It was rightfully so because there were guys playing in the big leagues—five-, six-year veterans— that didn't make the money I was making.

But overall it was quite well because I was a hard worker, had a good attitude, and kept my mouth shut. I would say maybe five or ten percent made sharp criticisms, innuendos, but that soon left. I was only subjected to that for three, three and a half months, 'cause then I went in the service.

*Mike Higgins was your manager.*

JP: He was very receptive. And Rudy York was hitting instructor, Mickey Owen was the catching instructor. They were great. They worked my tail off.

In spring training in '60, Williams' last year, he really got me over the hump and personally helped me in my hitting, which was great. I was a dead pull hitter and he got me to hitting the ball straight away with power, which was terrific.

*Were the other players helpful?*

JP: Absolutely! It depends on the team and it depends on your personal attitude, too.

*You rejoined Boston in 1960 and were in the majors to stay.*

JP: Right. I went out and played minor league ball in '58 and '59 and part of '60. I went up to the big leagues, I think, in July of '60.

*You were essentially the regular catcher the next two years and then you were traded to Pittsburgh. What did you think of that?*

JP: I was a pretty fierce competitor. I just felt that the management style of the Red Sox was one of ... well, I think I expected a little more attention to the details of the game.

I found that, when I went over to Pittsburgh, they played a tighter game of baseball because it was a low-strike league. Consequently, the dynamics of the game changes because of the low strike as opposed to the American League's high strike. A tighter game is played and you learn the finer details of the game in the National League.

*The Red Sox during the time you were there appeared to be underachievers.*

JP: That's well said.

*Was this due to management's attitude?*

JP: Like any corporation in business, I think it all starts from the top. Tom Yawkey, God rest his soul, was absolutely *wonderful* as far as treating his players first class. Guys would have mediocre to sub-par years and they would have a raise, whereas with other organizations at the time, you'd take a severe cut.

I know I had my best years at Pittsburgh and had a tough general manager in Joe Brown. I had to fight tooth and nail, even in good years, to get what I felt I deserved only because he was a tough general manager. That was not the case when I was with Boston.

*Are you happy with your overall career?*

JP: Yeah, I am.

Of course, I had a back injury; I had two discs removed in my cervical area. That occurred in '66; I had the operation in '67 and I was able to play two more years. That's the only thing. I think I have some regrets, but you have no control over that. That could have appeared in the beginning of my career.

Overall, I've always felt blessed. It's helped me in the business world in the sense that it gives me a pretty good backbone for what's after. I'm very thrilled with it. We — my wife and family — still have an enormous amount of friends across the country we still communicate with. I'm one of these guys that feels *very* grateful having done what I did. I feel that there's a lot of people out there that wish they could have played.

I feel sorry, with a tremendous amount of regret, for those ballplayers that have some animosity or some bitterness or left the game with that type of framework that something or someone owes them something. Instead, they should say I was very fortunate, it taught me something it gave me a background to go on.

*On August 13, 1955, you played your only game as a Bonus Baby.*

JP: (Laughs) I caught one inning and got a sacrifice fly. It was against the Washington Senators. I hit a ball to left-center and Tom Umphlett ran it down. I thought I hit it off the wall but it was right against the wall and I got a sacrifice fly. It was against Mickey McDermott. He was a character.

*Is there one game that stands out in your memory?*

JP: There's so many anecdotes to the game. The best year, the most exciting year, was the year that we — the Pirates— were in first place all year, battling the Dodgers. Unfortunately, we lost the pennant in the last four games of the year in '66. The Giants came into Forbes Field and beat us four straight. But that year was really an incredible year, playing with [Bill] Mazeroski and Clemente and [Willie] Stargell and Bob Veale. It was a great year. That stands out in my mind more than anything — that particular year — as opposed to one particular game.

*Who was the best player you saw?*

JP: Gosh, I was very fortunate in playing with or against seven or eight of the guys that are in the top ten or 12 in home runs— you know, 500 home runs plus. Willie Mays, Killebrew, Aaron, even Joe DiMaggio was our coach in Oakland, Billy Williams, McCovey, Clemente.

I think the two most exciting players I was ever around — bar none — were Willie Mays and Roberto Clemente. I think they had the same cat-like instincts in running the bases; it was almost like the game was created for them. It was such a natural God-given ability and you'd watch 'em in awe. Of course, I played with Clemente for five years so I really lean that way because I saw him every day, but Mays hit more home runs than Clemente. I think that was the separation point. Those were the two most *exciting* people I've ever seen in the game.

The greatest hitter I was ever around was Ted Williams. That is solidified by Stan Musial, Mickey Mantle, Hank Aaron — guys that played against him, they all say without question the greatest technical hitter of all time was Ted Williams. Even DiMaggio will say the best technical hitter, the best *controlled* hitter, was Ted Williams.

I called a lot of these great hitters' home runs— Mantle, Aaron, Killebrew, right on down the line. They all had it: compact swing, wrists, putting it all together.

*And a little bit of God-given ability.*

JP: Yeah. Nothing to it. (Laughs)

*If you suspected the outcome of the average Bonus Baby, would you do it the same way?*

JP: If all things were equal, yeah, I would. My parents didn't have nay money. My dad worked his heart out. He was from the old country and I saw the money as relieving my dad of some lifetime obligations, which weren't much, but he was such a hard worker that, bar anything, I wanted to help him out there.

At the time, I was one of those guys that would have paid to play, but since it was coming my way ... absolutely, I'd take it again.

*What's your opinion of the bonus rule?*

JP: I think it was an economic mechanism to prevent clubs going out and spending a lot of money. I think it was just a real simple design.

*Were you aware of under-the-table payments?*

JP: Yeah. I don't think it would be fair to elaborate, but I don't think it was done to a high degree, a high degree or a high degree of dollars. If somebody wanted to wave $5,000 in cash in front of somebody, that was a lot of money back then.

*The bonus rule did not hurt you, but do you think it was detrimental to others?*

JP: I think it hurt Billy Consolo and I say that because I was with him and around him. That's the only thing I can reflect on.

### James Vincent Pagliaroni
Born December 8, 1937, Dearborn, MI
Ht. 6'4" Wt. 210 Batted and Threw Right

| Year | Team, Lg. | G | AB | R | H | 2B | 3B | HR | RBI | BA |
|---|---|---|---|---|---|---|---|---|---|---|
| 1955 | Boston, AL | 1 | 0 | 0 | 0 | 0 | 0 | 0 | 1 | .000 |
| 1956-57 | | | | Military service | | | | | | |
| 1958 | Allentown, EL | 50 | 140 | 23 | 36 | 7 | 0 | 5 | 23 | .257 |
| | Memphis, SA | 44 | 119 | 15 | 27 | 6 | 0 | 5 | 20 | .227 |
| 1959 | Vancouver, PCL | 80 | 223 | 20 | 48 | 9 | 0 | 8 | 33 | .215 |
| 1960 | Boston, AL | 28 | 62 | 7 | 19 | 5 | 2 | 2 | 9 | .306 |
| | Spokane, PCL | 57 | 161 | 27 | 47 | 5 | 1 | 10 | 51 | .295 |
| 1961 | Boston, AL | 120 | 376 | 50 | 91 | 17 | 0 | 16 | 58 | .242 |
| 1962 | Boston, AL | 90 | 260 | 39 | 67 | 14 | 0 | 11 | 37 | .258 |
| 1963 | Pittsburgh, NL | 82 | 252 | 27 | 58 | 5 | 0 | 11 | 26 | .230 |
| 1964 | Pittsburgh, NL | 97 | 302 | 33 | 89 | 12 | 3 | 10 | 36 | .295 |
| 1965 | Pittsburgh, NL | 134 | 403 | 42 | 108 | 15 | 0 | 17 | 65 | .268 |
| 1966 | Pittsburgh, NL | 123 | 374 | 32 | 88 | 20 | 2 | 11 | 49 | .235 |
| 1967 | Pittsburgh, NL | 44 | 100 | 4 | 20 | 1 | 1 | 0 | 9 | .200 |
| 1968 | Oakland, AL | 66 | 199 | 19 | 49 | 4 | 0 | 6 | 20 | .246 |
| 1969 | Oakland-Seattle, AL | 54 | 137 | 11 | 33 | 5 | 1 | 6 | 16 | .241 |
| **Major Lg. Totals** | | 849 | 2465 | 269 | 622 | 98 | 7 | 90 | 326 | .252 |

# 14 Jim Pyburn

*Jim Pyburn received $48,000 from the Orioles in 1955. He had been an All-American football player at Auburn.*

BRENT KELLEY: *Didn't your son, Jeff, sign a baseball contract?*
JIM PYBURN: He played four years with San Diego's chain. He played Double-A ball for two years and Triple-A ball for two years. He hurt his knee badly in college and he had two or three more scopes while he was playing baseball, so he ended up going to law school out in Phoenix, actually in Tempe — Arizona State — so he lives out there.

He was drafted in football, too, and he had thought about going with Buffalo. In fact, he went to spring practice with Buffalo and worked out good and was running first team safety for 'em and that's when he had another scope operation. He ended up with a bad knee.

*What was your bonus?*
JP: Mine was $48,000 and it was sort of tied in with bonus and salary. My salary after the first two years was negotiable.

*Who scouted you for the Orioles?*
JP: Luman Harris came down and watched me play in college.

*Were other teams after you?*
JP: At that time, there wasn't any draft or anything. There was no other offer at that time, so I accepted that offer from the Orioles.

*Why did you choose baseball over football?*
JP: I had always liked baseball. I was raised from a family of four and my daddy worked in the steel mill. Then, that type of money — $48,000 — it doesn't seem like much today, but at that time one of the biggest bonuses in the South was Pig House that signed for $60,000. If you figured on what money would go for today, it probably would be $3- or $400,000. it was big money at the time and that was a factor without question.

*Do you know whose roster spot you took?*
JP: When I went up with 'em, I was sort of a utility player. I started

out playing third base but I ended up playing some in the outfield, so I really didn't take anybody's spot. [Paul] Richards had a combination of young players and old-timers there, guys that were sort of in-between being over the hill and having a year or two left.

*Richards loved young players.*

JP: Yeah, he did, but I don't think he knew how to handle young players. (Laughs) He didn't play the young players. Of course, that bonus rule was not a good rule because a guy had to stay with the parent club for two years. They were trying to discourage the bonus contract. I think I would have been better off playing down in the minor leagues.

*The Orioles roster had 20 percent Bonus Babies at one point.*

JP: There wasn't but three bonus players on the team that first year, then they signed a couple the next year. One of the guys, Tommy Gastall, got killed in an airplane crash. Had another guy named Bruce Swango, a boy that came from out west, and he had a little wildness problem. Of course, Wayne Causey wound up staying in the major leagues and playing for a good long time.

Jim Pyburn

*What kind of reception did you have from your teammates?*

JP: I didn't have any problem. I don't think many of the players up there had any hard feelings toward the guys that came in with a bonus. I think having the bonus contract and having to keep 'em on the major league roster discouraged the bonus contracts.

I really never did notice it. If it was there, I just didn't notice it. I think a lot of times if you want to find fault or find problems, you can find it anywhere you want to. I was up there to play ball, so it never really crossed my mind. It could have been there, but I didn't notice it.

*Was the adjustment difficult?*

JP: No. I roomed with a couple of guys. One was a guy

named Gil Coan that had been in the major leagues a long time and if I had any problems about tipping or what to do, he helped. He always went to the clubhouse early every day, so I went with him and we ate together.

If you get in with a guy that's been around, it sort of takes care of itself. It worked out that way because I don't think any of the bonus guys roomed together. I never roomed with any of 'em. The three years that I was with the Orioles, I roomed with Gil Coan most of the time and a guy named Chuck Diering.

*How was the coaching?*

JP: I think Richards, him and his coaches—Luman Harris and Harry Brecheen—I think they had a pretty good coaching staff. I think Richards, in my opinion, was highly overrated as a handler of people. I think he had a pretty good baseball mind, but I'm not sure how well he handled young players. He really wasn't a motivator. I think he expected some of the young players to have some of the savvy and some of the experience that the older heads had and it just wasn't there.

*Where did you go when they sent you down?*

JP: I went to Louisville in the American Association. That was Triple-A ball and I really enjoyed it.

During that third year, I played half the season with the Orioles, then I played a little bit with San Antonio and a little bit with Louisville, then the fourth year when I went completely away from the ballclub I went with Louisville. They had a ten-player working agreement [with Baltimore]. Del Wilber was the manager.

*How long did you play after that?*

JP: That was it—four years. I coached in high school several years and then, of course, I ended up in '64 going to [University of] Georgia [as a coach].

*How do you think the bonus rule affected you?*

JP: I think it took a couple years away that I could have probably been preparing myself for the major leagues. I think that's the worst thing that it did because there's not any guy hardly that can step out of college or high school and start playing regular with guys that have the experience— the Mantles and Ted Williams and Hank Bauers and those kind of guys— and the pitching staffs these teams had. It was just a situation that you played as a spot player and most of the experience you got would have been actually getting batting practice and working out in extra workouts. A lot of times, young players went out and worked out in the mornings.

I think I lost two years of baseball by the bonus rule. And I think all the players basically did. I think it hurt all the bonus players, maybe with the exception of a player or two like Al Kaline.

*If you went back and realized what the situation would be, would you do it the same way or would you try to get a minor league contract?*

JP: That's really a hard question to answer. (Laughs) I had no idea, when I went up there, how much I would play or how little I would play.

*There were widespread rumors of under-the-table payments. Were you aware of any of this?*

JP: I'm sure that went on. It's the same thing as college recruiting. I coached in college for a lot of years; I never was involved in cheating in recruiting, but I know of some people that had gotten involved in it. There were things given under the table to certain athletes and I'm sure there were a lot of players that played in the minor leagues that got more than the $4,000. I'm sure that was true.

That was just a club's way of dealing with it, is working under the table. I wasn't conscious of it. A lot of times, when you're 19-, 20-, 21-years-old, you just aren't conscious of those things like somebody else might be. You're another ballclub competing against them and knowing that they're doing that, you might be tempted to turn 'em in to the commissioner.

*Do you regret signing a bonus contract?*

JP: No. I never have looked back in anything. You have choices to make and you make those choices and you either do good at 'em or it doesn't work out, but it was a choice that I made at the time. I had a choice to go into pro baseball or stay and play my last year at Auburn.

I don't look back on it with any regret. In that four years I had a lot of *great* experience and met a lot of great guys and got to see a lot of great players play in the major leagues. I don't have any regrets. None at all.

*Who was the best player you saw?*

JP: I think Ted Williams, when you get to basic hitting skills, he was probably the best that's played in the modern era of baseball. I don't think there's any question about a pure hitter.

Of course, [Mickey] Mantle was in his heyday when I was with the Orioles. We played against [Willie] Mays in spring practice when we were out in Phoenix. The Giants trained out in Phoenix and we were training in Scottsdale. I think Mays and Mantle were the two most complete ballplayers at the time I was up there. 'Course, I played more against Mantle.

Whitey Ford had a terrific pitching career with New York. I was always fortunate to play against him a good bit 'cause I was a righthanded hitter and he was a lefthanded pitcher and I enjoyed the competition and had some good games.

There were guys when I went up there that I had read about through my teens and you kinda looked at 'em in awe.

I enjoyed my career and I wish it had been a better career, but I gave it my shot and there's no regrets about it.

### James Edward Pyburn

Born November 1, 1932, Fairfield, AL
Ht. 6' Wt. 190 Batted and Threw Right

| Year | Team. Lg. | G | AB | R | H | 2B | 3B | HR | RBI | BA |
|---|---|---|---|---|---|---|---|---|---|---|
| 1955 | Baltimore, AL | 39 | 98 | 5 | 20 | 2 | 2 | 0 | 7 | .204 |
| 1956 | Baltimore, AL | 84 | 156 | 23 | 27 | 3 | 3 | 2 | 11 | .173 |
| 1957 | Baltimore, AL | 35 | 40 | 8 | 9 | 0 | 0 | 1 | 2 | .225 |
|  | Knoxville, SAL | 49 | 163 | 26 | 44 | 4 | 4 | 3 | 9 | .270 |
|  | San Antonio, TxL | 26 | 82 | 6 | 15 | 0 | 1 | 1 | 4 | .183 |
| 1958 | Louisville, AA | 139 | 457 | 44 | 131 | 20 | 5 | 4 | 46 | .287 |
| **Major Lg. Totals** |  | 158 | 294 | 36 | 56 | 5 | 5 | 3 | 20 | .190 |

# 15 Jim Small

*The Tigers signed Jim Small to a $30,000 bonus in 1955.*

BRENT KELLEY: *You were required to stay with the team for two years under the bonus rule. How did it affect you?*

JIM SMALL: You're young and you're enthusiastic and [Al] Kaline had gone through it and been allowed to play and then in '56 I played quite a bit and looked like I was on my way. At that point, I thought it was probably the best thing for me to do, but I guess, in looking back, there was an awful lot I needed to learn about hitting and the relative lack of activity for two years was probably not a good thing for me.

It took me a couple of years [in the minors] and all of a sudden I learned how to hit and then I ended up getting rheumatic fever and I was done for baseball. I was traded at the end of the '61 season to Cincinnati. I'd played in the Texas League—first time I'd stayed healthy for a year—and I made the minor league all-star team and hit .319 at Albuquerque. I drove in about a hundred runs and just had a bang-up year. Then I got traded to Cincinnati and got rheumatic fever.

It [the bonus rule] slowed my progress down. I think there's people who can overcome it. I felt at one time in '57 in spring training—I had a big spring after I hit .300 for 'em in 58 games in '56—I thought I'd won the job and they said they're not going to play me right off the bat. So after the next 60 days I've gone to bat 11 times and I go to Charleston in the [American] Association. I wasn't happy being there. I thought I'd got a raw deal, but I hit over .300 and they brought me right back. I was there [Charleston] for about 45 days and I didn't play that much again [back in Detroit] and then they traded me to Kansas City.

I guess it probably would have been better for me not to have had to go through the bonus rule. I'd probably been better off going right into a [class] B league or something and spending two or three years down. Would I do it over again any differently? No. (Laughs)

*In '56 you really had a heck of a year. You batted .319 and had a great year pinch hitting. And you were extremely fast. With all this going for you, and the Tigers not going anywhere in those days, it seems as if you'd have been given a better shot. How did your managers look at you?*

JS: In '56 it was Bucky Harris and Bucky let me play quite a little bit. There were a couple guys who got hurt and that's how I got a chance to play. [Charlie] Maxwell and Kaline both got hurt on a trip; they both ran into the wall.

I screwed up a few times in the outfield. At that time, Harvey Kuenn was the team captain and in '56 we had a shot for fourth-place money and they were afraid that I'd screw up in the outfield and cost them a ballgame or two, so towards the end of the season they sat me down again.

Jim Small

But in '57 when I had the big spring, I think the only one who out-hit me was Maxwell and I was second to him in RBIs. Jack Tighe was the manager at that time and Jack was scared of his job. As it turned out, he had every right to be; he only lasted a year or so. I think he was probably fearful, and justifiably so, of putting me in the starting lineup. I'd just turned 19 years of age and I don't think he thought he could hardly go wring by using [Bill] Tuttle rather than some kid who might screw up.

When I was sent out, I think I'd been to bat only 11 times and I don't think I had a hit. They sent me to Charleston and John McHale was the farm director at that time and he said, "I'm not going to take sides, but I'll tell you what. If you go down there and do a good job, I'll have you back."

At the end of 45 days in the American Association, I was hitting about .320 and he brought me back. I think after I came back I hit .280-something, so I ended up two-something for the year. But, once again, it was periodically—in and out. Then, of course, they got rid of me over to Kansas City.

*What did you think of the trade?*

JS: It was a big disappointment to me because as a kid — hell, I was still a kid — all I wanted to do was play in Detroit. I'd turned down more money to go with Detroit. Baltimore had offered me damn bear twice as much, but I wanted to play in Detroit. And I'd been offered money under the table by a couple of other ballclubs to go to the minor leagues and play, but I wanted to play in Detroit.

It [the trade] was a shock. It's a time in your life where you seem to forget how you *did* feel. It's almost like it never happened, I guess.

*How did the Tigers become the team you wanted to play for?*

JS: Just as a kid growing up — [Hal] Newhouser, George Kell were my heroes. I was asked, "Why did you turn down more money to go to Baltimore?" I said, "I didn't like their hats." (Laughs) And I didn't.

Of course, Kaline's success figured in. And I'd played in the United States All-Star game in New York two years after he did. Reno Bertoia was a teammate of mine in that all-star game, and Reno signed with Detroit. There were different things that influenced me, plus they had followed me and wined and dined me, so to speak, since just after my freshman year in high school. They'd been *very* active. Then Charlie Gehringer was my coach when I was with the all-star team, so there were a lot of good connections there.

*The Tigers were very active in signing Bonus Babies: you, Kaline, Bertoia, Jim Brady, Bob G. Miller, Steve Boros, and George Thomas. Was Walt Streuli a Bonus Baby?*

JS: Walter? I doubt it. I'm sure Walter got some money, but it was probably under the table. Big, strong kid, great arm, tended to be lazy.

*Is there one game that stands out in your memory?*

JS: Oh, gee. I guess maybe my first big league hit — off Bob Lemon. That was a thrill.

Another thing I remember. (Laughs) I didn't get to do it, but I figured if I had to make an out it might as well be the last one. The last year Bob Feller pitched, he pitched the last game of the season against us and I made the *next* to last out of the game against him. I wish I'd been the last out he'd gotten. Might as well be a trivia answer.

*Who was the best hitter you saw?*

JS: [Ted] Williams. No doubt. That guy was incredible.

*How about the best overall player?*

JS: The most talented guy had to be [Mickey] Mantle. He had a year in '56; nobody could afford to pay him today. That was an incredible year.

Baseball was very strong at that time. There was a lot of identity and there weren't so many clubs. Baseball, I think, from the early '50s to the early '60s, quality-wise, may have been the best it's ever been.

I would suspect that in the '50s and *early* '60s, and, for that matter, the late '40s, you go through the American League and you might find five guys that struck out a hundred times. It wasn't really an acceptable thing in those days. Now you'll have five or six on every ballclub that strike out a hundred times. It's a different game.

Everybody's a weight-lifter now and they muscle up and it's just accepted. Now they're saying, "We're lucky this guy strikes out 'cause he doesn't hit into a double play." (Laughs) It's all in the way you look at it.

*The San Francisco Bay Area produced a lot of top ballplayers back in the '50s.*

JS: J. W. Porter was probably five years older than I was, but he was from the Bay Area. He was with the Emeryville [Oakland] American Legion teams that twice went to Cincinnati and won the national championships. He was a *legend* in the Bay Area.

We all played high school ball against each other — Vada Pinson, Frank Robinson, all of us. It was quite a hot spot.

I remember we'd go up and play Sacred Heart [High School] at Big Rec Park in San Francisco. His last year in high school, [Jim] Gentile hit about a hundred-and-fifty because everybody played about 400 feet back — there were no fences — and they caught everything he hit. (Laughs)

*Who was the best pitcher you saw?*

JS: I gotta believe Herb Score was. For those few years I was around, he seemed to be a notch above. He had a great fastball and a great curve and he threw strikes. And he was a tough competitor. [Jim] Bunning was a good pitcher. Of course, Frank Lary was good.

Probably the best arm I ever saw was a kid in the Oriole organization that never made it, and that's Steve Dalkowski. I hit against him a couple of times and the guy was incredible. Just incredible.

*No control.*

JS: No. None whatsoever. Didn't care. (Laughs) He was a beauty. And I don't know of anybody that's ever thrown the ball any harder and he wasn't that big a kid. Great arm.

*What did you think of your managers? You had Harris and Tighe in Detroit and Harry Craft in Kansas City.*

JS: Harry Craft was a lot like Bucky Harris — very quiet. Bucky was just a nice guy. You'd lose and he'd leave the clubhouse whistling; you'd win, he'd leave the clubhouse whistling. He had a job in baseball his whole life and apparently that was one of the reasons. I guess he'd get fired, he'd walk in, shake everybody's hands. He was never angry. Nice guy. He didn't say much. Never said too much to me; never got on my case, either.

Jack Tighe was a coach when I first came on the ballclub and an awfully nice fellow as a coach, but once he got the manager's job he became different. And I don't blame Jack. He was nervous about his job and he had every right to be. He was done in a year or so.

Best managers I ever played for would have been in the minors. That was John McNamara and Bill Norman. I played for John for two years; just a great guy to play for and so was Bill.

I came across John at a time that I probably needed a lot of help mentally and John was just great for me. I jumped the ballclub at Hawaii. I left and came back home and Kansas City didn't have anybody to take me. Finally, they got McNamara to take me on in Lewiston in the Northwest League. I went out and played for John a half a season and he turned me around. I think I played 50 games and drove in around 60 runs for him and got my confidence built up. The next year I went in the Texas League and that's when I had the good year there. I learned a lot just because he built my confidence back up.

I played for Norman at Charleston when they [Detroit] sent me down. I was down at the time and Bill would sit and talk and wouldn't let me leave the clubhouse without it. He said, "You're gonna play a lot of years in the big leagues." He was good for young kids.

*Did you save any memorabilia?*

JS: Do you remember a sports cartoonist with the [Detroit] *Free Press* by the name of Frank Williams? Back in the late '40s and early '50s, Frank did all the caricatures on the sports page. He moved up to where I lived and I got to know him over the years and he gave me a number of the original drawings that he did.

You know, back in those days, Newhouser and Feller always pitched on Sunday and they'd have the match-up between 'em. One of them [drawings] that he did showed the two of 'em and they still had the patch on their sleeves they wore right after the war years—the flag. I hosted the alumni golf tournament here for three years and Newhouser would come up, so I got him to sign it. Feller was at a card show in Detroit a few years ago, so I went down there and had him sign it. I had to pay five bucks.

I go to the alumni meetings down in Detroit and this is all they talk about; how much they're gonna get paid. I know one individual who has *never* returned or signed anything, keeps everything. Just obsessed with not getting paid, so he keeps everything.

*You said earlier that if you were 18 you'd do it all again the same way. Any regrets?*

JS: Yeah, that I didn't work harder at what I was doing. In a way, it came too easy for me early on. I had good ability. I had a lot of things going for me.

You think you're such a big shot at that age. My god, I look back now and I was just a flat-out baby! (Laughs) It's almost overwhelming to think what I was doing when I was 18 years of age. I was so incredibly young. I got out of high school and three days later I'm in Detroit and two days later I'm in New York. I wasn't allowed to stay out after nine o'clock at night at home and all of a sudden I'm tipping porters to carry my suitcase and eating at the finest restaurants.

In fact, back in those days if there'd been a school that they could send you to to indoctrinate you, I think it would've been a good thing. They could let you know what to expect.

## James Arthur Small

Born May 8, 1937, Portland, OR
Ht. 6'1½" Wt. 180 Batted and Threw Left

| Year | Team, Lg. | G | AB | R | H | 2B | 3B | HR | RBI | BA |
|---|---|---|---|---|---|---|---|---|---|---|
| 1955 | Detroit, AL | 12 | 4 | 2 | 0 | 0 | 0 | 0 | 0 | .000 |
| 1956 | Detroit, AL | 58 | 91 | 13 | 29 | 4 | 2 | 0 | 10 | .319 |
| 1957 | Detroit, AL | 36 | 42 | 7 | 9 | 2 | 0 | 0 | 0 | .214 |
|  | Charleston, AA | 36 | 134 | 19 | 48 | 7 | 2 | 1 | 17 | .321 |
| 1958 | Kansas City, AL | 2 | 4 | 0 | 0 | 0 | 0 | 0 | 0 | .000 |
|  | Buffalo, IL | 47 | 120 | 12 | 26 | 4 | 1 | 1 | 7 | .217 |
|  | Birmingham, SA | 86 | 307 | 49 | 81 | 10 | 4 | 2 | 23 | .264 |
| 1959 | Shreveport, SA | 85 | 268 | 46 | 74 | 19 | 1 | 3 | 34 | .276 |
| 1960 | Shreveport, SA | 65 | 164 | 30 | 38 | 14 | 2 | 2 | 13 | .232 |
|  | Lewiston, NWL | 19 | 29 | 5 | 8 | 1 | 1 | 0 | 2 | .276 |
| 1961 | Lewiston, NWL | 65 | 201 | 37 | 65 | 11 | 2 | 9 | 50 | .323 |
|  | Hawaii, PCL | 58 | 172 | 31 | 39 | 9 | 0 | 3 | 14 | .227 |
| 1962 | Albuquerque, TxL | 127 | 435 | 92 | 138 | 10 | 11 | 13 | 82 | .317 |
| **Major Lg. Totals** |  | 108 | 141 | 22 | 38 | 6 | 2 | 0 | 10 | .270 |

# 1956

The fewest (four) bonus signings took place this year, but the quality was good. The New York Giants gave Mike McCormick $50,000 and he went on to win a Cy Young Award. Moe Drabowsky (Chicago Cubs, $50,000) had a long and productive career, and Jerry Kindall (Cubs, $50,000) was a solid infielder for a number of years.

# 16 Jerry Kindall

*The Cubs signed Jerry Kendall after his junior year at the University of Minnesota, when he had been a first-team All-American selection.*

BRENT KELLEY: *How much did you receive for signing?*

JERRY KINDALL: It was quoted as a $50,000 bonus for three years; that is, it was a three-year contract, but in actuality it was a $32,000 bonus spread out over three years and then $6,000 minimum major league salary for three years. A total of $50,000, but $18 of that was salary. The bonus was $32.

I don't say that the Cubs misled the public or the media when they said $50,000 because they said it was a $50,000 package and I'm not sure that they said $50,000 bonus. I never did and my parents never did because we understood that there was 18 of that in salary. Now, they maybe said $50,000 package and the media picked up 'bonus.' I'm not ascribing any kind of misleading that the Cubs did.

In fact, I have tremendous regard for the Cubs. I was six years with the Cubs, four years with the big league club and two years in their minor league system. It was a tremendous experience. I have *great* regard for the Cubs.

*You were attending the University of Minnesota when you signed.*

JK: I had played shortstop for the Gophers for two years, as a sophomore and junior. At that time, freshmen weren't eligible. I was on the freshman team in the spring of '54 and then played the spring of '55 and '56 with the Gophers as the shortstop. We won the national championship in 1956.

Of course, this was before the draft so I could sign at any time and be signed by any club; it was a free market. I had a good year in '56 and our team, of course, had a terrific year in winning the national championship in Omaha, so I had a lot of attention because our team was doing well and I hit some home runs and I could run pretty good. A good many teams were talking to me and asking me to sign, but I wanted to go back to school. I was also a varsity basketball player for Minnesota and I had played as a sophomore and junior and was looking forward to my senior year in basketball.

My parents were *very*, very intent on my getting a degree. I was, too, but not nearly as much as they were. (Laughs) They had a better perspective; my vision was rather short at that time.

It was going to take a pretty good offer to get me to sign because I was aware of the Paul Pettits and the Don Kaisers, the Don Buddins. I knew that the money was available and if they wanted to sign me that badly and have me forsake my last year of school, why then it would have to be a pretty good offer.

I'd always loved the Cubs. My first major league game that I saw as high school player was at Wrigley Field — the Cubs and the Dodgers. In St. Paul, we had the Dodger minor league farm club, the St. Paul Saints, and in Minneapolis we had the Giants' minor league club, the Minneapolis Millers, so I had an affinity for them, too.

There was an old-time Yankee scout that followed me a lot and was very, very kind and gracious to me, gave me a bat that said 'Yankees' on it. That was Joe McDermott. So I had an affinity for the Yankees, but I think the Cubs, because I had been in Wrigley Field, the only major league game I had seen up to that point — no, I take that back, I had been in Comiskey, also, to see a doubleheader — but the Cubs were dear to my heart.

So when the Cubs

**Jerry Kindall (courtesy Jerry Kindall)**

came in with their offer, we decided to sign and it was a good offer, some people say a lot more than I deserved. (Laughs) With the permission of my parents and my college coach, the late Dick Siebert at Minnesota, I signed.

*How many teams made offers to you?*

JK: The Cleveland Indians, the Pittsburgh Pirates, both the Dodgers and the Giants because their scouts and their minor league front office personnel were right there in my backyard. By the way, they were all very, very good to me, too. Mel Jones, the general manager for the St. Paul Saints, allowed me to work out with the Saints as a high school and college player — you know, come to practice with them in the summer, put on the uniform, and take batting and infield. And the Millers did the same thing; they both wanted to sign me.

In fact, when I came to negotiate with the Cubs in our living room on June 30, 1956, and they made their offer, I said to Wid Matthews, who was the general manager of the Cubs, and Vedie Himsl, who was their chief scout, "I should make a call to the Dodgers and the Giants because they've been so good to me and they would like to sign me." They said, "Don't sign until you hear from us," and that kind of thing.

They [the Cubs' representatives] said, and very rightly so, "Son, if you want to do that, then we withdraw our offer." (Laughs) That wasn't unreasonable.

My mother and dad and I conferred for another ten minutes or so and realized that that was a fair response from the Cubs because, at that point, they had come on to the table with a very good offer and for me to begin bartering with them, or using these other clubs, wasn't fair. I truly didn't intend to try to up the offer; by that; I was trying to honor what the Giants and the Dodgers had requested. So I signed with the Cubs.

There were other teams. The Yankees were interested. I don't think any one of those clubs wanted the bonus rule of $4,000. Perhaps if we had gotten into some kind of serious bidding kind of thing, which I wanted to avoid, they would have come up with a comparable offer, but they all wanted me to go to the minor leagues, which is really where I belonged out of college. But I wasn't going to do that.

Without identifying the teams, there were several teams that wanted to provide equal things but not in money. For my parents, for instance. We were a very, very low income family and they said, "We'll take care of your folks. We'll take care of your dad," and that kind of thing, never with such specific information that we could really hang our hat on, and we recognized that that was not legal. My dad — he's dead now — was a man of great honor and integrity and he would not listen to those, other than just broaching the subject. He would close the door on it right away.

*There was a lot of suspected cheating. No one admits to it today, but there were too many rumors for it to be unfounded.*

JK: We never got into any details on that and the subject was just broached — what do they say? — to just float a balloon to see how the Kindall family reacted to that, but my father closed the door on those offers right away.

*Do you know whose roster spot you took when you joined the Cubs?*

JK: Yes. I do. That was a painful thing for me. It was a very popular infielder named Eddie Winceniak, who was a fine player, a utility man, but a good, solid player and very popular with the other Cubs. When I came in as a bonus player and reported July first, 1956, that meant that Eddie had to go. I had to take one of the 25 spots on the roster. I wasn't really aware then of some of the resentment toward me because of that.

I got to know Eddie Winceniak the next spring in spring training and to Eddie's credit — and I'll always appreciate this — he did not make it an obvious feeling of resentment. I know he was disappointed — heck, he had to leave the big leagues — but he was still friendly and gracious toward me the next year in spring training.

And, in time, the Cub players accepted me, too, but there was that first couple weeks because, heck, I wasn't going to move Ernie Banks out of the lineup and all the Cubs knew that. (Laughs) I was just excess baggage. I could pinch run a little bit, maybe go in to play the last two innings defensively if we were way ahead way behind to give Ernie a little rest, but he was an iron man and obviously one of the two or three best players in the big leagues at that time.

The other players had every reason to think, "What's he doing here? He's not adding anything to our winning effort." But, in time, I think they recognized this was all a business deal, too.

We had three bonus players on the roster and we all had to fight through that period of adjustment of some resentment from the older players.

*Were there any particular overt problems or was it just underlying resentment?*

JK: Nothing overt. There was never any verbal abuse. I kept my mouth shut; I was smart enough not to do anything other than just mind my own business and be friendly toward them.

I'll tell you who helped make the transition into being accepted and then finally as a member of the team was Yosh Kiwano, clubhouse man, who I just think the world of, and the trainer at that time, Al Schuneman. I knew Doc — Al — because he lived in St. Paul and he had been, for a long time, trainer for the St. Paul Saints. I had gotten to know him when I was working out with the Saints as a high school player. He helped me and Yosh Kiwano kind of took me under his wing to see that I did not offend anyone.

*Were there any players who went out of their way to help you?*

JK: Yes. Ernie Banks, bless his heart. Of course, he's friendly to everyone and I think it's a genuine response from Ernie. He's a terrific guy; he made me feel welcome. I don't think he saw me as any threat, believe me. (Laughs)

Walt Moryn, he was a St. Paul native. I knew him from the winter times at the Hot Stove League banquets and he was an accepted and acknowledged big leaguer at that time and he helped me over the hump.

Then, of course, the three of us — Don Kaiser, Moe Drabowsky, and myself — we kind of gravitated to one another. That was helpful.

*Your first manager was Stan Hack and then you had Bob Scheffing. What were their attitudes toward you? A lot of managers didn't like this idea at all.*

JK: And I don't blame them. All of us — the Kaisers and the Drabowskys and the Kindalls — could have profited by going directly to the minor leagues and putting in their apprenticeships right away. Of course, Moe Drabowsky became an outstanding pitcher in time, and so did Don Kaiser. Don was a high school kid off the farm in Oklahoma — big, long stringbean kind of guy — and he had *terrific* stuff, but we all had a period of adjustment in '56 and we could've helped ourselves better by being in the minor leagues and playing every day and pitching every day. I'm certain that Stan Hack and Bob Scheffing would liked to have had an experienced big league player in our place.

Stan Hack was very friendly. He didn't play me very much; if you look in the record, in that first half-year, 55 at bats. But he was very friendly and tolerant of me.

Bob Scheffing came in in '57 and Bob was also good. He retired in Scottsdale so I saw quite a bit of Bob after I came here to Arizona years ago. Bob had brought his group from Los Angeles. In '56, the Los Angeles Angels in the Pacific Coast League under Bob Scheffing had won the Pacific Coast League pennant with a lot of outstanding players: Casey Wise, Dick Drott, Bob Anderson, Bob Speake, and on and on. He brought in his own group; the Cubs gave him the freedom to play his own players and he did. I got to play a little bit more that year, I think.

Bob was patient and tolerant with me, but he chose to go with his own infielders: Casey Wise, and Gene Baker was still with the club, I believe, and Ernie played short, obviously. Gene Freese was another infielder he brought in and he played third base most of the year. He was an experienced big league infielder, had been with the Phillies and the Cardinals, as I recall. Bobby Adams, also, a good experienced guy.

So Bob Scheffing went with either his own players that he had managed at Los Angeles or the big leaguers we had made trades for. I was just yearning at that time, and so were the Cubs, for that two years to be up so I could go to the minor leagues and learn my trade a little better. They rescinded the rule of two years on the roster that winter, so I went right to Fort Worth out of spring training in '58.

*You didn't hit for a high average, but you had a good power year.*

JK: I hit .229 and I made the all-star team. We won the pennant down there in the Texas League; we won it by a lot. I played every game. How many at bats did I have?

*You had 512 that year and 610 in 1959.*

JK: I played just about every game, except for a few minor injuries.

That was what I needed. College and pro ball — there's quite a difference. It was good for me to go into a bus league and play with younger players my age. There were some former major leaguers down there on the way down but most of us were on our way up. That was really good experience.

And then in '59 I went back to Fort Worth but now it's in the American Association — we're up a level — and played Triple-A ball and had another good year. And then I was ready for the big leagues.

*Back to your first two years. A universal complaint from the pitchers is that coaching ranged from bad to terrible while the position players seemed to have received good coaching.*

JK: I got good coaching. I came from a college program I think was the best coaching of all. To this day, I don't think there's a better instructor, a better teacher, than I could have been under than Dick Siebert — the late Dick Siebert — at the University of Minnesota. I don't know if you know much about Dick, but he had played for Connie Mack's Philadelphia A's, had played with the Cardinals. He was 10–12 years in the big leagues himself.

Dick coached at Minnesota for something like 35 years. Dick was a *terrific* teacher, so I had the fundamentals in place. I knew the fundamentals and techniques of infield play and hitting and so on.

Then, when I got up to the Cubs, I think the Cubs recognized that and that's why they signed me, because many of the coaches and managers that I had there in the early years, they knew Dick. They'd played against him and played with him. They respected me because I'd played for Dick. They respected my ability and they built on that.

The first year, in '56, Pepper Martin was the infield coach. That was a wonderful experience to get to know Pepper. We had Ray Blades, who was kind of a hitting coach; we had Freddie Fitzsimmons, who was the pitching coach. And then Stan Hack was the manager. Those guys all paid attention to me, especially Pepper.

I have no complaint at all about the coaching I received, but I also want to say for the record that the coaching in college starting with Dick Siebert and continuing on into the present day and among the leading programs in the country in college, I think is every bit as good for the programs that I've been around as the coach, and I'm not blowing my own horn here — I have some associates here on my staff that are just *terrific* teachers — and then the other programs against whom I play out here in the west — I'm talking about USC, Stanford, Arizona State, then you go into Texas and there's Texas A&M, Mississippi State, Miami — there's a host of colleges and universities now that I think offer coaching every bit as good as the major leagues. Not particularly better — that's not the point — but I think we're every bit as good in how we instruct in the fundamentals.

*You returned to the majors in 1960 and were essentially a regular in Chicago and then in '62 you were traded to Cleveland, where you became an everyday player. How did you feel about the trade?*

JK: I was very disappointed.

I need to give you a little background here. At the end of the '61 season, and I'd had a pretty good year, I'd played a lot, I'd split time with Don Zimmer at second base and played a little shortstop when Ernie was given some time over at first base and then at the end of the season I'd hit some home runs and driven in some runs and I thought I'd had a pretty good year. I think I hit .244 or something like that. So for an infielder who could field and throw and run a little bit, that's a pretty good average. And the Cubs thought so, too, and they told me that,

At the end of the '61 season, they said, "Jerry, we're gonna make the move of Ernie Banks to first base and you're gonna be our shortstop next year. Ernie's agreed to that." And it appeared in the papers and *The Sporting News* and all of those things. I was so excited that I would get a shot at my favorite position. I'd been pretty much second base from '58 on.

I went back to school; I was still working on my degree than. I was on my graduate degree, I was in school in November and I called my wife to tell her I was on my way home and could I bring her anything and she said, "Boy, you better hurry home. You had a call from Gabe Paul in Cleveland." And just that morning on my way to school, I picked up *The Sporting News* and there was a big article: "Kindall to shortstop, Banks to first." I was really feeling pretty good about it all and that very day they traded me. (Laughs)

So Gabe Paul had put in the call from Cleveland and I returned the call when I got home. He said, "We just made a trade for you. We want you to be our second baseman."

I was disappointed 'cause I loved the Cubs—still do—but that was my first trade.

*The Cubs put Andre Rodgers at short who couldn't stop a ground ball with a net.*

JK: They felt like they needed pitching, I guess, and the trade was for Bobby Locke. Locke was a very promising young pitcher with a great arm, but apparently he hurt his arm or whatever and never really developed much after that.

So they gave Andre the shortstop job and Andre could hit. He was a good hitter.

I went on to Cleveland in the American League and Cleveland made me feel very much at home. I feel like Gabe Paul is a terrific general manager. I get a lot of dispute on that among the players, but in my mind Gabe was a terrific boss.

*A strong case can be made for you being the top defensive second baseman in the American League while you were with Cleveland.*

JK: In '62 I played every day. I missed, I think, three or four games when my mother died and I went home to St. Paul for the funeral, but other than that I started every game. I believe—you'll have to check the record—I led the American League in assists and putouts. That was one of my contract negotiating points for the next year. (Laughs) And we were way up there in double plays and I hit pretty well. I drove in some runs; I think I had 55 or 57 RBIs or something like that.

I could cover a lot of ground then. I remember that the first baseman for the Indians was Tito Francona and he was a very, very good fielding first baseman, so we had that side of the infield pretty well covered.

We had a good year. The Indians moved into first place in June by beating the Yankees in a four-game series—middle of June—and we hung on to first place for a while. Then our pitching kind of failed us.

But that was a good year for me and I was very, very happy at Cleveland, after getting over the disappointment of getting traded from the Cubs. I was very happy in Cleveland for the next two-and-a-half years.

*Then you went home.*

JK: Yeah, then I was traded to the Twins in '64 and that was the biggest blessing of all. My family was growing; we had three small children and my wife was pregnant with our fourth child in the summer of '64 and she was unable to travel, so my family was not with me in Cleveland in '64. They were with me in spring training, but then they went home to await the birth of Martha and I was just desperately lonesome. I was really struggling and hurting by not being with my family, and they were struggling and hurting by not having their daddy home.

So when I was traded on June 13th or 14th, just before the deadline, to the Minnesota Twins, that was the biggest blessing of my entire baseball career. I got to spend the last two years at home with the Twins.

I went to spring training in '66 and I was released just before the season began. Calvin Griffith made a trade for Chuck Schilling from the Boston Red Sox and Chuck and I were very much the same kind of players at that time: good defensive players but couldn't hit very much. (Laughs) I did not hit very well with the Twins.

Calvin called me in in Orlando, Florida, that morning and said, "We're giving you your release; we just made a trade for Schilling. We don't need both of you." (Laughs) I don't know whether he could have optioned me out or not—I really don't know—to the minor leagues, but, he said, he wasn't gonna do that because he knew that I was eight years in the big leagues by that time and I probably wouldn't want to do that, so I could cut a deal for myself. So he released me.

*Did you go into coaching then?*

JK: I had my family with me in spring training in '66 and we went back to Minnesota *very,* very disappointed and discouraged. I didn't expect to be released. I thought I had played a pretty significant role in the pennant-winning team of '65. I didn't hit very well—.196—but I had played quite a lot and then I had been injured with about six weeks to go in the season and never did recover from that injury. I was wiped out at second base on a double play. I thought that I had played a significant role and I was having a good spring training, too—swinging the bat okay and doing my thing in the field—and so I was *very* surprised.

We went home to Minnesota, pretty discouraged, and I made three calls to see if I could hook on with the White Sox, the Indians, and the Angels. I made those three calls, but it was the worst time to try to get on a big league roster because they were cutting down to the opening day limit, so none of those teams could use me.

Then, I had been assistant basketball coach at Minnesota—freshman coach—for two winters leading up to that time. Up until the time I had left for spring training, I had the freshman team in basketball. The athletic director at Minnesota offered me a job to come on as assistant basketball coach and fundraiser for the athletic department. And I did and I am *so* glad that I did that.

You know, I had other possibilities: to go into business and go into teaching. I was working on my Master's degree at the time; I was just a few credits away. I could have gone into teaching at the high school level;

I'm trained as an English teacher. So I had those options and my wife and I prayed a great deal about it. I had always wanted to be a coach. I admired Dick Siebert a great deal, and, although I wasn't coming on as assistant baseball coach because that position was filled by a very capable guy, who also I learned a lot of baseball from, but there was a position open as assistant basketball coach. So we prayed about it and I took it at a *significant* decrease in salary from my big league salary down to an entry-level job in college.

*When did you get into baseball coaching?*

JK: Three years later.

The assistant baseball coach resigned to go into physical therapy. He was also a trainer; he was a physical therapist and assistant baseball coach and he went into a clinic in Minneapolis. So then I became, for one year, both assistant basketball and baseball coach.

*That kept you busy.*

JK: Oh, it was impossible! And I was also chairman of the Williams Scholarship Fund, which was the fundraising arm. It was an impossible job, especially because the new basketball coach that came in at that time, Bill Fitch, who, of course, went on to the NBA not long after that, demanded a *great* deal of his assistant coaches. There were two of us and here I am in the spring out there as assistant baseball coach. It was not a good situation.

Bill Fitch asked me at the end of that first year, "What do you wanna be, a baseball coach or a basketball coach?"

I said, "There's no question. I want to be a baseball coach."

So I sat down with the athletic director, with Dick Siebert and Bill Fitch, and we worked out some additional duties in the athletic department and I became a full-time baseball coach and fundraiser and some other things, and I got out of basketball. We [Siebert and Kindall] were a good team. I was a young coach and eager and enthusiastic and he was a terrific teacher. Like I say, I think he was the best ever.

I've been at baseball ever since. I worked for Dick as his assistant for five years and then came here to Arizona.

*Back to your playing days. In 1960, you tried switch-hitting.*

JK: Oh, yes. That happened under Lou Boudreau. An interesting chapter in my life, I still wonder what would have happened if I'd pursued that.

Toward the end of the '60 season, Lou was the manager and he suggested — because I had pretty good speed — "Why don't you take some batting practice from the left side?" I thought, "Oh, no, has it come to this? Am I that bad a hitter?" (Laughs)

But I did. I fooled around with it in batting practice and the last series of the season, out in the Coliseum against the Dodgers, of 1960 I batted lefthanded against Don Drysdale and Roger Craig and one other. I had six official at bats as a lefthanded hitter. I walked a couple times and I had a sacrifice bunt, so I think I was up there nine times lefthanded, and, although I didn't get a hit, I had a sacrifice fly and I put the ball in play. I think I only struck out once, against Drysdale. You know, he could strike me out righthanded pretty easily, along with a lot of other people.

I was real encouraged about my lefthanded hitting. Maury Wills was my inspiration because he had just come up to the Dodgers from Spokane and he was becoming a big league star at that time. He credited it to the fact that he became a switch hitter in Triple-A ball. I thought, "Gosh, if he could do it at that rather late stage of his career, I can do it, too."

I practiced all winter hitting lefthanded down in my basement in Minneapolis and I went to spring training in '61 fully intending to be a switch hitter and enthused about it. At that time, we instituted the college of coaches. The Cubs had the infamous college of coaches, so Lou Boudreau was gone and these guys were very skeptical about my ability to bat lefthanded, 'these guys' meaning the eight or 12 or however many there were.

I switch-hit in spring training and I did get some hits. I wasn't doing too badly in the exhibition games. But then, toward the end of spring training, the college of coaches called me in and said, "We want you to give up switch hitting. We have plans to play you a lot"—which they did in '61—"and we want you to be our regular second baseman. You have some power righthanded and we need that from the right side, so drop that lefthanded hitting."

I protested. I said, "No. I want to keep it up. I want to continue. It's going to be a help to my career." So we argued a little bit. (Laughs) And they said, "Okay, if you wanna be a switch hitter you can go down to Des Moines." (Laughs) I said, "Oh, wait a minute! Let's talk more about this." (Laughs)

I relented and dropped the switch hitting and became again strictly a righthanded hitter and I had a pretty good year in '61, which led to my trade to Cleveland.

*It makes you wonder, though.*

JK: Yeah, I've always wondered and I gave a great deal of patience and understanding to the college players that came in and said, "Hey, coach, I think I'd like to try switch hitting." I said, "Okay, let's give it a shot."

*What is your opinion of the onus rule and how do you think it affected your career?*

JK: I'm ambivalent about that because we needed the money. We always had food on the table, but my dad was working two jobs. My mother was very ill with multiple sclerosis. She was in a wheel chair and my dad worked two jobs for as ling as I can remember, up until Mother died in '62, to support the family and to pay the medical bills.

So $32,000 cash was a *huge* amount of money and were it not for that — and then I shared that with my parents — it would have been very, very difficult for the family. I'm very grateful for the bonus money and the Cubs were very generous with me.

Now, my baseball development I think, if not retarded for the year-and-a-half, it was put on hold. I didn't progress as rapidly as I would have had I gone down to Double-A ball right away and then played a year or two and then come back up. I'd have been more prepared to cope with major league pitching and major league life.

So that year-and-a-half under the bonus rule was kind of a tread-water period for me. I don't think I necessarily went a long way backward in my development, but I didn't progress, either.

*You were a little older. Many of the 18- and 19-year-olds feel they lost ground.*

JK: Yeah, I think they did. I had the three years of college ball under a terrific teacher and in good competition. The Big 10 was a *very* very strong league then, and still is. When we got into the playoffs and went to the college world series in Omaha; we were playing against the cream of college talent. So I had that talent to hold my skills so I was ahead of those other guys like Don Kaiser, for instance, or Don Buddin when they came out of high school. I was ahead of other guys by two years in age and experience, so I could handle it a little bit better.

*How did you find the adjustment?*

JK: The other part of my being able to handle the adjustment was my parents. I came from a *strong* Christian background. My mother and dad were very upright and very, very Godly people and so they had imbued in me a strong sense of right and wrong — biblical sense of right and wrong — and so the bright lights and fast living kind of thing did not overcome me because of my mother and dad.

When you're thrown right into the big league mix and living in these plush hotels and having a lot of money in your pocket and a lot of time on your hands, that can be a deterrent to your career, and oftentimes it is. I'm not saying it was for Jim Small or any of the others; that would be for them to say.

The bonus rule, then, worked both ways. It was both an advantage and a disadvantage to the player and certainly to the club, too. It depends on how you handle it.

*Would you do it the same way again?*

JK: Yes, because we needed the money and also because of the club that I signed with. The Cubs were *very,* very good to me and the six years I was in their organization I have nothing but positive reinforcement of the Cubs.

You never know, it's just conjecture, but if I had gone directly to the minor leagues and developed the normal way — quote, unquote — I might have stuck in the big leagues longer, but I still had eight years in the big leagues.

*A couple of fellows have said that they're glad they did it and maybe they didn't turn out the way they had hoped, but had they gone on to college they may never have developed, may have regressed, may have been hurt and then never had the opportunity. By doing this, they received an opportunity they don't know they would have had otherwise.*

JK: If pro ball and the bonus rule prevented guys from going to college, then I've got to wonder if it was right for them. I think college is the best choice, by far, in most cases today and then, too, to get a college degree and to prepare yourself for something other than baseball, because the money, no matter how much it is, is soon gone. The career training in something other than baseball and the college degree — the credential — is going to sustain you for the rest of your life.

If it came down to choosing — if I had to choose out of high school to go to pro ball or to college — I would have said college, by all means. No matter how much money. Now, I didn't have the foresight then that I have now in hindsight, but my parents did and the adults in my life who really loved me did.

But college is the best option. Now, if you can have both — college and professional baseball — that's the best of two worlds. I can be grateful that I had that, but if I hadn't gone to college, if the bonus offer had been given to me out of high school and I had taken it — because you don't get back to college once you go into pro ball. Very, very rarely does a high school player signing a pro contract ever get a college degree.

*One of the benefits of the bonus rule seems to have been a higher college attendance level by the players.*

JK: It provided a means for them to get to college.

Attendance in college for a year or two is not the degree and pro baseball is not compatible with going to college. Anyone that says that it is is using a fallacious argument. You just don't have the time and pretty soon you have a wife and you have several children and you have more obligations, more bills. (Laughs) So in the winter, instead of going back to college, you need a job. That's the overwhelming truth.

*Minnesota became a baseball powerhouse.*

JK: Dick Siebert points to the advent of Paul Giel as the turnaround of the Minnesota baseball program. Paul was a senior when I was a freshman so I didn't play with him. I was on the freshman team, but, boy, did I admire him and watch him. He was an All-American in football, All-American in baseball.

When he came on in baseball, he gave the charisma and the ability to turn the Minnesota baseball program around at that point and from there on Dick went on to three national championships. The Gophers won in '56, in '60, and in '64. And that's a snowbelt school. To have done that, it's just unprecedented.

People began to pay attention, come to our games. You know, here's an All-American football player — Hey! He's also a pitcher! — let's go watch him. Striking out people right and left and scouts are coming in and they're winning games. So Dick Siebert said Paul was the key man. He's a fine person and one of the all-time greats in Minnesota.

*Do you have any regrets from your career?*

JK: No. Wonderful experience and I could enjoy it and really relish it at the time because I had a college education and knowing that when baseball was over I could go on to something that would meet the needs of my family and give me some satisfaction.

There were *so* many of my teammates who didn't have that assurance and so hanging on in professional baseball and hanging on to their big league jobs became an obsession. I had the comfort of a degree and the knowledge that I could do something after baseball.

I'm grateful to the Lord. I've been a Christian all these years and recognizing that God, I feel, has had control of my life if I'm faithful and He has provided blessing after blessing.

## Gerald Donald Kindall

Born May 27, 1935, St. Paul, MN
Ht. 6'2½" Wt. 175 Batted and Threw Right

| Year | Team, Lg. | G | AB | R | H | 2B | 3B | HR | RBI | BA |
|---|---|---|---|---|---|---|---|---|---|---|
| 1956 | Chicago, NL | 32 | 55 | 7 | 9 | 1 | 1 | 0 | 0 | .164 |
| 1957 | Chicago, NL | 72 | 181 | 18 | 23 | 3 | 0 | 6 | 12 | .160 |
| 1958 | Chicago, NL | 3 | 6 | 0 | 1 | 1 | 0 | 0 | 0 | .167 |
|  | Ft. Worth, TxL | 143 | 512 | 60 | 117 | 23 | 9 | 16 | 65 | .229 |
| 1959 | Ft. Worth, AA | 153 | 610 | 70 | 144 | 31 | 5 | 7 | 42 | .236 |
| 1960 | Houston, AA | 27 | 112 | 14 | 26 | 4 | 0 | 3 | 9 | .232 |
|  | Chicago, NL | 89 | 246 | 17 | 59 | 16 | 0 | 2 | 23 | .240 |
| 1961 | Chicago, NL | 96 | 310 | 37 | 75 | 22 | 3 | 9 | 44 | .242 |

| Year | Team, Lg. | G | AB | R | H | 2B | 3B | HR | RBI | BA |
|---|---|---|---|---|---|---|---|---|---|---|
| 1962 | Cleveland, AL | 154 | 530 | 51s | 123 | 21 | 1 | 13 | 55 | .232 |
| 1963 | Cleveland, AL | 86 | 234 | 27 | 48 | 4 | 1 | 5 | 20 | .205 |
| 1964 | Cleveland-Minnesota, AL | 85 | 153 | 13 | 28 | 3 | 0 | 3 | 8 | .183 |
| 1965 | Minnesota, AL | 125 | 342 | 41 | 67 | 12 | 1 | 6 | 36 | .196 |
| Major Lg. Totals | | 742 | 2057 | 211 | 439 | 83 | 9 | 44 | 109 | .213 |

# 17 Mike McCormick

*Mike McCormick signed with the New York Giants in 1978 for a $50,000 bonus. He won the National League Cy Young Award in 1967 and was a two-time All-Star.*

BRENT KELLEY: *Your bonus was reported as both $50,000 and $65,000. Which was it?*
MIKE McCORMICK: It was $50,000. Most of the papers at that time had $65. Through the years I never denied that it was $50.
*Who scouted you?*
MM: The one that got credit for it was Dutch Ruether, the old left-handed pitcher.
*What other teams were after you?*
MM: The Yankees were after me, but they wouldn't offer a bonus, even though I found out after the fact they paid some players under the table. I think Deron Johnson, who signed at the same time I did, got some money under the table. I've never been able to confirm that. We grew up in the same area and kind of competed against each other in high school. We had some pretty good players out in southern California in those days.

If everything would have been equal, I would have signed with the Pirates. Growing up as a kid in L.A., the Hollywood Stars, which was the Pirates' Triple-A team, let me come out whenever they were home — like every Thursday night — and pitch batting practice and kinda work out with 'em. And even though I was an L.A. Angel fan — this is the old Pacific Coast League — the Angels never extended that opportunity to me. It was really done through my American Legion and high school coach.

I pitched batting practice from my sophomore through my junior year once a week to the old Stars. [Bill] Mazeroski was there and Bobby Bragan was the manager.

When the Giants made me the official offer, we called Bragan and ultimately got to Joe Brown [Pittsburgh general manager] and advised them that all they had to do was match it and I would sign with the Pirates. I used to see Joe Brown as I played through the years and he used to always make it a point to come up and tell me that in all his years and experience, *nobody* had ever given him that opportunity.

I felt I kind of had an allegiance there. I didn't know one team from the other. I didn't even know what the major leagues were, never seen a game and all at once I was there.

He [Brown] told my father, 'cause he had to do the negotiating, that they were really weighted with bonus boys. I had everybody scouting me as a kid, but when it came time to come forward with offers, it was really [only] the Giants.

Mike McCormick

*What was your amateur record?*

MM: I know in American Legion it was like 49-and-4. Maybe 30-and-4 in high school, something like that. I guess I was so wrapped in what I was doing and doing it so well as a kid, that I didn't pay a lot of attention to the record. Today in the age of the computer, they can tell you anything you want to know; records are stressed so much more.

*Whose spot did you take when you joined the Giants?*

MM: I may not have taken anybody's at the moment because I think the official date that I went on the roster was like September first, when they could expand it to 40. It wouldn't have been 'til the next spring that somebody didn't make the club on account of me. They signed me in late August. My dad and I flew back there because he had to sign the contract. I wasn't of age; I was 17.

*How was the reception by your teammates?*

MM: As I recall, and I guess maybe being so doggone young I could have been oblivious to some things, they seemed to receive me pretty well. I think the fact that I came in September helped; I didn't bump somebody off the roster. The Giants at that time were an old organization and even into the next year, into '57, it was just a bad old club. They made major changes when they came West.

They played a lot of practical jokes on me. Don Mueller and Whitey

Lockman, some of those guys, nailed my shoes to the clubhouse floor, tied my glove to the hook in the dugout, put a couple of New York [telephone] directories in my duffle bag when I was traveling — I guess things they would do to any new young player.

But I think I was pretty well received. Wes Westrum really took me under his wing. He was closer to my father's age than he was to me. He and his family kind of took me under his wing and saw that I got settled okay in New York. He's a real fine man.

The first maybe half a year I was there, they had me room with Bucky Walters, the pitching coach. He was probably older than my father.

*Did you find the adjustment difficult?*

MM: I think the hardest part was all the free time I had alone. I guess you could say I was lonesome. I *really* valued my time at the ballpark because that was the only time I was able to feel like I was part of something. When the game ended, because of the age discrepancy, guys would go drinking or something and I didn't know what alcohol was. This was on the road.

Then at home they had families, so I spent an inordinate amount of time by myself. I guess the only good fortune was, at least in those days, for the most part, you could walk the cities without being mugged. I did a lot of that. I ate by myself, went to a lot of movies, just did things to keep busy, looking forward to going to the park.

*Did you have a roommate in New York?*

MM: No. I lived at the hotel on 57th and Columbus Circle.

Then I got married young, so the first year we were there my wife and I had an apartment in the same complex where Wes Westrum and his family lived. I didn't have a car so I was able to commute with him.

*That* was an experience. When you come from suburban California where everything's kind of Heinz 57 and go into the ethnic neighborhoods of New York City — I'd never seen anything like that. We happened to be in what was primarily a Jewish neighborhood with one quote Protestant housing project. When we went out shopping it was interesting but it was certainly different, with the Kosher food and the way they sold vegetables and fruit. We bought everything by the pound in California; they sold it by the piece.

My perception of the world was pretty small anyway. I hadn't been on an airplane 'til I went to New York.

*How did Bill Rigney, your manager, accept you?*

MM: Pretty good. I don't remember ever having any problems with him. I think he just was looking for anything that might be a breath of fresh air. The team was old. They were some hard-nosed guys, too. They were good guys to me, but you take your Hank Thompsons and Dusty Rhodes, Marv Grissoms—there were some old, salty guys.

*Rigney was your manager for a long time.*

MM: The last game he managed with the Giants I pitched. He and I sat in the training room—I was getting a rubdown—and he and I and the trainer were the only ones there and he told me, "I'm gonna lose my job tonight."

Here I am pitching and I think, "Well, that's great. What am I gonna do—get bombed?"

What happened was, he had been having run-ins with [Giants' owner Horace] Stoneham about [Orlando] Cepeda and [Willie] McCovey playing left and first. Bill wanted to do it one way, 'cause he felt the other way was weakening two positions, and Horace didn't want it that way. He [Rigney] said, "I'm gonna do it my way and it's gonna cost me my job." [Rigney wanted Cepeda at first and McCovey in left.]

And, sure enough, we won the game and when we came to the ballpark the next day he'd been fired.

*Rigney and Stoneham had other problems over the years. For one, Stoneham wanted Andre Rodgers to play shortstop and Rigney didn't.*

MM: Nor did the fans. He had a great arm, great range, but terrible hands.

Horace was good to me, but he was just a tough guy. He was an alcoholic and he ran the club based on whim—how he felt at the time. If he was in one of his drinking moods and he got down on you, man, you were *gone*. People used to say the Giants made such terrible trades; that was the basis for a lot of 'em.

Great guy. He took care of his players, but he was a drinker and when he got on one of those binges, you could be the best player in the world and he'd get rid of you. You can look back at some of the trades he made. They didn't make sense.

He almost bankrupted the team in New York and his salvation was to come to San Francisco and they were on the verge of bankruptcy there when the league took it over and he sold it. He was a nice man, but certainly not a good businessman. He had a lot of hangers-on.

*What kind of coaching did you receive?*

MM: I can't remember getting an awful lot, even though they did take some film of me in spring training one year. Bucky Walters gave it to me and said, "If you ever get off track, go back and look at this because this is where you're throwing at what I would say is the truest of forms."

But there wasn't a lot of coaching, not only as a kid but I think even all the way through my career. I never felt that I got a lot of one-on-one coaching. Someone was there to try to keep you in shape and keep you busy, but not instruct. I always tell people that all the years I played with the Giants, which was a lot, not *once* did Carl Hubbell come up to me and share with me how he threw his screwball or ask me how I threw mine. Here's a guy that was famous, worked in the organization, was always around—but I think that's just the way it was.

I think why you didn't get the training—you weren't part of their plans at the moment, so they spent more time with the guys they were gonna try to run out there every day.

*Do you remember your first game?*

MM: Oh, yeah.

The first game I came in in relief against the Phillies on Labor Day weekend and I pitched to—I don't remember the exact order—Del Ennis, Jim Greengrass, and Stan Lopata, had three ground balls to second base. I thought, "Boy, this league's not gonna be so tough."

That was like Monday and I started a game, I think, Thursday night in Philadelphia. I went to the fourth or fifth inning, but I was wilder'n a March hare. I think it happened so quick on Labor Day I didn't have a chance to get nervous, but when they told me I was gonna start and gave me a couple days' preparation I had a chance to get nervous. I was never wild or one to have any control problems, but I sure had 'em there. If you look at my whole career, even with all the arm problems I had, I still never walked many players.

I pitched against Curt Simmons in that game. I don't remember whether we won or lost; I know I didn't get a decision.

I was 0-and-1 that year. I lost a game in the Polo Grounds against the Cardinals, I think—whatever team Alvin Dark was on.

*Even though you were able to be sent down at the start of 1958, you were in the rotation then.*

MM: I pitched enough in '57—I say enough, I guess I pitched around a hundred innings—and they just wanted to make a major change. I think they wanted to start in San Francisco with a young ballclub. I was still the extreme, but that's when they brought in Cepeda and [Jim] Davenport and a lot of young players. I think they saw at least an equal value in me as some of the old guys they had, so they just let 'em go.

*The '58 Giants were a good team.*

MM: Yeah. We had nothing but good teams, we just couldn't win [the pennant]. We were always the best second place team.

*In 1959, you pitched a rain-shortened, five-inning ho-hitter and the rule change on no-hitters took it away.*

MM: I was driving in my car and I heard it. I thought, "There goes my asterisk." (Laughs)

## 17. Mike McCormick

I shouldn't have had a no-hitter, anyway. The records will reflect that Richie Ashburn got a hit in the sixth inning and it got washed out. I think some of the other guys maybe are being slighted or shorted [by the ruling].

I don't know the rationale behind some of these things. They [the rules committee] have got to have better things to do.

*You were traded to Baltimore in 1963.*

MM: The '62 season was probably the most difficult one in my career because I had been among the leaders of the Giants' pitching for three or four years and then came up with a sore arm.

Actually, my arm started bothering me at the end of the '61 season, but when I went to spring training in '62 I could just never get it in shape and come out of it. I was in some ways useless on the club that year. I won a couple of important games at the time for them, but I never really felt part of that team.

I think your first trade, you view as nobody wants you—"They're getting rid of me." You don't think, "There's always somebody on the other side that's accepting you." The Orioles kind of made it an easy transition for me.

That [the trade] was hard. I had settled into the Bay Area, I was from California, the Giants were the only organization I had known. To have somebody say, "We don't want you anymore," was hard.

But after that you start to learn that you're just a commodity and you go where they send you or you go home.

*You struggled in Baltimore.*

MM: The '62 and '63 seasons were very difficult times for me. The Orioles sent me to Rochester. You could call it a rehab, you could call it whatever you want, but I was sent there to find out if I could pitch. I still had some arm problems, but I pitched pretty well.

Hank Bauer [Baltimore manager] was never a great fan of mine, or me of him. He really liked those hard throwers, and they had 'em. [Jim] Palmer had come up and they had [Dave] McNally and [Steve] Barber and [Milt] Pappas and Wally Bunker and I was certainly expendable, so in the spring of '65, toward the end of the spring, I was traded to the Senators.

I did really well there. I was not a regular starter; I was kind of a jack-of-all-trades. I started, relieved—short relief, long relief—did a little bit of everything, and, as a result, created a market for myself again. I wound up going back to the Giants. It was like coming home. (Laughs)

*By this time, you were a heck of a pitcher.*

MM: I was certainly a more refined pitcher than I had been. I still was never as talented as I was before I hurt my shoulder, but I learned a lot. I was able to continue to have good control and savvy and be left-handed, which was always a plus.

*Overall, your career was probably second only to Koufax among Bonus Baby pitchers.*

MM: People say, "If you could do it over, would you do it differently?" I wouldn't do anything differently. I just would have loved to play that same period of time healthy. They were talking about the next Warren Spahn and that was certainly being put in select company. I always felt I was blessed with a lot of God-given talent and then I had that doggone shoulder thing. It really set me back.

*Did you have surgery?*

MM: No. I worked it out. I went the cortisone route and I pitched some games I probably shouldn't have, taking pain pills. The shoulder never was, and still isn't, the same, but you learn to get by. I became a short-armer, not by design — that's just what happened. Your whole method and mode of pitching just changes. Fortunately, I was able to survive. Most guys didn't.

I saw some of those that had surgery and, boy, you talk about layered out! In elbow surgery, those guys had nine, ten inch incisions. In shoulder surgery, they literally went right through everything. Surgery today has advanced so much. It's saved a lot of guys' careers.

*You suffered much less than most from the bonus rule. What is your opinion of the rule?*

MM: If you look at the rule itself, it probably was not a good one. It was a hindrance to all of us. I happened to be the right guy in the right organization. They [the Giants] relocated and wanted to go young and I fit in to all of that.

I used to talk to some of the bonus players. We probably didn't have a lot of other people to talk to, or at least we had something in common to talk about. Some of those guys were just frustrated as hell because they were given *no* opportunity to see if they *couldn't* make it. They were just there. At least I got a chance to spot pitch an inning here, an inning there, start once in a while.

*Any regrets?*

MM: No, only that I wasn't healthy. That's all.

On any given day, or parts of any given season, you had differences with somebody, but by and large I got along with just about everybody I ever played with or worked under as a player. I was a player rep a lot, so I had a taste of dealing with management. I had good relationships with everybody; I don't think there's anybody out there that would say I was a lousy guy.

## Michael Francis McCormick

Born September 29, 1938, Pasadena, CA
Ht. 6'2" Wt. 195 Batted and Threw Left

| Year | Team, Lg. | G | IP | W | L | Pct | SO | BB | G | ERA |
|---|---|---|---|---|---|---|---|---|---|---|
| 1956 | New York, NL | 3 | 7 | 0 | 1 | .000 | 4 | 10 | 7 | 9.00 |
| 1957 | New York, NL | 24 | 75 | 3 | 1 | .750 | 50 | 32 | 79 | 4.08 |
| 1958 | San Francisco, NL | 42 | 175 | 11 | 8 | .579 | 82 | 60 | 192 | 4.60 |
| 1959 | San Francisco, NL | 47 | 226 | 12 | 16 | .429 | 151 | 86 | 213 | 3.98 |
| 1960 | San Francisco, NL | 40 | 253 | 15 | 12 | .556 | 154 | 65 | 228 | 2.70 |
| 1961 | San Francisco, NL | 40 | 250 | 13 | 16 | .448 | 163 | 75 | 235 | 3.20 |
| 1962 | San Francisco, NL | 28 | 99 | 5 | 5 | .500 | 42 | 45 | 112 | 5.86 |
| 1963 | Baltimore, AL | 25 | 136 | 6 | 8 | .429 | 75 | 66 | 132 | 4.30 |
| 1964 | Baltimore, AL | 4 | 17 | 0 | 2 | .000 | 13 | 8 | 21 | 5.29 |
|  | Rochester, IL | 29 | 186 | 12 | 8 | .600 | 129 | 54 | 183 | 3.29 |
| 1965 | Washington, AL | 44 | 158 | 8 | 8 | .500 | 88 | 36 | 158 | 3.36 |
| 1966 | Washington, AL | 41 | 216 | 11 | 14 | .440 | 101 | 51 | 193 | 3.46 |
| 1967 | San Francisco, NL | 40 | 262 | 22 | 10 | .688 | 150 | 81 | 220 | 2.85 |
| 1968 | San Francisco, NL | 38 | 198 | 12 | 14 | .462 | 121 | 49 | 196 | 3.59 |
| 1969 | San Francisco, NL | 32 | 197 | 11 | 9 | .550 | 76 | 77 | 175 | 3.34 |
| 1970 | San Francisco, NL | 23 | 78 | 3 | 4 | .429 | 37 | 36 | 80 | 6.23 |
| 1971 | Kansas City, AL | 4 | 10 | 0 | 0 | .000 | 2 | 5 | 14 | 9.00 |
| 1972 | Phoenix-Hawaii, PCL | 27 | 190 | 14 | 9 | .609 | 104 | 59 | 183 | 3.51 |
| 1973 | Hawaii-Tacoma, PCL | 30 | 204 | 8 | 14 | .364 | 83 | 70 | 223 | 3.75 |
| Major Lg. Totals |  | 484 | 1281 | 134 | 128 | .511 | 1321 | 795 | 1281 | 3.73 |

# 1957

The Bonus Rule was scrapped after this season. The 14 signees marked the second most signed in one year, and the quality was down.

The Milwaukee Braves paid out the two highest bonuses given under the rule: Bib "Hawk" Taylor received $112,000 and John DeMerit got $100,000.

Useful major leaguers signed this year include Steve Boros (Tigers, $26,000), Jay Hook (Cincinnati, $65,000), Don Pavletich (also Cincinnati, $30,000), Bob L. Miller (Cardinals, $25,000), and Jerry Walker (Baltimore, $20,000).

# 18 Steve Boros

*Steve Boros signed in 1957, the last year of the bonus rule.*

BRENT KELLEY: *Several of the announced bonuses were not the actual amounts. Yours was announced as $25,000.*

STEVE BOROS: Mine was accurate. Actually, it was $26,000. Everybody in my hometown speculated that it was more than that, but that was the amount of the bonus.

*Who was the signing scout? Pat Mullin scouted you part of the time, at least.*

SB: I think maybe Ed Katalinas and Pat Mullin got credit, and they might have mentioned Gene Desautels, too, who was the Tigers scout who lived in Flint, Michigan, at the time.

*How many teams were after you?*

SB: It's hard to say because a number of them had talked to me but we had kind of discouraged them because I didn't think I was gonna sign. I really thought I was gonna go back for my senior year in college. I just didn't think I was gonna be able to get a bonus contract from the Tigers and when it happened, I just simply signed. I didn't want to go anyplace else — I'd been raised in Flint, I'd been a Tigers fan all my life, so had my parents — and we just didn't want to really consider any other offers. Once we found out the Tigers were willing to go beyond the $4,000 that put you in the category of being a bonus player, we just kinda sat down with Mr. [John] McHale and threw a few figures around. It wasn't that no one else even knew that I was even thinking about signing. In fact, when I signed with the Tigers it wasn't the kind of piece negotiating that would make a text on negotiating at the Harvard business school. I wanted to get a home for my family, I wanted to get myself through school, I wanted to get my brother through school, and I wanted to get a car and we added those figures up and we came up with $26.000.

No one else even knew that I was even thinking about signing. In fact, when I signed, I told the Tigers I would appreciate it if they would just write a brief note to all the scouting directors because I think I talked to almost every major league club in baseball at some time and I knew a lot of scouts might get in trouble if I signed because their parent organizations would say, "Well, how come you weren't in on this?" and "How come you didn't know that Steve Boros was gonna sign?" I didn't wanna get those scouts in trouble; I'd been scouted enough to know that those scouts are supposed to keep track of boys and get a handle on whether they're thinking about signing and, if they are, how much would it take to sign them.

But this thing with the Tigers happened so quickly and all they had been talking about for a long time had been a minor league contract, that when they finally said they'd be wiling to pay a bonus, like I said, in a few minutes we came up with some figures and that was it. But, as I said, part of the arrangement I made with them was I wanted the Tigers to notify by wire all the parent organizations and the scouting directors that I'd signed with the Tigers (and) no one else was really in the hunt and that the decision was final and I really wasn't ready to consider any other team.

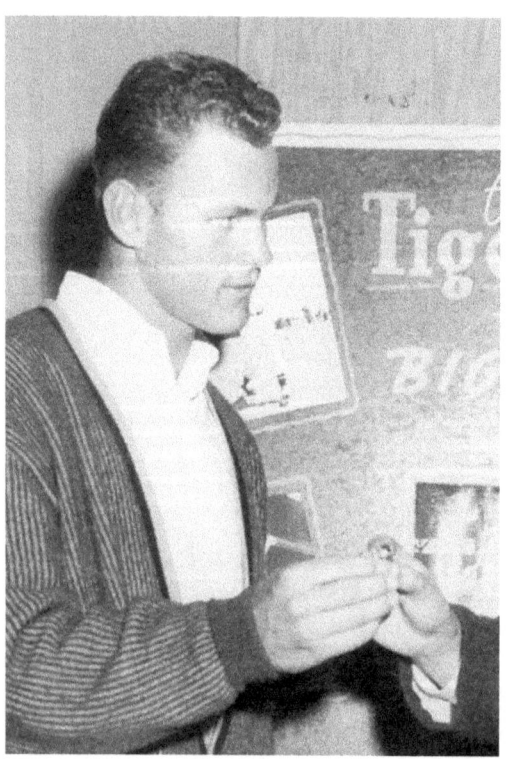

Steve Boros (courtesy Detroit Tigers)

*You have almost a squeaky clean reputation. Some fellows would have surprised me to have said something like this, but not you.*

SB: It was something that I had to do because I knew, as I said, that I could possibly get some people in trouble because I signed with the Tigers, signed so quickly. There weren't any repercussions, or none that I heard of. I don't think any scouts got in trouble because of that.

*You gave up your last year of college eligibility.*

SB: Yeah, but the only way my parents would sign the contract — I was only 20 at the time and I needed their signatures—is I promised them that, when I made the big leagues, I would go back and get my last year of college. My father only had a sixth-grade education, my mother had an eighth-grade education. I was the oldest, I had already got three years in and it was their dream to put all their kids through college, so I promised them that when I made the major leagues I would go back to school and that's indeed what I did.

I got a degree in English literature. I thought I was gonna play in the big leagues for 20 years, make the Hall of Fame, and become independently wealthy when I finished my career and it didn't matter that I would major in anything so impractical as English literature. (Laughs) It didn't quite work out that way, but I'm not sorry. I really enjoyed my last year of college.

I was in Liberal Arts school my sophomore year. I started out in Pharmacy a year, then Liberal Arts, then I switched to Business school. My father kind of panicked 'cause he didn't see how I could get a degree that would have any practical value if I was a Liberal Arts major.

Then the last year, when I paid my own freight through school, I went back and met with my counselor and decided that my favorite subjects in school had been literature courses, so I went back and became an English major that last year and I'm not sorry at all about it.

*Whose roster spot did you take when you joined the Tigers?*

SB: Karl Olson. I felt badly. Here I was activated on about June 15 of '57 and he had to get sent to the minors.

*What kind of reception did you get from your teammates?*

SB: They were great to me, although they [the Tigers] had a tradition of bonus players, like Harvey Kuenn, Al Kaline; they turned out pretty well.

I got a *very* nice reception. I remember that I joined the Tigers and I was wearing all this Ivy League stuff. Remember the trousers with the little belt in the back? And a lot of tweed. I'm dating myself. I got on that bus and made that first chartered air flight with the Tigers and Ray Boone saw all this stuff and says, "Hey, bush. We're gonna have to get you some clothes when you get to New York."

And the first trip took us to New York and, if I remember right, Isenberg and Isenberg was a men's clothing store in New York where all the big league players got their clothes. They got a pretty good rate on suits and sports coats and slacks. Ray Boone went with me and kinda showed me around and I bought a new outfit over there. The pants with the little belts in the back and the tweed jackets and that got put to the back of the closet.

He [Boone] was a great clutch hitter and a great guy.

*Did the players try to help you?*

SB: Yeah, they did. Really, they were very cooperative. I remember Reno Bertoia was on the club; he was an ex-bonus player. He was very nice to me. George Thomas joined as a bonus player about a month after I signed, so both of us were on the club.

Jim Brady was there. Jim Small. There were a lot of us. Bob [G.] Miller. We knew each other. Bonus players were just well-received in the Tigers organization. I had no problems whatsoever.

I remember Dave Philley used to growl at me every once in a while, but that might have to do with the fact that the first time I took infield in Tiger Stadium — in college, after you took the throw from the catcher at second base, where you were a middle infielder, you threw it to the first baseman. Well, in pro ball you throw it to the third baseman. I threw the ball to first base, Dave Philley wasn't looking, I hit him right in the middle of the forehead. He dropped right over backwards.

Actually, he was pretty nice to me, but he was kind of a gruff guy who didn't like young ballplayers who made careless mistakes and didn't know how to play the game and weren't veterans. Even so, he did it in a good-natured way.

My reception there was very favorable. I was very comfortable with those guys. I never felt like I was out of place and that they made me feel like I wasn't a part of the team.

*What about your manager, Jack Tighe?*

SB: He saw me in a tryout camp three years before and I was a high school senior and he suggested I go to college. He said, "You're not ready to go play pro ball. You go to college and put on some weight and hit the books and then maybe you'll be ready for pro ball." I was already thinking about going to [University of] Michigan.

Two years later the Tigers gave me a bonus contract and it was so unusual because the fellow who ran the tryout camp for the Tigers was Jack Tighe and now he was the big league manager. He knew me and I really liked Jack Tighe.

I remember the second day I was with them. I made my major league debut; I pinch hit against Tom Sturdivant and fouled a fastball and a curve and a slider and I felt pretty comfortable. I was ready to break in my first time with a hit and then he threw me a knuckleball and that thing danced back and forth three or four times. I barely fouled it off and I remember getting out of the box and saying something to myself, "What in the world are you doing here?" Then I popped up the next pitch.

Then I think we got beat three in a row in New York. We went to Baltimore and lost another game. The club had been struggling and I remember walking out of the hotel after the Friday night game we lost in Baltimore and Jack Tighe was walking in. He says, "Hey, kid. You think you can hit big league pitching?"

And I said something like, "Yup." He says, "What kind of answer is that?" and I said, "Yes, sir!" And I thought he might put me in the lineup tomorrow night and, as it turned out, he did. I started and the first time up I singled off of Billy O'Dell. Al Kaline singled in about the twelfth inning and won the ballgame for us, 2-to-1.

I played a few more games in Baltimore and a couple in Washington and then they found out pretty much I had trouble with changeups and slow curveballs. When they got onto that, then Jack took me out of the lineup. Then basically I just had spot starts the rest of the way.

*How was the coaching you received?*

SB: I think the feeling was that you were supposedly a pretty good player and they didn't want to mess you up. They felt like a lot of coaching might mess you up.

I know that Tommy Henrich was a coach with the Tigers. He gave me some tips. Billy Hitchcock worked with me a little bit, but you didn't get coaching, especially with hitting, to the extent that you do nowadays. The feeling pretty much was: "Hey, this guy was supposed to be able to do something. Leave him alone and let him see how he does rather than confuse him or change him and perhaps foul him up. The scout saw something in this young guy, they gave him this money, he's been in college — just let him play. He must be able to do something right."

*You were a couple of years older than some of the Bonus Babies and had been to college. Was the adjustment difficult?*

SB: No, not really. There is a protocol that you follow in the big leagues as far as tipping people, dressing, how you behave, and you gotta know your place in that clubhouse and on the bench and on the team in general, but I didn't have any problem with that. Like I said, I felt very comfortable right from the word go. That was something I'd been shooting for ever since I was a young kid who could dream about being a ballplayer and the players made me feel comfortable and I felt pretty much at ease. I wish I'd have hit a little better, not only then but later on.

*The bonus rule was rescinded after the '57 season and you were able to be sent down. You made the most of this.*

SB: I wanted to play. I felt like I could play in the big leagues right away. Al Kaline had done that, Harvey Kuenn had done it. I had just hit .400 in the Big 10 and I thought I could play right away and I found out soon that I couldn't, that I needed some experience. I had to go learn some things.

As a matter of fact, the last week on the season in Detroit, John McHale called George Thomas and I into his office and said that if we wanted to, Willis Hudlin was going to manage a team in the winter league in Mexico City and George and I could go down there and play if we wanted. We both jumped at the opportunity to go down to Mexico to play in winter ball.

Then when I found out that the bonus rule had been changed over the winter and that they made it apply to bonus players signed the previous year and that we could go to the minors, I was really very pleased about it. I got a taste of the big leagues and I liked being in the big leagues, but I found out very soon that I needed to go to the minors and learn my trade.

I struggled my first year in the minors; I hit about .260 in A ball. I started in Double-A and I was over my head there, especially defensively, and then I went to Triple-A just for eight days to help 'em out — they were short-handed. Then I ended up in A ball and I hit .260 there and hit 14, 15, 16 home runs, something like that, but really had a terrible time with the slider and had a tough time with my defense.

The next year at Birmingham, I hit .305, I think. Basically, what I did that summer is I learned to hit the slider and I had to because I'd have never survived if I hadn't. Once I learned how to deal with the breaking ball — the slider in particular — then the next year at Denver in that ballpark that was really suited for hitting, I really put together a good year. [Boros was named league MVP.]

*You came back to Detroit and took over at third base.*

SB: Yeah. I had a tough spring. I didn't hit well in the spring. I hit 30 home runs at Denver the year before, but that park was suited to that, and I had to survive so I kind of changed my batting philosophy towards the end of spring training and started hitting the ball up the middle and thinking about hitting strikes and staying with the pitch and I had a good year. It's a shame I got beaned and then I broke my collarbone or I might have had a real shot at being Rookie of the Year that year.

But at the end of the year, even though I'd hit .270, hit 5 home runs, and driven in 62 runs and I missed something like seven weeks of the season with the broken collarbone and the beaning, I felt disappointed that I didn't hit more home runs. I *wanted* to hit more home runs.

I went back to school that winter at Michigan to pick up a semester I needed and then I went to spring training with Detroit. I was determined to hit with more power and I had a great spring. I hit .320, I hit four or five home runs in the spring, and I just felt I was gonna hit with power and hit home runs and pull the ball more. Then the season started and I got off to s horrendous start, never got squared away, hit 16 home runs but struck out too much, hit .220, and had a really bad year.

Then that winter, even though I went to Japan with the club and hit

.300 on the trip trying to get back to my old style of hitting the ball up the middle, they decided they wanted to make a trade and the trade was made and I went to the Cubs [for Bob Anderson].

*You never established yourself with the Cubs, but the next year [1964] with the Reds you were essentially the everyday third baseman for them.*

SB: Yeah. Chico Ruiz struggled at the plate early and I got sent out Opening Day. It was between me and Ed Dickson, a pitcher, and they sent me out. I went to Triple-A, hit .300, and Chico Ruiz had a terrible time, so they brought me up and I just got off to a great start. I went 50 games without an error which set a record for a Cincinnati Red third baseman; it had been held by Heinie Groh. That might have been my biggest thrill in baseball. And I hit pretty well. I tailed of a little towards the end.

At the end, when we made a run at the Phillies and the Cardinals, Chico Ruiz got hot. He stole home against the Phillies. In fact, that is a play that Phillies' fan haven't forgotten yet — how Chico Ruiz stole home to beat them, 1-to-nothing, in a ballgame that either started them on their losing streak or really kept 'em going. Chico had been playing well, doing well, so he basically finished out the season at third base, 'cause we'd been on a losing streak and he had been a part of that. Until that last ten days of the season, basically I'd been the starting third baseman at Cincinnati, but I only hit two home runs.

I used playoff money and some money I'd saved and I went to Europe. I'd gotten my degree the previous December and I'd always wanted to go to Europe. I had to choose between going to Europe and going to the University of Chicago graduate school. I'd been accepted there in the English Master's program and I decided to go to Europe instead. While I was in Europe I read in *The Sporting News* where Dick Sisler, who took over for Freddie Hutchinson, was disappointed that they didn't have more power production at third base and they were going to try Deron Johnson at third base and let Gordy Coleman play first. That basically pushed me into the utility man role, which was the role that I served in for the first month of the season in '65. Then I was sent to Triple-A and I never did get back to the big leagues after that.

*How long did you play after that?*

SB: I played through the '69 season and then started managing in the minors for the Royals in 1970. I managed in A ball for five years at San Jose and Waterloo. Then I got back to the big leagues as a coach for the Royals for Jack McKeon and when he got fired Whitey Herzog kept me on. I coached for the Royals for five years, then Whitey and the coaches all got fired and I went to the Expos organization. I managed in their minor league system for one year and then I got put on their big league coaching staff in '81 and '82.

In '83 I was appointed the manager of the A's and I was there in '83 and part of '84 and I got fired there. Then in '85 I was field coordinator for the minor league system of the Padres and did that for one year. Then when Dick Williams resigned one day into spring training in '86, they didn't have anybody available to grab that job and I had big league experience and knew the Padre players, so they appointed me to manage for one year.

After one year I went back to being field coordinator. That was in '87. Then I got fired by Chub Feeney, who had come over as president of the Padres. That's when I joined the Dodgers for three years.

*By the time you signed in 1957, you had seen the Bonus Babies and most of them had failed. Did this give you any reservations about signing a bonus contract?*

SB: No. I just felt certain I was gonna make it and make it big time. Like I said, I thought I was gonna play for 20 years and be an all-star player, maybe even get in the Hall of Fame. You feel that way when you're 19-, 20-years-old and you hit .400 in the Big 10 and doing pretty much what you want on a ball field.

Then you get into a league where everyone around you did that and then you start to realize that there's special gifts, special skills that go with being an all-star caliber major league player.

But I thought I was gonna do it. I really did. And I'm sure all those young players felt the same way. As a minor league field coordinator responsible for the instruction of 200 players — they all feel like they can do it, too, and you realize that only about five percent of the kids who sign will make the major leagues. You start to realize what a rare combination of talent, luck, perseverance, mental discipline — all of it, the whole package — how rare it is to find it in one player.

*Every one of those kids was a star at home.*

SB: That's right.

*You've gotta stay healthy and be lucky if you're gonna play 10, 15 years and be the top guy at your position in this league.*

*Walt Masterson, the former pitcher, said that the best players aren't in the major leagues, the survivors are.*

SB: They're the survivors and they've got mental skills to match their physical skills. To me, the mental aspect is the thing that comes into play more and more, especially when you get to the upper echelon of major league players.

*What is your opinion of the bonus rule?*

SB: I liked the rule. I felt that I could play in the major leagues. I think that putting the requirement that the player stay two years in the major leagues was a necessary one at the time. Before the draft, I think they had to put some limitation on the players. There were teams out there that could simply out-spend you and it was a way to make the thing a little more fair. The draft wasn't in existence at the time and it seemed to me the fairest way to do it.

I'm glad that they changed it. I'm glad I was able to go back and play in the minor leagues, but under the circumstances, with some clubs in big markets with big money to spend, they could simply go tie up all the players, give 'em big money, and send 'em to the minor leagues and basically make a mockery of scouting and the whole process of signing and developing players.

*There were rumors of cheating and under-the-table payments.*

SB: I heard those rumors. No one approached me and offered me that kind of a deal, but I heard the stories and heard the rumors. I know that no one that talked to me offered me that kind of a deal and I talked to a lot of ballclubs.

*Knowing what you know now, if you were 20 again would you sign a bonus contract?*

SB: Yes, I would. I felt confident I'd go back and get my last year of college, I felt I could play at the major league level, I wanted to get started playing. I'd just hit .400 in the Big 10; I didn't know what else I could prove. I could've gone back to college and sprained an ankle, tore up a knee, hurt my shoulder — who knows what all — and I was very comfortable with the fact that I wanted to sign, *but* it had to be a major league contract. I was wrong at the time, but looking back on my mind-set at that time, I just felt I could play at the major league level and I wasn't about to take a minor league contract.

But when they changed the rule, I scurried back to the minors happily 'cause I'd got a taste of the major leagues and I knew very well that I had to polish up my skills a little bit.

I can't complain [about my career]. Fortunately, the coaching and the managing aspect of it — I had more success at that. I'm very happy with my career in baseball and obviously I love the game or I wouldn't have chosen to stay in it. It's been very good to me.

### Stephen Boros

Born September 3, 1936, Flint, MI
Ht. 6' Wt. 185 Batted and Threw Right

| Year | Team, Lg. | G | AB | R | H | 2B | 3B | HR | RBI | BA |
|---|---|---|---|---|---|---|---|---|---|---|
| 1957 | Detroit, AL | 24 | 41 | 4 | 6 | 1 | 0 | 0 | 0 | .146 |
| 1958 | Detroit, AL | 6 | 2 | 0 | 0 | 0 | 0 | 0 | 0 | .000 |

| Year | Team, Lg. | G | AB | R | H | 2B | 3B | HR | RBI | BA |
|---|---|---|---|---|---|---|---|---|---|---|
| 1958 | Charleston, AA | 6 | 13 | 0 | 1 | 0 | 0 | 0 | 0 | .077 |
| | Augusta, SAL | 77 | 269 | 53 | 69 | 7 | 2 | 14 | 36 | .257 |
| | Birmingham, SA | 44 | 138 | 24 | 36 | 3 | 2 | 6 | 15 | .261 |
| 1959 | Birmingham, SA | 147 | 522 | 89 | 159 | 24 | 7 | 16 | 85 | .305 |
| 1960 | Denver, AA | 151 | 571 | 108 | 181 | 42 | 8 | 30 | 119 | .317 |
| 1961 | Detroit, AL | 116 | 396 | 51 | 197 | 18 | 2 | 5 | 62 | .270 |
| 1962 | Detroit, AL | 116 | 356 | 46 | 81 | 14 | 1 | 16 | 47 | .228 |
| 1963 | Chicago, NL | 41 | 90 | 9 | 19 | 5 | 1 | 3 | 7 | .211 |
| 1964 | Cincinnati, NL | 117 | 370 | 31 | 95 | 12 | 3 | 2 | 31 | .257 |
| | San Diego, PCL | 26 | 100 | 18 | 39 | 8 | 0 | 3 | 15 | .300 |
| 1965 | Cincinnati, NL | 2 | 0 | 0 | 0 | 0 | 0 | 0 | 0 | .000 |
| | San Diego, PCL | 117 | 420 | 73 | 113 | 28 | 6 | 12 | 30 | .269 |
| 1966 | Buffalo, IL | 106 | 330 | 51 | 92 | 16 | 1 | 13 | 40 | .279 |
| 1967 | Buffalo, IL | 107 | 290 | 29 | 55 | 5 | 0 | 10 | 23 | .190 |
| 1968 | Indianapolis-Vancouver, PCL | 100 | 320 | 24 | 85 | 15 | 0 | 1 | 32 | .266 |
| 1969 | Omaha, AA | 103 | 309 | 56 | 84 | 13 | 5 | 4 | 53 | .272 |
| **Major Lg. Totals** | | 422 | 1255 | 141 | 308 | 50 | 7 | 26 | 149 | .245 |

# 19 John DeMerit

*The Milwaukee Braves signed John DeMerit in 1957 out of the University of Wisconsin for a $100,000 bonus.*

BRENT KELLEY: *The Braves were your home team. Was that a factor in your signing with them?*

JOHN DEMERIT: They were 25 miles down the road. I was in the stands watching these guys a couple of years earlier. It was important in their minds, too, to sign somebody from the state to this kind of contract.

*You went to the University of Wisconsin on a basketball scholarship.*

JD: Yes, if you call $200 a year a basketball scholarship. (Laughs) But at that time, the tuition was $90 a semester. That was a help. A bigger help was the ability of the athletic department to get me a job; that was more sustaining.

*Do you know whose roster spot you took when you joined the Braves?*

JD: Ultimately, the person to leave was Chuck Tanner.

*Fred Haney was the manager. What was his attitude toward Bonus Babies?*

JD: I thought a little reserved. Obviously, ultimately the responsibility of operating the team was his, subject to management above him, but I was probably received better and encouraged more by some of the coaches on the staff.

Fred was his own manager and obviously a good one, but he went with the big boys and played for the big inning, really protected his pitching staff with the Big Three he had. I didn't fit into those plans at that time, obviously.

*You and Bob Taylor were signed at the same time, but you got much more playing time than he did. He was just out of high school and you had been to college. Was the adjustment for you difficult?*

JD: It wasn't much of a problem. I didn't stay in any big hotels and tip people and things like that until I got involved at the professional level, but I had been exposed to traveling, playing on the road, playing on different fields—I think that helped, plus being a little older. I was away from home for three years [in college]; it wasn't like just walking out of your house into instant baseball. I think that was probably an advantage that I would have over Bob Taylor, who came right in from wherever he lived. I had at least some preparation; probably not classified as a 'city boy,' *per se*, out of a town of 5,000, but it was the metropolitan Milwaukee area.

*Do you recall your first game?*

JD: Yes. It was against the New York Giants; I'm not sure what date it was [6–17–57]. It was shortly after I got there. I pinch hit in one of the later innings of the game, got a scratch single off of Stu Miller, who threw the ball about 70 miles an hour.

*That's a good start.*

JD: Yeah, it was. I was nervous, obviously. After I got on base, I was more nervous than standing at the plate. (Laughs) I started realizing what was going on.

*The Braves were a good team. Did you get a World Series share?*

JD: Yes. That was interesting. I had been there most of the year, outside of spring training and the first month-and-a-half, and was not involved in any major effort by the team. I was given a third share.

I was really forced onto the [World Series] roster. I would have not been on the roster had there not been an injury to Bill Bruton. That was a matter for the commissioner's office in the end. By nature of being on the roster, obviously something was forthcoming and a third, I thought, was reasonably generous.

*You pinch ran in the Series for Del Rice.*

JD: I think it was kind of a token effort to make sure I got in a game. I had no problem with that.

*Do you feel you got the proper opportunity in your career?*

JD: Yes and no. (Laughs)

John DeMerit

That's a hard question because if someone plays professional sports for five years there certainly should be an opportunity. That's plenty of time under most circumstances, but I felt that people who were involved with making some of the decisions were experimenting.

I got to Atlanta [in 1958], got off to a pretty reasonable start, walked into a very political situation, which I obviously had *no* idea of what was happening. Atlanta was probably the most fickle sports town in the USA, maybe still is.

Long-time owner [Earl Mann] reluctantly working with a major league team, taking some players but making his own decisions — buying players, etc. — it was really a volatile thing. And expectations in Atlanta were very high and the team wasn't fulfilling them and the fans weren't turning out, the wheels were constantly turning, and you're advised "You better start pulling the ball more" and this and that.

Those were the things I thought affected me. If I had been left to do the things the way I'd gotten there — by fooling around with your stance or fooling around with your approach to batting, pretty soon you're not doing anything. I had several stretches during that season which were bad and this was the response.

*The Mets drafted you for their inaugural season. How was that experience?*

JD: That *was* an experience, but not so much on the field. For example, I'd never gone anywhere in my five years in baseball where you didn't get some assistance in looking for housing. We got to New York and they said, "Buy a newspaper." (Laughs)

I could not believe it — the lack of organization, I guess some of it would be rightfully so, but their efforts were entirely different. Houston and New York joined at the same time and it struck me how much the drafting and later the playing was so different. Houston went after younger ballplayers for the long term and New York went after names to get people in the park. They really didn't have to do that; that ballpark was sitting in Harlem where, at any time, you were gonna get 20,000 people because there was nothing else to do anyway. But they were really under the gun.

Casey Stengel — I don't know what he was at his peak — but he was an interesting character when he was there. It was too much for him, though. It was just beyond him.

*Warren Spahn said he was the only man who played for Stengel both before and after he was a genius.*

JD: Yeah. (Laughs) That's about right.

The guy would come out in centerfield and start talking about some rock that was out there when he was playing in 19-whatever. It wasn't a passing comment, it was a five-minute discussion.

He fell asleep in the dugout one night. We almost had to carry him off a plane in Houston because it was a late flight. I felt sorry for him.

*He was there to draw fans, too.*

JD: I think he was doing a favor to George Weiss, of course. It was a *strange* time.

*Rogers Hornsby was the hitting coach. He had a rough reputation.*

JD: (Laughs) I didn't know him from Adam except from reading about him for many, many years and admiring him from afar, but my admiration took a pretty good dip after getting to know him. The guy had one thing on his mind according to what we could see: watching the batting cage, watching batting practice, and going to sit down, and if you didn't like that, tough luck. If you were in his way when he sat on the bench, he'd yell at you. He was not contributing anything to anything, that I could see, except maybe filling a contract obligation.

We had a whole bunch of people like that, people who were really cast in the wrong roles. Ex-managers and ex-all-stars. Solly Hemus and Cookie Lavagetto, a whole crew of people who were pretty good at second-guessing Stengel and explaining what he meant after he had a clubhouse meeting and left. (Laughs) If you could have taped it all, it would have been hilarious. It was a strange place.

The old guys were just hanging on. [Richie] Ashburn and [Gil] Hodges and names like this were in a deep decline in their careers and they were playing. Gus Bell was hitting about a hundred-and-ten. These were all nice guys but over the hill and they were hanging with 'em early in the season and getting pounded.

*That was your last professional season.*

JD: Right. There were real interesting circumstances with regard to that because when I was cut from the roster I had no options left. You had three options, so it was a situation where I would have to cut a deal with Syracuse, where they were trying to send me, and I had held out for ten grand to go to spring training. I was told before I left Los Angeles that night that if I wanted to go to Syracuse it was for five grand. (Laughs) I was supposed to be going right to Toronto to meet Syracuse and I got my ticket changed and came home to sit on that little idea for a while.

They brought a guy in to replace me on the roster who was under the diathermy machine when I left. I don't know if he ever pitched for the Mets the whole time he was there. I don't remember his name.

Stengel was very apologetic. "Oh, you'll be back in September," and all that, but I never got answered to why I was leaving. Certainly, getting a guy to replace me who can't pitch was not much of an answer. It was just juggling to say you're doing something.

So, anyway, I stayed home and went to summer school back at Madison and started work on advanced credits and was kind of waiting out to see what happened in regards to contract offers.

They did call me after September when they could expand their roster and said they'd put me back on the roster if I wanted. I didn't know quite what they meant and that would have really screwed up some things I was doing at home here, so I passed. And that was the last of it.

In September of the year I joined the Equitable, the firm that has the major league pension, and stayed with them for about seven years. I had picked up my degree a couple of years earlier so I had that, but I was working on an advanced degree. I went back to school nights in '61 and then summer school in '62. I was about half-way to a Master's degree, but I didn't work any further on it.

The last many years I've been the Park and Recreation Director here in the city of Port Washington [Wisconsin]. It was a situation I thought needed a little bit better control to begin with. I was close to the situation, having lived here, and it was an area very much akin to my school experience. There's a lot of flexibility and a seasonal turnover, so there's not the same old thing every day — a lot of advantages to keeping your mind intact.

*In your opinion, did the bonus rule hurt you?*

JD: Probably yes from the standpoint that if I had been signed and probably, say, gone to [Class] A ball and made the next step over a couple of years it would have been a smarter approach.

But that's hard to say. It isn't that you don't learn things at the major league level, being around. You probably lose some of the edge in your skills if you're not playing and you have no way of improving them. Coming right out of college where you've been active for three years this probably, in retrospect, was a drawback. It hurts development.

That's the thing that a lot of people were putting in my mind, and I'm sure other people's, too: What have you got to lose? What you have to lose is possibly the chance of long-term playing in the major leagues, which should be a bigger benefit.

I remember my dad saying, "That's more money than I've made in 20-something years." You get encouragement: "You want to be doing something better than I did," "These guys want you," "It's their money; they do what they want with it. What's the difference?" It's hard not to bend to that, you know. Not that you don't have reservations about it; we discussed it heavily a number of times, but you still have to make a decision. You hope you can just fly right by there.

## John Stephen DeMerit

Born January 8, 1936, West Bend, WI
Ht. 6' 1½" Wt. 195 Batted R Threw R

| Year | Team, Lg. | G | AB | R | H | 2B | 3B | HR | RBI | BA |
|---|---|---|---|---|---|---|---|---|---|---|
| 1957 | Milwaukee, NL | 33 | 34 | 8 | 5 | 0 | 0 | 0 | 1 | .147 |
| 1958 | Milwaukee, NL | 2 | 3 | 1 | 2 | 0 | 0 | 0 | 0 | .667 |
|  | Atlanta, SA | 136 | 506 | 72 | 130 | 20 | 8 | 13 | 70 | .257 |
| 1959 | Jacksonville, SAL | 126 | 475 | 68 | 119 | 14 | 5 | 14 | 48 | .251 |
|  | Atlanta, SA | 9 | 28 |  | 7 |  |  |  | 1 | .250 |
| 1960 | Louisville, AA | 126 | 352 | 47 | 95 | 20 | 2 | 12 | 50 | .270 |
| 1961 | Milwaukee, NL | 32 | 74 | 5 | 12 | 2 | 0 | 2 | 5 | .162 |
| 1962 | New York, NL | 14 | 16 | 3 | 3 | 0 | 0 | 1 | 1 | .188 |
| **Major Lg. Totals** |  | 90 | 132 | 21 | 23 | 3 | 0 | 3 | 7 | .174 |

**World Series Record**

| 1957 | Milwaukee, NL | 1 | 0 | 0 | 0 | 0 | 0 | 0 | 0 | .000 |

# 20 Von McDaniel

*The Cardinals signed Von McDaniel in 1957 for a $50,000 bonus. He holds the modern National League record for wins by an 18-year-old with 7.*

BRENT KELLEY: *Fred Hahn scouted all the McDaniel buys for the Cardinals. How many teams were after you?*
VON MCDANIEL: Basically, only about four: The Phillies and the Red Sox and the Cardinals and the Orioles.
*The Red Sox were after a lot of the Bonus Babies, but they signed very few.*
VM: I think it's because they had a scout down here in Oklahoma and Texas where a lot of players were and they were paying attention to him, I guess, until they got ready to put the money.
*Did any of the other teams make offers to you?*
VM: No, they really couldn't do that. See, I signed the night I graduated from high school so I didn't give 'em, any chance to make offers, except Freddie Hahn.
*Do you know your high school record?*
VM: Yeah, hitting and pitching both. My batting average was about .613 and we played a spring and fall season of baseball down here in Oklahoma. My senior year record was, I believe, 13-and-1.
*How long was your schedule?*
VM: I think we played about 30 games. My total victories in high school, I'm not sure about that. I think I only lost about three games.
*What was your American Legion record?*
VM: We won the state championship in American Legion. We went to the Nationals, but St. Louis beat us and they won the Nationals. I think my record in American Legion was about four losses in three years and probably about 30 wins—25, 30 wins.
*You were valedictorian of your class, so you pretty well had it knocked any way you looked at it.*
VM: I had some scholarships offered to me in basketball, too.

*Were you tempted?*

VM: Yeah, a little bit. Abe Lemmons was the coach at Oklahoma State University and that was pretty tempting. And, of course, I had scholarship offers at the University of Texas because Darrell Royal was my dad's first cousin. They had a good baseball team down there and if I didn't go pro I probably would have done that.

*Did you go to college?*

VM: Yes, I went to college. I graduated from UTA [University of Texas at Arlington] and I've got about 120 hours of college altogether. Accounting and Economics and Finance.

*A much higher percentage of Bonus Babies attended college than did the non–Bonus Babies.*

VM: It could be that the parents got the kids to say they'd go to school for allowing them to sign the bonus.

*Do you know whose roster spot you took when you joined the Cardinals?*

VM: I signed under the bonus rule in 1957. In 1958 it went out. In '57 I have no idea unless it was some pitcher somewhere. I came up in the middle of June, right after I graduated.

*What kind of reception did you receive from the veteran players when you joined the team?*

VM: Pretty good. Probably a better reception after I became active. The ones who didn't get to play much, they didn't like it too much. I was able to pitch in, I think, 13–14 games—something like that—and I was 7-and-5 my first year.

*Your manager was Fred Hutchinson. He'd*

**Lindy (left) and Von McDaniel**

been over in Detroit and he'd had all those Bonus Babies they'd signed and most people credit Al Kaline's early success to him — the fact that he was given an opportunity to play — and he came to St. Louis and had Dick Schofield and your brother Lindy. He was a very stern, quick-tempered man, but everyone loved him. What was your opinion and how did he work with you?

VM: A very good opinion, but he didn't hesitate to tell you what was on his mind. He was that way, but you understood that. I think he was kind of a father figure to most of the players except the ones that were just as old as he was, like Walker Cooper or some of those. He had the authority; there was nobody that would buck him.

*Was he helpful?*

VM: Oh, yes, he was. Very patient and he seemed to me to manage for the long run — the season — rather than just short-term. Some managers kind of manage for short-term, you know, but he knew what a player had to go through during the whole season.

*One of the complaints from the Bonus Baby pitchers was that the pitching coaches weren't helpful.*

VM: [Al] Hollingsworth was the coach. He was good. I think I was helped because Freddie Hutchinson was a pitcher, too. Even though he was manager, he actually was a pitcher, so I think that helped me.

Probably in another situation they were hurt more because the manager himself wasn't a pitcher.

*You were in a game pretty quickly.*

VM: We were so far behind in the game there wasn't any reason to be scared, as far as the game was concerned. It didn't look like we had a chance to win it and, of course, I was able to keep the ball low and throw strikes. That's all they told me to do and it worked.

*You came back a few days later and got a win.*

VM: That was a relief appearance, too. We were still on the road trip and I came in in relief and that was completely an accident. We were behind six runs and they started warming me up in the bullpen and then [Stan] Musial hit a home run and then [Ken] Boyer hit a home run and then all of a sudden the game was tied up and the manager looked and I was the only one warming up. So I came in and he ran another pitcher out there — Larry Jackson, I think — and he was throwing real quick, you know.

The umpire said, "Nothing doing. You can't do that." So I went in the game. I guess if I had let the first guy get on he'd have probably pulled me out 'cause by the end of the game it was tied. The Cardinals had rallied up. I think Musial had hit a grand slam or something.

So I kept getting 'em out and then I'd come in and go back out and I kept getting 'em out and then finally they got a double off of me and he didn't take me out. He let me pitch and I got four innings in and won the game.

*What about your first start?*

VM: That was against the Dodgers. We came home and I got to start about a week or so later against them. Duke Snider got a bunt single and one other player got a hit. I think it might have been that old second baseman they had,. Not Charlie Neal, but [Jim] Gilliam, the one that got so many doubles. Gilliam got one and Duke Snider bunted him over and bunted for a single.

*Later you one-hit the Pirates.*

VM: About a month-and-a-half later. Gene Baker got the hit.

*Is there a game that stands out?*

VM: It was probably the game against the Pirates because I'd lost a couple of games 'fore I won that one. To come back in that one and pitch a one-hitter was pretty exciting. It was the second game of a doubleheader; I believe it was on a Sunday afternoon.

*You came up with a back injury. What happened?*

VM: I went to college that winter and I was always active in high school, you know, playing basketball in the wintertime, and I got busy studying a lot and I was not very active, so when I went to spring training it wasn't that I was out of shape or overweight or anything, but I probably was not as strong as I normally was.

So I started having some back trouble about the middle of spring training and it was very unusual 'cause I'd not experienced that before and a lot of people said it was just a matter of me growing older and larger and bigger and so forth. It could be some of that, but I did notice that I did have a back problem that plagued me for a long time after that. That caused most of it.

It was way in the lower back. I do have a small vertebra on one side and it could be the more mature I got then the more problems I had with my back as far as twisting on the mound.

*When were you sent to the minors?*

VM: I was sent to the minor leagues about cut-down date in 1958.

*How did you perform there?*

VM: I didn't do very well 'cause I stayed as a pitcher. I think I went to Houston first and then to Winston-Salem before the end of the year. I think I won about two or three games or something.

In '59 they decided to get me more active and let me play infield as well as pitch. I did that in [class] D ball in Daytona Beach, Florida, in the Florida State League and I did very well. I hit 300-and-13 as a regular player, with about 70 RBIs, and my record was 13–5 pitching, so I had a good season.

*Was your back still bothering you?*

VM: It didn't bother me as much when I stayed active like that, but I was not able to relax on the mound like I used to when I was younger, so the pitching never really came back like it was earlier.

*You eventually went to spring training with the Astros as an infielder.*

VM: Yeah. Third baseman.

*Was there a chance to make it?*

VM: Yes, except they had paid a lot money for a lot of players in front of me. [Bob] Aspromonte was in front of me at third base; they had bought him from the Dodgers and paid a lot of money for him, so it probably hurt me a little bit on being able to stick with the Astros.

*How long did you stay in the minor leagues?*

VM: I played nine years in the minor leagues, mostly Double-A. I played one year of D ball and one year of C ball and then the rest of 'em were in Double-A and Triple-A.

*Did you and Lindy ever pitch in the same game?*

VM: It's possible we did in Milwaukee in 1957. It seems like I came in to relieve late in a game that we were behind in and then we rallied up and won the ballgame in extra innings or something. I wasn't the winner, but I did get to pitch.

*What is your opinion of the bonus rule?*

VM: I think it hurt the players. It was a punitive action against the players for signing for a bonus. That's what it was.

Of course, all of baseball had it. it wasn't just one team decided to do it, so I'm not blaming the Cardinals or anything. It was an action that made the players inactive and it couldn't do anything except hurt the players.

*You started off so well. Did it hurt you?*

VM: No, it probably didn't hurt me. It probably didn't because I was able to play, but I'm sure it hurt some that had to sit there. I think it hurt Bob [L.] Miller because he didn't get much action except to mop up games and you don't feel too good doing that.

*Some of the boys only played in a handful of games in the two years. It's hard to stay sharp that way.*

VM: You wouldn't be in the game very much. Your mind wouldn't be in the game, there's no doubt about that.

I was more fortunate in that I had an older brother on the same team, so that probably made it easier for me. He was my first roommate.

*Do you think you'd sign a bonus contract if you had it to do over again?*

VM: Yes, except the rule is kind of tough , you know. You had to go to the major leagues. When you're 18-years-old you're better off not having to go to the major leagues.

*Did you find the adjustment from home to the major leagues difficult?*

VM: Not as much as probably other people because I had my brother there. He warned me about a lot of the adjustments. You know. I think that first year, as far as when I was home in St. Louis, I stayed in the hotel about, what, three or four blocks from the ballpark. I stayed there all the time. 'Course, he'd come by and pick me up and we'd go places and so forth. I didn't have a car my first year until that fall when I went to school.

*Other than the injury, do you have any regrets?*

VM: No. I enjoyed it and I probably would have enjoyed just being in professional baseball that first year rather than the major leagues, though. Because of what occurred and the fact that I did have pretty good control of my pitches, it probably was easier for me.

I guess the strong, real hard-throwing kids it would be the hardest on, you know, like Sandy Koufax was. He had a lot of problems getting the ball over the plate and that was frustrating.

## Max Von McDaniel

Born April 18, 1939, Hollis, OK — Died August 20, 1995, Lawton, OK
Ht. 6' 2½" Wt. 180 Batted and Threw Right

### Pitching Record

| Year | Team, Lg. | G | IP | W | L | Pct | SO | BB | H | ERA |
|---|---|---|---|---|---|---|---|---|---|---|
| 1957 | St. Louis, NL | 17 | 87 | 7 | 5 | .583 | 45 | 31 | 71 | 3.22 |
| 1958 | St. Louis, NL | 2 | 2 | 0 | 0 | .000 | 0 | 5 | 5 | 13.50 |
|  | Winston-Salem, CarL | 6 |  | 0 | 0 | .000 |  |  |  |  |
|  | Houston, TxL | 6 |  | 1 | 2 | .333 |  |  |  |  |
| 1959 | Daytona Beach, FSL | 21 | 147 | 13 | 5 | .722 | 84 | 34 | 154 | 3.49 |
| 1960 | Tulsa, TxL | 12 | 32 | 1 | 0 | 1.000 | 17 | 14 | 39 | 7.50 |
|  | Winnipeg, NoL |  |  | 0 | 0 | .000 |  |  |  |  |
| 1963 | Oklahoma City, PCL | 6 | 9 | 0 | 0 | .000 | 6 | 0 | 17 | 10.00 |
| 1964 | San Antonio, TxL | 1 | 5 | 0 | 0 | .000 | 0 | 0 | 3 | 0.00 |
| Major Lg. Totals |  | 19 | 89 | 7 | 5 | .583 | 45 | 36 | 76 | 3.45 |

### Batting Record

| Year | Team, Lg. | G | AB | R | H | 2B | 3B | HR | RBI | BA |
|---|---|---|---|---|---|---|---|---|---|---|
| 1957 | St. Louis, NL | 17 | 26 | 0 | 0 | 0 | 0 | 0 | 0 | .000 |
| 1958 | St. Louis, NL | 2 | 0 | 0 | 0 | 0 | 0 | 0 | 0 | .000 |
| 1959 | Daytona Beach, FSL | 104 | 342 | 63 | 107 | 12 | 1 | 10 | 71 | .313 |
| 1960 | Tulsa, TxL | 12 | 13 | 2 | 3 | 1 | 0 | 0 | 2 | .231 |
|  | Winnipeg, NoL | 71 | 283 | 53 | 79 | 16 | 3 | 10 | 72 | .279 |
| 1961 | Tulsa, TxL | 130 | 455 | 67 | 121 | 21 | 3 | 15 | 64 | .266 |
| 1962 | Oklahoma City, AA | 134 | 458 | 54 | 113 | 25 | 4 | 14 | 70 | .247 |

## 20. Von McDaniel

| Year | Team, Lg. | G | AB | R | H | 2B | 3B | HR | RBI | BA |
|---|---|---|---|---|---|---|---|---|---|---|
| 1963 | Oklahoma City, PCL | 69 | 163 | 16 | 35 | 4 | 4 | 5 | 22 | .215 |
| 1964 | Oklahoma City, PCL | 13 | 41 | 3 | 8 | 0 | 0 | 1 | 3 | .195 |
|  | San Antonio, TxL | 113 | 405 | 61 | 106 | 27 | 3 | 17 | 74 | .262 |
| 1965 | Dallas-Fort Worth, TxL | 104 | 352 | 37 | 77 | 18 | 1 | 7 | 41 | .219 |
| 1966 | Dallas-Fort Worth, TxL | 109 | 326 | 29 | 73 | 8 | 1 | 4 | 40 | .224 |
| **Major Lg. Totals** |  | **19** | **26** | **0** | **0** | **0** | **0** | **0** | **0** | **.000** |

# 21 Don Pavletich

*The Cincinnati Reds signed Don Pavletich in 1957 for a bonus of $30,000.*

BRENT KELLEY: *Were your actual bonus and the amount announced the same?*
DON PAVLETICH: The bonus was $30,000; it was announced as $20,000.
*Who scouted you for the Reds?*
DP: Phil Seghi.
*How many teams were after you?*
DP: I'm gonna take a guess. Maybe ten.
*Were there any other bonus offers?*
DP: Baltimore talked about a bonus offer.
*You joined the Reds in spring training of 1957. When did you sign?*
DP: I signed in August of '56. I didn't join them then. I went to spring training with them in '57.

What happened with me was, I went to spring training with Cincinnati and I had to be on the club because I signed a bonus and they — a kind of unique situation here — actually wanted me to go into the service to get some playing time and I would get my service out of the way in the meantime, 'cause they were drafting people at that time. And they wanted to have, I believe it was George Crowe, if I'm not mistaken, was the fellow they wanted to keep on the roster because they were going for the pennant at that time. We had Ed Bailey and Smokey Burgess and I wasn't gonna catch at all. Bailey was catching and Burgess was a pinch hitter and catcher at different times, so I wasn't gonna play. I knew that, so I went in the service and I was in for two years.

*Did the time in the service count on your bonus time?*
DP: It counted on your pension. It counted against the two years because I came out in 1959, went to spring training with Cincinnati, and then I went to Topeka, Kansas, right away.
*You pinch hit in 1957 before you left for the service.*

DP: I hit for Don Newcombe. I walked.

*How long were you with the team?*

DP: I was there until May of '57 and I went right in the service from there. Then I was in the service in '58 and I got out in February of '59. I got out three months early. I enlisted for two years; you could get out up to three months early. I was considered hardship because I was gonna make it to spring training and it was my livelihood.

*How did your teammates receive you when you joined the Reds in 1957?*

DP: For the brief time that I was there, fine. There was no problem. I just came out of high school and I had some pretty good credentials. I had a lot to learn. I was accepted fine.

Don Pavletich

*Was anyone in particular helpful?*

DP: Over the years, Frank Robinson was probably the most help to me. He was probably the most help as far as hitting. I don't recall anybody specifically in those first couple months, but over the time I was in Cincinnati. Robinson was the most helpful.

*Several Bonus Babies mentioned the lack of coaching.*

DP: I wasn't there long enough to realize it, but Birdie Tebbetts was the manager. He was a catcher plus a psychologist — he had a major in psychology — so I saw where he handled the ballplayers in that short length of time quite uniquely — I would say that's the word to use — plus he knew his things about catching. I found them to be okay, no problems.

*Tebbetts had a reputation for liking young players.*

DP: I think he liked me, maybe because he was a catcher and that's what I was.

*Was the adjustment difficult?*

DP: Oh, definitely! You go from high school and you end up with a few bucks in your pocket, not that I had that much money. You're traveling with the big boys now and it was quite an adjustment.

*Did the veterans help you with the adjustment?*

DP: Yeah. I don't recall any problems with any of the ballplayers. They would tell me how to act, they would tell me how to dress. (Laughs) The whole shot—what you should wear and what you shouldn't wear. They were very helpful.

*You did well when you went to the minor leagues in 1959. Do you think this is where you belonged in the first place?*

DP: Not necessarily 'cause everything worked out quite well really 'cause I knew, being the fact that they had Bailey and Burgess, that I was not going to play. The chances were very slim, I figured that if I did go in the service and I think at that time the service ball was compared to like [class] B ball, and I figured I can play two years of minor league ball and come out. In '59 I came out and played minor league in '60, '61, and in '62 I was up in the major leagues.

So after coming out of the service I spent three years in the minor leagues and went from [class] B—Topeka—went to Columbia, ,South Carolina—[class] A—then I was at San Diego for a little while, which was Triple-A, and then Indianapolis, Triple-A.

The way it all worked out, I didn't second-guess myself that I did anything wrong.

*That's not a typical answer. Many had second thoughts.*

DP: As to what?

*As to signing the bonus contract and rusting for two years.*

DP: They sat for two years where I was playing ball and getting some experience where I figured I was not gonna play. It probably worked out for the best. And, I might add, I did get a few bucks for going in the service.

*What is your opinion of the bonus rule in general, not specifically as it applied to you?*

DP: I don't think there should ever be a bonus rule. If the guy can get the money and regardless if they have him at the major league level or the minor league level, whatever it may be, just because he can get X amount of dollars over a certain amount means that he's gotta be in the major leagues, I don't think that's in the best interest of the ballplayer. I think that's kinda what you've been hearing from the guys because they got more than 4,000 they had to sit on their rear ends for two years, which to them was not helpful whatsoever. I don't think there should even be a bonus rule.

*So you feel that the rule was detrimental?*

DP: Yeah. Like in my case, it worked out. That wasn't the thing I wanted to do—go into the service and not be a major league ballplayer—

but after I talked about it with my mother and dad, a few other people, I figured it might not be too bad an idea 'cause at least I'd be playing ball there. We had some pretty good competition. I went over to Europe and I played ball all summer over there. Didn't put a [Army] uniform on through the whole summer. A few people were a little angry about that, but we had some pretty good competition over there. I think that may have helped.

*So you didn't have all the disadvantages of the bonus rule, but had all the advantages.*

DP: After I go back and think about it, it worked out fine. I was in the service when I was 18-years-old and I grew up real quick.

*When you came back up to the Reds, you backed up Johnny Edwards for a while, then you platooned. Later on with the White Sox, it looked as if you were going to be a regular and then you got injured.*

DP: I broke my hand. That was pretty much the whole year right there. I did come back and play and then they traded me to Boston the next year.

## Donald Stephen Pavletich

Born July 13, 1938, Milwaukee, WI
Ht. 5'11" Wt. 190 Batted and Threw Right

| Year | Team, Lg. | G | AB | R | H | 2B | 3B | HR | RBI | BA |
|---|---|---|---|---|---|---|---|---|---|---|
| 1957 | Cincinnati, NL | 1 | 1 | 0 | 0 | 0 | 0 | 0 | 0 | .000 |
| 1958 | Military service | | | | | | | | | |
| 1959 | Cincinnati, NL | 1 | 0 | 1 | 0 | 0 | 0 | 0 | 0 | .000 |
| | Topeka, III | 69 | 242 | 38 | 67 | 12 | 0 | 12 | 50 | .277 |
| 1960 | Columbia, SAL | 15 | 43 | 7 | 12 | 2 | 0 | 0 | 10 | .279 |
| | Topeka, III | 89 | 324 | 52 | 92 | 18 | 2 | 10 | 65 | .284 |
| 1961 | Indianapolis. AA | 142 | 511 | 76 | 151 | 28 | 2 | 22 | 78 | .295 |
| 1962 | Cincinnati, NL | 34 | 63 | 7 | 14 | 3 | 0 | 1 | 7 | .222 |
| 1963 | Cincinnati, NL | 71 | 183 | 18 | 38 | 11 | 0 | 5 | 18 | .208 |
| | San Diego, PCL | 30 | 121 | 19 | 35 | 5 | 2 | 6 | 19 | .289 |
| 1964 | Cincinnati, NL | 34 | 91 | 12 | 22 | 4 | 0 | 5 | 11 | .242 |
| | San Diego, PCL | 71 | 235 | 51 | 71 | 15 | 2 | 12 | 40 | .302 |
| 1965 | Cincinnati, NL | 68 | 191 | 25 | 61 | 11 | 1 | 8 | 32 | .319 |
| 1966 | Cincinnati, NL | 83 | 235 | 29 | 69 | 13 | 2 | 12 | 38 | .294 |
| 1967 | Cincinnati, NL | 74 | 231 | 25 | 55 | 14 | 3 | 6 | 34 | .238 |
| 1968 | Cincinnati, NL | 46 | 98 | 11 | 28 | 3 | 1 | 2 | 11 | .286 |
| 1969 | Chicago, AL | 78 | 188 | 26 | 46 | 12 | 1 | 6 | 33 | .245 |
| 1970 | Boston, AL | 32 | 65 | 4 | 9 | 1 | 1 | 0 | 6 | .138 |
| 1971 | Boston, AL | 13 | 27 | 5 | 7 | 1 | 0 | 1 | 3 | .259 |
| **Major Lg. Totals** | | 536 | 1373 | 163 | 349 | 73 | 8 | 46 | 193 | .254 |

# 22 Buddy Pritchard

*Buddy Pritchard signed with the Pirates in 1957 for a bonus of $30,000.*

*BRENT KELLEY: What was your bonus announced as?*
BUDDY PRITCHARD: It was announced at $50,000. Actually, with my salary it was around that, but the actual bonus was only $30,000.
*Who signed you?*
BP: Joe Brown.
*How many teams were after you?*
BP: I don't know. Playing at [University of] Southern California I was contacted by several through the years, but I wasn't eligible to be signed. And then Pittsburgh just, more or less out of the blue, they worked me out. I didn't really want to leave SC at that time; I'd been voted captain of the team and I was to graduate and all that, so they asked me what it would take to sign me and I gave what I thought was a ridiculous figure and they said all right. (Laughs) I think, actually, nobody really anticipated me signing until after my senior year.
*Did you return to school later and get your degree?*
BP: Yeah, I went back and got my Bachelor's and my Master's degrees.
*A much higher percentage of Bonus Babies have college educations.*
BP: I think a lot of the college players, at least around my area, do go back and get their degrees. I don't know what the percentage is.
Right now I scout for the major league scouting bureau and I'd say the majority of the [college] players that sign, regardless of what kind of money they get, come back and do finish up. I think most of the kids that are coming back and finishing, though, are juniors and, at least up until this point, they can't sign 'til they're juniors, so a lot of 'em only have a year to go.
*Are many of the boys who sign out of high school going on to college?*
BP: Yeah. In fact, it's getting tougher to sign high school kids. I would say, as far as the good ones are concerned, unless they get an astronomical

amount of money, most of 'em are going on to college. It's really competitive between the schools and professional baseball.

The colleges do a good job of scouting. They know who's out there. The reason that the rounds [in the draft] aren't announced is because of the agents. That doesn't prevent them from finding out either, though.

A lot of kids, what they do, they go on to school; if they're fringe-type prospects they're not gonna be offered a great deal of money so they go on to school and they sign after their senior year. They've got their education and they give pro ball a shot and most of 'em don't make it, but at least they had the opportunity.

Buddy Pritchard (Courtesy Buddy Pritchard)

*How was the reception from your teammates when you joined the team?*

BP: I felt comfortable right off the bat and there wasn't any animosity or anything. I had read some things in the paper about the fact that, as a result of—and Pittsburgh had signed several bonus players—there were some comments about having to play with a limited roster and that type thing, but as far as individuals themselves, there was no problem. I played that one year with Pittsburgh; I played about eight years in the organization and then I managed for them and over the period of close to 15 years I really never met anybody in the whole organization I didn't like or get along with.

I always like to say I started at the top and worked my way down. (Laughs) I don't have any regrets because, between SC and Pittsburgh, everything I've got I basically owe them. It was a real experience.

*Some of the older players were kind of rough on some of the Bonus Babies.*

BP: Nah. Never once did I have any incidents like that. Seems like the bigger the stars, the friendlier they were. You know, Roberto Clemente and Vernon Law and Dick Groat used to help me all the time. [Bill] Mazeroski was my roommate. I got all the help I could get. It was just the fact that I didn't get to play very much.

*Your managers were Bobby Bragan for two-thirds of the year and then Danny Murtaugh. It's been said that Bragan was not particularly thrilled with young players.*

BP: He never made that evident to me. He made some comments in the papers that were flattering, as far as I was concerned. 'Course, he also made some comments comparing the fact that I was a bonus player compared to Mazeroski, who wasn't. He never did anything that was negative or anything like that.

Murtaugh was great. He was just a good baseball man and he was a funny Irishman — had a lot of stories and everything — and he had his own way of dealing with things. He was great with the press. He just did a good job.

When I managed with Pittsburgh and scouted for 'em, I'd run into Danny all the time and he was just like he always was. Like I say, I didn't run into anybody in the whole Pirate organization who I ever disliked or anything. And Joe Brown [general manager], he's the one that signed me and stuck his neck out for me and to this day we see each other and are friendly. He scouts the same area I do and he's always kidding me about wanting me to give the money back. (Laughs)

*How was the coaching you received? Many Bonus Babies say it was insufficient.*

BP: I think that's the individual player's fault. Obviously, they're not going to spend as much with a Bonus Baby. For example, I was a shortstop and Dick Groat, he was always willing to help me. You get a lot of help from various people, a lot of advice, and you've gotta be smart enough to pick out *what* can help you and apply it and overlook the other advice.

I don't think I ever asked a player or coach to help me that he didn't help me. I think oftentimes, at least if I'm a coach, it's difficult to get through to a guy that doesn't want help. No, I don't have any complaints from that area. I think that's the way you learn in baseball, from other players, particularly veteran players.

Groat, he was an outstanding player and a very intelligent guy and I've always been surprised he didn't wind up being a major league manager. I think it's just because he didn't wanna go down in the minor leagues and manage. He never played in the minor leagues. I think it might have been an ego thing that he didn't wanna go down and manage and work his way up. He was really an intelligent player and I've often wondered why he never wound up managing.

*How did you find the adjustment?*

BP: I think probably it's one of the most difficult things for a player. When I was managing, that's one of the things you have to look out for. You get kids that it's their first time away from home and they either go wild or they're just real homesick.

The biggest adjustment I had to make wasn't *off* the field, it was on the field. I was used to being the big fish in a little pond and now all of a sudden I'm playing with guys that are better than I am. Probably that is the biggest adjustment I had to make and I think that's probably a big adjustment for all kids coming out of high school and college.

I realized that my ability was limited. I didn't have any false ideas about that, but I just was used to playing all the time and I didn't get to play much so that was a big adjustment for me.

*Do you remember your base hit?*

BP: Yeah. I got it off Don Newcombe in a game against Brooklyn at Forbes Field.

My first at bat we were playing Milwaukee and it was off T-Bone Phillips. I hit a line drive to right-center and I thought, "Crime, this is a piece of cake," you know, base hit first time up. Billy Bruton came out of nowhere and sucked it in. (Laughs) Right then I figured this is gonna be a little tougher than I thought.

*You signed in the last year of the bonus rule. For four years, you had seen the boys sign and sit on the bench and rust from disuse. Did you have any reservations about signing a bonus contract?*

BP: No, not really. I was cocky enough to think that wasn't going to be a problem for me. (Laughs)

My only reservation was the fact I enjoyed playing for [coach Rod] Dedeaux at SC and I really would've liked to play my last year. Like I say, Pittsburgh asked me what I wanted and I told 'em a figure I thought was a little out of line, but they said okay, so there wasn't much else I could do.

*When somebody hands you more money than you've ever seen, you have to take it.*

BP: Especially when I was only a semester away from graduation.

*In retrospect, would you do it again or would you choose to go to the minor leagues?*

BP: I don't know. Obviously, after I've thought of that, I really don't know. Maybe if I would've started in Class D or C ball, maybe I'd have never got out of it. Then again, maybe I would've wound up being a major league player.

The problem with me was, I really didn't have a whole lot of ability.

I just was one of those guys that hustled and did what you had to do to be effective.

I really don't have any regrets. I enjoyed my time at SC playing for Dedeaux and I've enjoyed all the people from the Pittsburgh organization. Obviously, I would've preferred to have stayed in the major leagues longer. But I got to manage for Pittsburgh and I've been scouting now for more than 20 years, so I'm still involved in the game. I don't have any complaints.

You often wonder — you know, there are about ten more clubs than there were then — so probably everybody in my situation feels if I'd have come along at this time rather than then you'd have had a whole lot better chance of making the big leagues. At that time, as I see it, I spent most of my career in Triple-A. Triple-A at that time was probably the equivalent of second division clubs in the major leagues right now.

I played against most of the good ones somewhere along the line, at least at that time. I played in the [Pacific] Coast League and the International League.

*Where in the Coast League?*

BP: For Salt Lake City and we won the pennant in 1959. It was the old Hollywood franchise and I played for 'em a year after they moved to Salt Lake. Then I played at Columbus in the International League for several years.

*Did you go to spring training with Pittsburgh?*

BP: Yeah, I spent two spring trainings with Pittsburgh.

*Did you consider switching positions to try to get back up? Shortstop and second base were pretty well covered.*

BP: I could play all the infield positions. Yeah, they had it pretty well covered with Groat and Mazeroski. Actually, I did pretty well in spring training the two springs I was there. I hit over .400 each time, but that would be early in the spring and then the veterans would start playing in the games and the extra guys usually would just go in and pick 'em up in the sixth and seventh inning.

*Who'd they carry as backups?*

BP: When I was with Pittsburgh, we had Gene Freese and Gene Baker and the O'Brien twins. Those were the extra infielders.

*What is your opinion of the bonus rule?*

BP: I think, in retrospect, it doesn't do the player justice because at that time you were supposed to spend two years in the major leagues and most of the bonus players weren't gonna be playing for the two years so that's gonna hamper their progress. If you have one or two bonus players on the club, that means you're limiting your roster by a couple guys that really aren't gonna help you, unless you're talking about an Al Kaline or something like that.

So all the way around, I didn't think the bonus rule was beneficial to either the club *or* the player.

*I think the Pirates had four or five Bonus Babies on their roster at one point.*

BP: We had four I remember when I was there: the O'Brien twins and Art Swanson and myself.

*The O'Briens bonus days were over then.*

BP: Yeah. Johnny stayed the whole year and they sent Eddie out.

*Johnny had become a pitcher by that time, hadn't he?*

BP: He was bouncing back and forth. That might have been the first year he started to pitch some. Basically, the year I was there he was an infielder.

We could have fielded a pretty good basketball team. With the O'Briens and Groat that's a pretty good nucleus.

*Some questioned a player's incentive after receiving a large bonus.*

BP: At least in my case, I didn't think anything about the money. The only thing the money meant to me was the fact it was kind of a prestige thing, but they could've given me a million dollars and I would have tried as hard as I could to make it. I really felt obligated to the Pirates because they reared me so well and they did have an investment in me. I wanted to make sure that I made it back to 'em. Joe Brown has told me, even though I didn't get back to the big leagues, he knows I tried as hard as I could and they feel they got their money's worth throughout the years.

'Course, the guys I see today in the big leagues, they're making thirty million dollars and I wouldn't have 'em on the club because some of 'em don't play hard, as far as I'm concerned. Maybe they're not motivated, but my problem was I played so hard I was hurt all the time and that's one of the reasons I didn't get back to the big leagues. I don't have much sympathy for guys that *don't* make the extra effort.

Individual major league baseball players have gotta be better than they were when I played because all other athletes are better, but the quality of teams aren't as hood because the talent is so diluted. I can't believe that the major league clubs are as good now as they were then. For one thing, there's not as much pitching. Like I said, I think probably the Triple-A clubs when I played might have been the equivalent of the second division clubs in the major leagues tight now.

I remember in the Coast League some of those guys signed contracts that they couldn't go to the big leagues. They preferred the Coast League. They made more money than they would in the big leagues.

## Harold William "Buddy" Pritchard

Born January 25, 1936, South Gate, CA
Ht. 6'1" Wt. 195 Batted and Threw Right

| Year | Team, Lg. | G | AB | R | H | 2B | 3B | HR | RBI | BA |
|---|---|---|---|---|---|---|---|---|---|---|
| 1957 | Pittsburgh, NL | 23 | 11 | 1 | 1 | 0 | 0 | 0 | 0 | .083 |
| 1958 | Salt Lake City, PCL | 11 | 18 | 0 | 2 | 0 | 0 | 0 | 0 | .111 |
|  | Lincoln, WL | 97 | 214 | 42 | 84 | 16 | 4 | 2 | 48 | .268 |
| 1959 | Salt Lake City, PCL | 69 | 201 | 29 | 50 | 6 | 3 | 4 | 18 | .249 |
| 1960 | Savannah, SAL | 115 | 403 | 51 | 102 | 14 | 3 | 12 | 51 | .253 |
| 1961 | Columbus, IL | 103 | 330 | 38 | 83 | 9 | 4 | 4 | 30 | .252 |
| 1962 | Columbus, IL | 72 | 247 | 27 | 68 | 8 | 0 | 3 | 30 | .275 |
| 1963 | Columbus, IL | 8 | 183 | 23 | 42 | 2 | 3 | 0 | 15 | .230 |
| 1964 | Asheville, SL | 47 | 135 | 17 | 41 | 4 | 0 | 5 | 13 | .304 |
| 1965 | Asheville, SL | 58 | 101 | 16 | 23 | 5 | 1 | 0 | 7 | .228 |

# 23 Jerry Walker

*Jerry Walker signed with the Orioles in 1957 for $20,000 salary plus bonus. He was an All-Star in 1959 and later in his career, he picked up the save in Early Wynn's 300th career victory and was the Tigers' general manager in the 1990s.*

BRENT KELLEY: You were the youngest starter and winner of an All-Star game [1959].

JERRY WALKER: That was very exciting. I remember the situation very well. I pitched in relief in a game in Cleveland on a Saturday prior to the All-Star game. Gus Triandos was the catcher and he was on the All-Star team and I threw a pitch and it was fouled off and it hit him on the back of the hand. Of course, he was unable to go to the All-Star game.

This was the second All-Star game that year, so the game was played on a Monday and there was no off-day. On Sunday we were sitting in the bullpen looking at the other games and seeing that a lot of the guys that were in the All-Star game were pitching on that day and wondering who was gonna pitch [in the All-Star game].

I went in after the game and they told me I was going to the All-Star game. I got on a plane in Cleveland and flew to Chicago and we spent the night there. The next morning I found out I was gonna start. We got to Los Angeles and got off the airplane and went directly to the Coliseum and I pitched. Really, it all happened before I knew what was going on — didn't have time to think about it.

*What happened after the game and the next season?*

JW: There is nothing that I can say. The All-Star game was in August and I think I was 8-and-5 at the time. I don't think I pitched much differently the rest of that year than I did up to that point.

I pitched a 16-inning ballgame that a lot of people say finished me, but I can't say that. I only threw 170 pitches or something and a lot of guys throw that many in a nine-inning game. I can't say that hurt me at all.

The next year, I remember early in the year I pitched some good ballgames and wound up with a lot of no-decisions. Then I had trouble with allergies and respiratory problems, which finally I had to get treatment for. Whether that was a big part of my problem, I don't know. By that time, we had all the other young pitchers and we were having a good year and winning and I just never got back in the rotation.

There's nothing I can put my finger on. Looking back at it from this end, having been a pitching instructor, I think the thing that happened to me Is the thing that happens to a lot of young guys. They come up and they throw the ball and let movement take care of location and they're not afraid to throw the ball over the plate. Then, after a while, they get to thinking, "I got it on the corner. I'm gonna throw this one just off the corner." Then they wind up thinking too much and get too fine.

Then I got to where I was getting behind and when I threw the ball over the plate, I got hit. When you throw the ball over the plate and get hit, you're afraid to throw it over the plate.

Jerry Walker

Looking at it 40 years down the road, I would say that, if anything was a problem, that's what my problem was.

*Back in 1957, you made three starts as an 18-year-old.*

JW: I made one that I didn't get through the first inning. The first game I pitched in I threw 11 pitches and ten of 'em were balls and then I pitched a couple of times and threw the ball over the plate. Then I got a start and didn't pitch very good, didn't get through the first inning. And then I pitched more in relief and my next start I pitched a one-nothing shutout, maybe ten innings.

*When you joined the Orioles, how were you received by your teammates?*

JW: I think very well. You

look back at it now and look at the circumstances and you wonder. I know when I signed there was a lot of talk about guys not treating the young fellows good, but I had no problem with it. I'd heard all that stuff—that the players wouldn't treat you good and wouldn't help you and all that—but it was definitely not that way with the Orioles.

*Your manager, Paul Richards, liked young players very much. How did you get along with him?*

JW: I got along with him fine. Paul Richards was a very businesslike manager and showed very little emotion. He didn't talk with the players a lot, especially during the game, but I just assumed that's the way it was. I had no problems at all with him.

*Did you receive adequate coaching?*

JW: Paul Richards was very much a pitcher's manager. He and Harry Brecheen spent time working with the pitchers. I think we got more attention than the other players.

Paul was a catcher and he made special note of the young pitchers. Whenever the young pitchers threw, he was always there with Harry. I think we got plenty of attention.

*Were the veteran pitchers on the staff helpful?*

JW: The pitchers were very helpful to me. Skinny Brown, in particular. Connie Johnson was there when I signed, Billy Loes, Ray Moore—all older pitchers and all of 'em very, very helpful to me.

I was very, very close to Skinny. I went back when they put him in the Orioles Hall of Fame, then I saw him at the end of the season at the auction they had to close out Memorial Stadium.

*You spent four years with Baltimore, then two years with Kansas City and two years with Cleveland. Your last year in the majors was 1964.*

JW: In '64 I went back to the minors. I was in the Cleveland organization at that time. They had [Sam] McDowell and [Luis] Tiant and those fellows. I think they were with Portland, so there wasn't room for me out there and they sent me to Jacksonville, which was the Cardinals' Triple-A club, on a loan. I spent the year there and then came back to Cleveland at the end of the year.

After that, they took me off the roster that winter and I pitched in '65 at Portland. At the end of that year, my contract was traded to the Yankees organization and I spent '66 in Triple-A ball with the Yankees and then in '67 I was a player-coach at Binghamton, Double-A ball. Then I started managing and I managed five years in the Yankee organization.

Then I scouted for the Yankees for a good while in different areas and wound up briefly as the Yankees pitching coach. I went to Houston in '83 for three years as pitching coach down there before I came to Detroit.

*By 1957, the year you signed, the fates of the earlier Bonus Babies had been seen. Did you have any second thoughts about signing and being kept on the major league roster for two years with possibly little chance to pitch?*

JW: No, I really didn't. I think everybody feels like they have the ability. Anybody that wants to play the game thinks they have the ability to survive and to contribute. Probably after I pitched a couple of games I may have doubted my ability, but before that, no, I had no doubts about my ability and didn't think anything at all because I knew that I wouldn't get to pitch a lot, but I'd get to pitch some and learn some things.

*Did the bonus rule hurt you?*

JW: I don't think so. If I'd had to sit there for two years, it might have hurt me. The first year I was there basically for three months—July, August, and September—and I learned a lot during that period of time. I pitched a little and I learned a lot. Then you played doubleheaders on Sundays and had Mondays off and I threw batting practice every Sunday after the doubleheaders if I didn't get to pitch. If they were close games and I didn't get to pitch, then after it was over I got to throw batting practice to Tito Francona and some other guys.

I learned a lot. Some guys can be around baseball all their lives and have a good time and never learn anything. I'm sure that some guys it *did* hurt, but I can't say it hurt me.

*When you look at the statistics, you find a much higher percentage of top ballplayers from the ranks of Bonus Babies than you do from those who did not receive bonuses. You wonder, of course, what would have come from the boys who played five games in two years and were never heard from again, if they had been allowed to develop.*

JW: That's a question you don't know. It's just like the draft now. You can take the players that are drafted in the first or second round and, percentage-wise, more of those guys wind up at the major league level than guys drafted down lower.

[Sandy] Koufax was a Bonus Baby, but how long was it before he really produced? Quite truthfully, if he was not a Bonus Baby, he might have been out pitching and hurt his arm and never pitched at all. You never know. It's just one of those things you can argue about 'til the sun goes down and you're still not gonna know the answer.

*The team is going to try a lot harder with the high draft choice or the Bonus Baby than it will with some kid it signed for bus fare.*

JW: They've got money in him. They're gonna try to find out if he *can* play or not. He's gonna have to prove that he *cannot*. A fellow that they don't have money in is gonna have to prove that he *can* play. That's a fact of life.

Just like the number one drafts now have to prove year after year that they *can't* play, where the kid that just wants a chance has got to keep proving every place he goes that he deserves to go to the next classification.

*You were a good hitting pitcher. One year you hit .368, tops in the major leagues for a pitcher, and for your career you hit .230 with four home runs.*

JW: I played other positions. In fact, Boston wanted to sign me as a third baseman, and the Cardinals wanted me as a catcher. I signed with Baltimore because, first off, they gave me the money, what was the equivalent of a major league contract. That's what it amounted to, I went to the big leagues. That was my objective. Money-wise, the actual bonus I got was just slightly over the $4,000. My total package was $20,000; that included salary for two years. That's really why I signed with Baltimore. The chances of making it to the big leagues were better that way than as a position player.

*You were also an excellent fielder. You went six years in a row without making an error.*

JW: I was fortunate to have a good high school baseball coach that knew how to teach baseball and teach discipline and knew what to do with the ball. We worked hard on fielding then.

I played third base and shortstop in high school and caught in Legion ball, so I knew how to play other positions. And back then we played pepper for hours and hours, even during the season.

*Other than the All-Star game and that first shutout against the Senators, is there a game that stands out?*

JW: I pitched a game against the White Sox in '59, the one I mentioned, the 16-inning shutout. I won that one, 1-to-nothing. I think that has to be the top game I ever pitched.

*Who was the best player or hitter you saw?*

JW: I played against the Mantles and the Marises and those type people. Other than spring training, I really didn't see Mays and McCovey and those very much. Mantle had probably the greatest ability of anybody I ever played against.

I did get to pitch against [Ted] Williams at the end of his career. Just watching him, I would have to say that he was the best hitter that I had seen. A year like George Brett had a few years ago, where he hit almost .400, was great, but Williams did it over a career.

*Who was the best pitcher you saw?*

JW: That's really a tough one. Probably the best year I saw anybody have was [Ron] Guidry's year [1978] with the Yankees, which was after I quit playing. Of course, I know that [Bob] Gibson and some other people have had years that were as great; any given year a pitcher can be outstanding.

*Did you save souvenirs from your career?*

JW: I saved some and our house burned several years ago. Most of 'em burned up. The house burned on the Fourth of July from the top down, evidently from a pop bottle rocket. I had most of my stuff in the attic and I salvaged none of that. I had a few things— a few baseballs and a few clippings— downstairs in a cabinet and they were saved.

## Jerry Allen Walker

Born February 12, 1939, Ada. OK
Ht. 6'1" Wt. 195 Batted Both, Threw Right

| Year | Team, Lg. | G | IP | W | L | Pct | SO | BB | H | ERA |
|---|---|---|---|---|---|---|---|---|---|---|
| 1957 | Baltimore, AL | 13 | 28 | 1 | 0 | 1.000 | 13 | 14 | 24 | 2.93 |
| 1958 | Baltimore, AL | 6 | 10 | 0 | 0 | .000 | 6 | 5 | 16 | 6.97 |
|  | Knoxville, SAL | 28 | 200 | 18 | 4 | .818 | 126 | 78 | 164 | 2.61 |
| 1959 | Baltimore, AL | 30 | 182 | 11 | 10 | .524 | 100 | 52 | 160 | 2.92 |
| 1960 | Baltimore, AL | 29 | 118 | 3 | 4 | .429 | 48 | 56 | 161 | 4.82 |
| 1961 | Kansas City, AL | 36 | 168 | 8 | 14 | .364 | 56 | 96 | 161 | 4.82 |
| 1962 | Kansas City, AL | 31 | 143 | 8 | 9 | .471 | 57 | 78 | 165 | 5.90 |
| 1963 | Cleveland, AL | 39 | 88 | 6 | 6 | .500 | 41 | 36 | 82 | 4.91 |
| 1964 | Cleveland, AL | 6 | 10 | 0 | 1 | .000 | 5 | 4 | 9 | 4.66 |
|  | Jacksonville, IL | 23 | 135 | 10 | 9 | .526 | 76 | 35 | 126 | 4.20 |
| 1965 | Portland, PCL | 56 | 95 | 6 | 8 | .429 | 76 | 49 | 90 | 3.79 |
| 1966 | Toledo, IL | 39 | 97 | 1 | 6 | .143 | 59 | 46 | 91 | 3.43 |
| 1967 | Binghamton, EL | 5 | 11 | 0 | 1 | .000 | 5 | 4 | 8 | 3.27 |
| **Major Lg. Totals** |  | 190 | 747 | 37 | 44 | .457 | 326 | 341 | 734 | 4.36 |

# 24 Frank Zupo

*The Orioles signed Frank Zupo to a $50,000 bonus in 1957.*

BRENT KELLEY: *What was your bonus announced as and what was it really?*
FRANK ZUPO: My bonus was $50,000. It was reported as $30,000.
*Who scouted you?*
FZ: Don McShane, who's gone now, and Freddie Hofmann, old Bootnose. I talked to Paul Richards over the telephone.
*Richards liked young players.*
FZ: Yeah, he did. My big problem there wasn't Richards, it was [Lee] MacPhail.
*Were other teams after you?*
FZ: Sixteen. The whole thing. And I had scholarships to Stanford, University of California — not on my grades, on baseball. But I didn't want to go to college. It was a little bit different then. You don't get a four-year scholarship anymore. I had a full deal, but I didn't want to go to school. I had enough of it in high school. I just wanted to get the hell out of there and play baseball.
*Do you know whose roster spot you took?*
FZ: I don't have any idea. I wanna say Jim Pyburn. His two years were up. I didn't have to do that, but I could've fought it. I wanted to get to the minors and get back to the big leagues.
We needed to be sent down. There was no doubt about it. No one was gonna get out of high school and go to play in the big leagues. The first night I got there I seen Billy Pierce strike out 14. I was hiding behind the water cooler. I never seen anybody throw a baseball so hard in my life!
*You were thrown out of a game before you got into one.*
FZ: We were playing the Yankees. In those days, the starting pitcher used to warm up right in front of the dugout. In Baltimore, the warning track was grey and it had been raining. It stopped raining and we had like

52,000 in the park and they weren't gonna let them get away. I was warming Billy Loes up and the catchers, whether it was wet or dry, we always used a towel down to kneel on 'cause that shale hurts your leg.

He was warming up and only had about another eight or ten pitches to throw. He was almost hot. The umpires had come out and they had the baseballs in their hands in their big leather bag. I didn't see 'em walking between me and Loes. I had just caught a pitch and I was gonna throw it back and I stopped it. Nobody moved except Ed Hurley; he went down on both knees and dropped the baseballs out of the bag. Maybe ten or 15 balls came out. They all wore black then and he got his pants all full of this grey stuff. It stuck to you like glue. It was clinging; I don't know what it was.

I think Loes threw three or four more pitches and I picked the towel up and I'm walking back toward the dugout and he [Hurley] was notorious for throwing rookies out and he's really jawing at me from home plate. Richards grabs me and says, "Hey, what'd you do?" He said, "He's gonna run you." I said, "No way." He's letting me have it and I finally yelled back. He walked over toward the dugout and I walk right up and finally he ran me. Before the game started, I got run, Richards got run, and Harry Brecheen got run. He got three of us, so we sat in Paul's office and watched it on TV.

Then after the ballgame there was a note in my locker to go down to the umpires' room. I went down there and he apologized. He says, "Frank, I shouldn't have done that. It was a mistake. We got off on the wrong foot and I don't want that to happen." He was a hard-nosed umpire, but he was a *good* umpire. And he says to me, "You get four strikes the rest of the year and all next year." Well, that was safe giving me four strikes 'cause I wasn't gonna play anyway.

But Opening Day the following season, I hit with the bases loaded against L.A. and Eli Grba was pitching and I just went up there and I did not take the bat off my shoulder and he walked me with the bases loaded and we scored the winning run. I took three pitches on the inside of the plate that could've been strikes as well as balls. He called four balls in a row.

Frank Zupo (courtesy Frank Zupo)

## 24. Frank Zupo

*How was the reception from your teammates?*

FZ: There was absolutely no animosity toward the [bonus] ballplayers at all, I think the reason being that it was a big bonus movement at the time.

They gave me the nickname "Noodles." That was Billy Gardner; he thought my name was "Supo," so he called me "Noodles." They had a big thing over my locker, "Welcome Noodles." I didn't know who "Noodles" was. I didn't know who they were talking about.

The first guy I met when I walked in the clubhouse was Bob Nelson. We used to call him "Babe." I lived with Brooks Robinson in Baltimore the whole time I was there. Brooks and I used to live in a private home about five or six blocks up from the ballpark. Mr. and Mrs. Groton. We had a room upstairs, me and Brooks and Skinny Brown.

*Was Richards helpful?*

FZ: Yes, he was very helpful. He never really put himself forth with me. On blocking some pitches, he would help me there — kind of smother the ball. Other than that, he never really said anything. He said, "There's nothing to tell you. You do everything pretty well and just try to improve on what you're doing."

*Were the other players helpful?*

FZ: If you asked the other ballplayers questions, 95 percent of 'em were helpful. Bob Nieman was a great help if you asked Bob anything about hitting.

Gus Triandos and I became *really* close friends. Even now; he's in San Jose. I never had a lot to do with Joe Ginsberg and I didn't get along very well with Dick Williams. I didn't like Dick Williams. If Richards would've stopped quick, he'd have broke his nose. He wanted to be a manager. He couldn't throw a ball 50 feet. He shouldn't have been in the big leagues.

Bob Boyd, Billy Goodman, George Kell. George Kell was kind of a loner, but he would help a rookie if you *asked* him. He wouldn't come forth with it. Brooks and I and Ronnie Hansen, we were all rookies. Willie Miranda, Billy Gardner took us to play golf and we went to the dog races with these guys in spring training. They accepted you.

I always played with older ballplayers all my life. I never played with kids my own age. Then when [Jim] Gentile showed, we'd been friends for so many years we roomed together.

There were some quiet guys. Wayne Causey was very quiet. Al Pilarcik — very quiet. Art Ceccarelli was there, and Kenny Lehman. All the pitchers were fine. No one would give you a hard time. Different personalities. Skinny Brown was quiet. Jack Harshman — very quiet. Billy O'Dell.

There wasn't a lot of guys I didn't get along with. I didn't get along good with Dick Williams.

I don't care for Earl Weaver. I never will care for Earl Weaver. He can come up here and shine my shoes and I wouldn't give him a tip. I don't like him, I refused to play for him, I had nothing to do with him. I didn't like the way he treated younger pitchers then, I don't like the way he did it in the minors. He had absolutely no credentials at all. Everywhere he went [in the minors], he had Baltimore's cream of the crop. He had [Paul] Blair, he had [Andy] Etchebarren. The shortstop, [Mark] Belanger. He had everything he wanted. He had Boog Powell. He never had [Brooks] Robinson; he was there. Brooks won't say much, but I know how he feels. They didn't get along. Give me five 20-game winners and I'll win a pennant, too. You ask [Jim] Palmer; he'll tell you how he felt.

We had a meeting down in the Arizona Rookie League. Richards was talking about signs. He had a famous expression: "A donkey can shake his head." If you don't wanna throw it, shake it off. We never got signs from the dugout. When we went out, we talked about hitters, how we were gonna pitch these guys in different situations, if we were behind or ahead.

Like with [Harmon] Killebrew. You pitched him one way when you were ahead in a ballgame, another way when you were behind in a ballgame. This is what you have to do. Mantle — he was a notorious high ball hitter righthanded, a notorious low ball hitter lefthanded. We knew what we were gonna do to these guys. Mantle — we used to try to throw junk on the inside part of the plate and let him pull it foul and then bust him away outside, eight, ten inches away when he would have to go after the ball.

Now they got guys calling the pitches from the dugout. I don't know how they know what kinda stuff the pitcher's got. When you get to that level of baseball, there is no higher classification than that; that's the ultimate. When you get to that level, you're supposed to know what the hell you're doing!

*Was the adjustment to big league life difficult?*

FZ: It was tough. I never got to run free. At ten o'clock I better be in the house or there better be a good reason why. My dad said ten, but he meant five to ten. And if it was five after, there was hell to pay.

I used to work in a gas station to make 15 dollars. I worked an hour a night for a dollar and then ten dollars on Saturday and I was going to school. We were a close Italian family.

It was a tremendous adjustment. You find yourself learning a lot of bad habits. You're watching these guys on television then all of a sudden the next day you're sitting on the field with 'em and you can't accept that. You're in awe; for the first month you don't know what the hell's going on. You go to these different towns, you don't know where to go, you don't know where to eat. I think at the time, the meal money was ten dollars a day. You have a sandwich at the hotel — it's gonna cost you three or four dollars. Then you have dinner that night. I'll never forget going to Goldie Aherne's in Washington with Bob Nieman — there were eight of us — dinner was 20 dollars a head and we only got ten!

But they kinda watch out for you. They never really let you get into a *lot* of trouble. Even in spring training in Scottsdale — I was only in Scottsdale one year — I got to be real good friends with Charlie Briley, the owner of the Pink Pony, and he'd sneak me a beer with dinner once in a while, but I couldn't sit at the bar and drink 'cause I was underage.

I grew up probably too fast. I was in Baltimore going to Pimlico. I was 18-years-old and I was at the racetrack. It's the survival of the fittest. I didn't know what else to do with myself. I was alone in Baltimore. I got married the next year; I got married at 18. She was here and I was there. My family was here and you get a little homesick. You've never been away before. The furthest north I was ever was Sacramento and the furthest south was Long Beach. I never went east.

The thing that I found the *hardest* was not really during the ballgame or before the ballgame, it was always after the ballgame. You don't know where to go. You try to find things to do and places to go. People — you don't know how to distinguish the phonies from the nice ones until after you've been around for a little while.

Billy Martin, we were really close. It tore me apart when he got killed. I couldn't believe it. he was one of the greatest people that ever played. He was a ballplayer's manager, believe me when I tell you that. I'd have played for that son of a bitch on crutches, or tried. He was that kind of guy — you wanted to play for him. He expected you to do what he did: break your ass out there. He was the kinda guy that, when you're alongside of him he's using a pick and shovel and he's not gonna ask you to do something that he didn't do. That's why he got respect. A lotta guys don't like that 'cause they don't like to be *told*.

What did [Pete] Rose do that was so bad? Ty Cobb and Pepper Martin and these guys, they were womanizers and gamblers and drinkers. They made an example of him. If they don't let this man back in baseball and in the Hall of Fame, they're doing a great injustice. Lou Piniella won with his [Rose's] ballclub. When the Giants won the pennant, Tom Haller built that ballclub, not [Al] Rosen.

*Where did you go when you were sent down in '58?*

FZ: I went to Knoxville first. I stayed there most of the year, Steve Dalkowski and I. I went from Knoxville to Wilson, North Carolina, then I played in Stockton with Billy DeMars. I was always with the big club in spring training and then the Triple-A club. I guess I kinda balked at that, not pout, but I'd get pissed off, didn't think I should be sent down. I told Richards the same thing, especially when they picked up [Clint] Courtney. You've got a guy here who can't throw the ball 35 feet. He couldn't hit me if I ran across the plate and here I'm trying to win a job and "Well, you need more seasoning. We'll send you back to where you can play." That didn't sit too good with me.

*How long did you play in the minors?*

FZ: I signed in '57 and I had, off and on, three-and-a-half years in the big leagues. I quit in '65. I was at Rochester, I was at Dallas; one year I went to six clubs. I went to Salem, Oregon; I pinch hit that night and beat Yakima and went to Yakima the next day with Hub Kittle. I was there a total of two days and then I finally called the front office and talked to MacPhail and said, "Look, you better get your hat on straight, pal, 'cause I've had it with this stuff." I couldn't take it anymore, I was moving around, I was like a piece of luggage.

Later on in my career, it got to where they had young pitchers is where they would send me, like at Stockton, and they wanted me to go to Elmira, where Weaver had Palmer, [Frank] Bertaina, Dalkowski, and that bunch of guys, and I wouldn't go. I wouldn't play for him. But I was always where there was younger pitchers 'cause I handled younger pitchers well.

I got into it with Weaver in the rookie league. I think it was Bertaina on the mound and he came out there screaming at him, "How the f*** can you throw that pitch!?" I said, "Hold it a minute. You wanna put the gear on? You put the gear on, otherwise you shut your f***ing mouth! I'm catching this ballgame, not you." He wasn't my manager, he didn't pay my salary. He just happened to be running the club that day 'cause Richards was playing golf or something. It was a constant turmoil between him and I. I didn't like the way he handled people. It was "Do as I say, don't do as I do." Well, that was bull. You gotta set examples for young ballplayers, you just can't go out and get drunk every night and not expect them to do the same thing.

*Were you ever given a fair shot?*

FZ: I never got a chance to play at Baltimore after my first or second year there. I'd come in in situations, like I pinch hit Opening Day or I'd catch the last two innings of this game. I started one game against Chicago. Jim Wilson pitched. I caught Don Ferrarese. We got beat, 1-to-nothing. That's the only full game I played.

First guy I hit against was a Yankee. I hit against Johnny Kucks in front of 56,000. I hit a double off of him and then I came in to pinch hit against Gaylord Perry's brother, Jim, with Cleveland.

What I didn't understand 'til I went to the minors again was that there was no rookie movement. Everything was veteran ballplayers. We finished fourth; I got voted in for a full share, which I think was $420, but the ballplayers voted me in for a full share.

I went to Rochester from Baltimore in '62, I think it was. The understanding I had with Richards was, they were coming in there [Rochester] to play us at the All-Star break. If I were hitting .300, I leave with the club. That was my verbal agreement with Paul Richards. That particular night, I hit two home runs off of Milt Pappas. I was hitting .311. Frank House was the other catcher; he gave me a tremendous amount of help, by the way; he was with Detroit all those years. Frank House was tremendous with younger ballplayers; he really helped me a lot. Clyde King was the manager. I don't wanna get into that. You can't even breathe the bad air or you're on his shit list. You can't smoke, you can't swear, you can't drink, you can't argue on a play. You can't, you can't, you can't. He took all the elements out of your hands, you know.

*Any regrets?*

FZ: Not really. I wish I'd have had a better chance to play. And I wish I'd never known Weaver.

### Frank Joseph "Noodles" Zupo

Born August 29, 1939, San Francisco, CA
Ht. 5'11" Wt. 182 Batted Left, Threw Right

| Year | Team, Lg. | G | AB | R | H | 2B | 3B | HR | RBI | BA |
|---|---|---|---|---|---|---|---|---|---|---|
| 1957 | Baltimore, AL | 10 | 12 | 2 | 1 | 0 | 0 | 0 | 0 | .083 |
| 1958 | Baltimore, AL | 1 | 2 | 0 | 0 | 0 | 0 | 0 | 0 | .000 |
| | Louisville, AA | 55 | 145 | 15 | 32 | 5 | 0 | 0 | 5 | .221 |
| | Wilson, CarL | 12 | 31 | 6 | 9 | 0 | 0 | 2 | 5 | .290 |
| | Knoxville, SAL | 35 | 106 | 10 | 29 | 3 | 0 | 2 | 16 | .274 |
| 1959 | Stockton, CalL | 43 | 103 | 22 | 20 | 4 | 1 | 2 | 10 | .194 |
| | Salem-Yakima, NWL | 25 | 69 | 11 | 15 | 2 | 1 | 2 | 5 | .217 |
| | Asheville, SAL | 7 | 16 | | 3 | | | | | .188 |
| 1960 | Stockton, CalL | 106 | 364 | 52 | 116 | 18 | 3 | 7 | 69 | .313 |
| 1961 | Baltimore, AL | 5 | 4 | 1 | 2 | 1 | 0 | 0 | 0 | .500 |
| | Rochester, IL | 40 | 107 | 12 | 22 | 6 | 1 | 0 | 8 | .206 |
| | Victoria-Ardmore, TxL | 29 | 67 | 7 | 22 | 5 | 0 | 1 | 9 | .328 |
| 1962 | Knoxville. SAL | 9 | 18 | 0 | 2 | 0 | 0 | 0 | 0 | .111 |
| | Austin, TxL | 26 | 75 | 6 | 19 | 6 | 0 | 0 | 6 | .253 |
| 1963 | York, EL | 89 | 284 | 27 | 77 | 12 | 1 | 3 | 41 | .271 |
| 1964 | Dallas, PCL | 106 | 297 | 27 | 76 | 11 | 2 | 6 | 30 | .256 |
| **Major Lg. Totals** | | 16 | 18 | 3 | 3 | 1 | 0 | 0 | 0 | .167 |

# Appendix: Players Signed Under the Bonus Rule of 1953–1957

## American League

| Team | Player | Year | Bonus |
|---|---|---|---|
| Baltimore | Billy O'Dell | 1954 | $24,000 |
| | Tom Borland | 1955 | 40,000 |
| | Wayne Causey | 1955 | 32,000 |
| | Tommy Gastall | 1955 | 30,000 |
| | Bob Nelson | 1955 | 40,000 |
| | Jim Pyburn | 1955 | 48,000 |
| | Bruce Swango | 1955 | 36,000 |
| | Jerry Walker | 1957 | 20,000 |
| | Frank Zupo | 1957 | 50,000 |
| Boston | Billy Consolo | 1953 | 65,000 |
| | Jim Pagliaroni | 1955 | 85,000 |
| Chicago | Ron Jackson | 1953 | 25,000 |
| | Bob Powell | 1955 | 36,000 |
| | Jim Derrington | 1956 | 78,000 |
| Cleveland | Kenny Kuhn | 1955 | 50,000 |
| Detroit | Reno Bertoia | 1953 | 23,000 |
| | Al Kaline | 1953 | 35,000 |
| | Bob G. Miller | 1953 | 60,000 |
| | Jim Brady | 1955 | 37,500 |
| | Jim Small | 1955 | 30,000 |
| | Steve Boros | 1957 | 26,000 |
| | George Thomas | 1957 | 25,000 |
| Kansas City | Clete Boyer | 1955 | 30,000 |
| | Dave Hill | 1957 | 30,000 |
| New York | Frank Leja | 1953 | 40,000 |
| | Tommy Carroll | 1955 | 62,000 |
| Washington | Harmon Killebrew | 1954 | 30,000 |
| | Jerry Schoonmaker | 1955 | 30,000 |
| | Ralph Lumenti | 1957 | 35,000 |

## National League

| Team | Player | Year | Bonus |
|---|---|---|---|
| Brooklyn | Sandy Koufax | 1955 | $24,000 |
| Chicago | Don Kaiser | 1955 | 27,000 |
| | Moe Drabowsky | 1956 | 50,000 |
| | Jerry Kindall | 1956 | 50,000 |
| Cincinnati | Al Silvera | 1955 | 20,000 |
| | Bobby Henrich | 1957 | 25,000 |
| | Jay Hook | 1957 | 65,000 |
| | Don Pavletich | 1957 | 30,000 |
| Milwaukee | Joey Jay | 1953 | 40,000 |
| | Mel Roach | 1953 | 45,000 |
| | John Edelman | 1955 | 20,000 |
| | John DeMerit | 1957 | 100,000 |
| | Bob "Hawk" Taylor | 1957 | 112,000 |
| New York | Joey Amalfitano | 1954 | 40,000 |
| | Paul Giel | 1954 | 60,000 |
| | Mike McCormick | 1956 | 50,000 |
| Philadelphia | Tommy Qualters | 1953 | 40,000 |
| | Mack Burk | 1955 | 40,000 |
| Pittsburgh | Vic Janowicz | 1953 | 25,000 |
| | Nick Koback | 1953 | 20,000 |
| | Eddie O'Brien | 1953 | 40,000 |
| | Johnny O'Brien | 1953 | 40,000 |
| | Laurin Pepper | 1954 | 35,000 |
| | Paul Martin | 1955 | 20,000 |
| | Red Swanson | 1955 | 20,000 |
| | Buddy Pritchard | 1957 | 48,000 |
| St. Louis | Dick Schofield | 1953 | 40,000 |
| | Lindy McDaniel | 1955 | 50,000 |
| | Von McDaniel | 1957 | 50,000 |
| | Bob L. Miller | 1957 | 25,000 |

# Index

Numbers in ***bold italics*** represent photographs.

Aaron, Henry 17, 109
Adams, Bobby 129
Aherne, Goldie 195
Alston, Walter 34
Amalfitano, Joey 43
Anderson, Andy 32
Anderson, Bob 129, 157
Aparicio, Luis 19, 81
Ashburn, Richie 29, 145, 164
Aspromonte, Bob 171

Bailey, Ed 174, 176
Baker, Gene 93, 129, 170, 182
Banks, Ernie 93, 128, 129, 131
Barber, Steve 145
Battey, Earl 19
Bauer, Hank 69, 71, 81, 113, 145
Belanger, Mark 194
Bell, Gus 164
Bella, Zeke 73
Bengough, Benny 15
Benson, Vern 33
Berra, Yogi 69
Berres, Ray 18
Bertaina, Frank 196
Bertoia, Reno 3, 5–9, 44, 52, 66, 81, 118, 153
Bierman, Bernie 45
Blades, Ray 130
Blair, Paul 194
Blanchard, John 73
Bolger, Jim 92
Boone, Ray 7, 153
Borland, Tom 2
Boros, Steve 6, 118, 149, 151–***152***, 153–160
Bouchee, Ed 29
Boudreau, Lou 64, 90, 135
Bowen, Rex 25
Boyd, Bob 193

Boyer, Clete 2, 53, 55
Boyer, Ken 34, 169
Brady, Jim 57–***58***, 59–63, 118, 154
Bragan, Bobby 140, 180
Brecheen, Harry 79, 113, 187, 192
Bressoud, Eddie 43
Brett, George 189
Briley, Charlie 195
Brodowski, Dick 58
Brooks, Herb 45
Brown, Joe 108, 140–141, 178, 180, 183
Brown, Skinny 187, 193
Bruton, Bill 162, 181
Buddin, Don 126, 136
Bunker, Wally 145
Burdette, Lou 27
Burgess, Smokey 174, 176
Burleson, Rick 105
Busch, August 97

Campanis, Al 67
Carey, Andy 69, 81
Carroll, Tom 64–***65***, 66–75
Causey, Wayne 30, 55, 76, ***77, 78***, 79–83, 112, 193
Ceccarelli, Art 193
Cepeda, Orlando 143, 144
Chakales, Bob 5
Charles, Ed 81
Clemente, Roberto 46, 109, 179
Coan, Gil 113
Cobb, Ty 195
Colavito, Rocky 52
Coleman, Gordy 157
Coleman, Jerry 69, 74
Collins, Joe 69
Comiskey, Charles 84, 86
Consolo, Billy 105, 107, 110
Cooper, Walker 20, 27, 92, 96, 98, 169

Courtney, Clint 196
Craft, Harry 119
Craig, Roger 135
Cronin, Joe 106
Crosetti, Frank 70
Crowe, George 174
Curry, Tony 29

Dalkowski, Steve 119, 195, 196
Dark, Alvin 34, 144
Davenport, Jim 77, 144
Dean, Dizzy 59, 93
Decker, Bob 67
Dedeaux, Rod 181, 182
DeMaestri, Joe 73
DeMars, Billy 195
DeMerit, John 28, 149, 161–*162*, 163–166
Derrington, Jim 84–*85*, 86–89
Desautels, Gene 151
Devine, Bing 96, 97
Dickey, Bill 70
Dickson, Ed 157
Dickson, Murry 96
Diering, Chuck 113
DiMaggio, Joe 66, 70, 109
Dixon, Sonny 51
Donovan, Dick 85
Drabowsky, Moe 94, 123, 129
Dressen, Charlie 49
Drews, Karl 15
Drott, Dick 94, 129
Drysdale, Don 135

Edwards, Johnny 177
English, Gil 25
Ennis, Del 144
Etchebarren, Andy 194
Evans, Dwight 105
Evers, Hoot 79

Feeney, Chub 158
Feller, Bob 118, 120
Ferrarese, Don 196
Finigan, Jim 7
Fitch, Bill 134
Fitzsimmons, Freddie 130
Fondy, Dee 93
Ford, Whitey 58, 70, 114
Fox, Nellie 19
Fox, Pete 5
Foytack, Paul 7
Francona, Tito 132, 188
Freese, Gene 129, 182
Fregosi, Jim 82
Friend, Bob 43

Gardner, Billy 193

Gastall, Tommy 78, 112
Gehringer, Charlie 118
Gentile, Jim 119, 193
Gibson, Bob 189
Giel, Paul 41–*42*, 43–47, 138
Gilliam, Jim 170
Ginsberg, Joe 193
Goodman, Billy 193
Gordon, Joe 81
Grba, Eli 192
Greengrass, Jim 144
Griffin, Archie 46
Griffith, Calvin 44, 133
Grimm, Charlie 28
Grissom, Marv 143
Groat, Dick 180, 182, 183
Groh, Heinie 157
Guidry, Ron 189

Hack, Stan 92, 129, 131
Hacker, Warren 91
Haddix, Harvey 32
Hahn, Fred 96, 167
Halas, George 41
Haller, Tommy 43, 195
Hamey, Roy 22, 23
Hamner, Granny 13
Haney, Fred 161
Hannan, Jim 58
Hansen, Ronnie 193
Harris, Bucky 49, 61, 117, 119
Harris, Luman 79, 111, 113
Harris, Stanley 61
Harshman, Jack 193
Hearn, Jim 33
Hemus, Solly 32, 164
Henrich, Tommy 155
Herzog, Whitey 157
Higgins, Mike 107
Himsl, Vedie 127
Hitchcock, Billy 6, 155
Hodge, Gil 164
Hoeft, Billy 51
Hofman, Freddie 191
Hollingsworth, Al 169
Hook, Jay 149
Hopp, Johnny 6
Hornsby, Rogers 164
Houk, Ralph 103
House, Frank 51, 197
Howser, Dick 81
Hubbell, Carl 144
Hudlin, Willis 155
Hudson, Sid 51
Huggins, Miller 66
Hurley, Ed 192
Hutchinson, Fred 6, 96–97, 157, 168

# Index

Jackson, Larry 169
Jackson, Randy 93
Jacobson, Rabbit 58
Janowicz, Vic 3, 43
Jay, Joey 3, 27, 94
Johnson, Connie 187
Johnson, Deron 140, 157
Johnson, Earl 48
Johnson, Roy "Hardrock" 90
Jones, Mel 127
Jones, Sam 91
Jones, Willie "Puddin' Head" 14, 76
Jorgenson, Spider 80

Kaiser, Don 90–*91,* 92–95, 126, 129, 136
Kaline, Al 3, 6, 8, 22, 66, 94, 102, 113, 116, 117, 118, 153, 155, 169, 183
Kasko, Eddie 35
Katalinas, Ed 151
Keane, Johnny 100
Kell, George 18, 193
Kellner, Alex 51
Kiely, Leo 58
Killebrew, Harmon 7, 39, 48–*49, 50,* 51–54, 109, 194
Kindall, Jerry 123, 125–*126,* 127–139
Kindall, Martha 132
King, Clyde 197
Kittle, Hub 196
Kiwano, Yosh 128, 129
Konstanty, Jim 13, 16
Koufax, Sandy 8, 22, 44, 55, 94, 96, 101, 146, 172, 188
Krichell, Paul 67
Kubek, Tony 59
Kucks, Johnny 58, 196
Kuenn, Harvey 117, 153, 155
Kuhn, Bowie 61
Kundla, John 45

Labate, Joe 65
Lary, Frank 119
Lattner, Johnny 42
Lavagetto, Cookie 49–50, 164
Law, Vernon 180
Lee, Bill 105
Lehman, Ken 29, 193
Leja, Frank 67, 71
Lemmons, Abe 168
Lemon, Bob 118
Lemon, Jim 49
Leonard, Dutch 91
Locke, Bobby 132
Lockman, Whitey 141–142
Loes, Billy 187, 192
Lollar, Sherm 19
Lopata, Stan 18, 144

Lopez, Al 15, 18, 19, 20, 86
Lowry, Peanuts 32
Lucadello, Tony 5
Lund, Pud 45
Lynn, Fred 105

Mack, Connie 130
MacPhail, Lee 73, 191, 196
Mann, Earl 163
Mantilla, Felix 29
Mantle, Mickey 69, 70, 109, 113, 114, 118, 189, 194
Marion, Marty 86
Maris, Roger 189
Martin, Billy 69, 71, 95, 195
Martin, Fred 100
Martin, Pepper 130–131, 195
Masterson, Walt 158
Mathes, Joe 96
Matthews, Wid 127
Mauch, Gene 29
Maxwell, Charlie 117
Mayo, Jackie 16
Mays, Willie 46, 93, 109, 114, 189
Mazeroski, Bill 109, 140, 180, 182
McCarren, Bill 58
McCormick, Mike 123, 140–*141,* 142–147
McCovey, Willie 43, 109, 143, 189
McCullough, Clyde 17, 92
McDaniel, Kerry 101
McDaniel, Lindy 55, 96–104, *168,* 169, 171
McDaniel, Von 101, 167–*168,* 169–173
McDermott, Mickey 108, 126
McDougald, Gil 69
McDowell, Sam 187
McHale, John 5, 6, 61, 117, 151, 155
McIlwain, Stover 88
McKeon, Jack 59, 157
McNally, Dave 145
McNamara, John 120
McShane, Don 191
Metro, Charlie 80
Meyer 96
Minner, Paul 91
Miller, Bob G. 11, 118, 154
Miller, Bob L. 16, 17, 149, 171
Miller, Stu 162
Miranda, Willie 80
Moore, Ray 18, 187
Moore, Terry 14, 15
Mory, Walt 129
Mueller, Don 20, 141
Mullin, Pat 6, 151
Murtaugh, Danny 34, 180
Musial, Stan 32, 109, 169

Neal, Charlie 170

## 204        Index

Nelson, Bob 78, 79, 193
Nelson, Cindy 45
Nettles, Graig 53
Newcombe, Don 58, 93, 175, 181
Newhouser, Hal 118, 120
Nieman, Bob 193, 195
Noren, Irv 71
Norman, Bill 120

O'Brien, Eddie 58, 182, 183
O'Brien, Johnny 58, 182, 183
O'Dell, Billy 39, 155, 193
Olson, Karl 153
O'Neill, Steve 11, 12, 14
Owen, Mickey 107
Oylers, Ray 8

Pagliaroni, Jim 55, 105–*106*, 107–110
Paige, Satchel 5, 17
Palmer, Jim 145, 194, 196
Pappas, Milt 145, 197
Parnell, Mel 51
Pasto, Harry 25
Paul, Gabe 131, 132
Pavletich, Don 149, 174–*175*, 176–177
Perry, Gaylord 196
Perry, Jim 196
Pesky, Johnny 6, 49, 52
Pettis, Paul 126
Philley, Dave 154
Phillips, T-Bone 181
Pierce, Billy 191
Pilarcik, Al 193
Piniella, Lou 195
Pinson, Vada 119
Pizarro, Juan 94
Poholsky, Tom 33
Pollet, Howie 98
Porter, J.W. 119
Posedel, Bill 98
Powell, Boog 194
Presko, Joe 33
Priddy, Gerry 6
Pritchard, Buddy 178–*179*, 180–184
Pyburn, Jeff 111
Pyburn, Jim 79, 111–*112*, 113–115, 191

Qualters, Tom 10–*11*, 12–24
Quinn, John 29

Rebollini, Jim 2
Reich, Herm 85
Rhodes, Dusty 143
Rice, Del 162
Rice, Wog 90
Richards, Paul 77, 79, 80, 112, 113, 187, 191, 192, 193, 194, 196, 197

Ridzik, Steve 73
Rigney, Bill 142, 143
Rizzuto, Phil 69, 71
Roach, Mel 25–*26*, 27–31
Roberts, Robin 1, 11, 13, 15, 16, 28
Robinson, Brooks 53, 193, 194
Robinson, Frank 119, 175
Rodgers, Andre 132, 143
Rose, Pete 195
Rosen, Al 195
Rowe, Schoolboy 61
Royal, Darrell 168
Ruel, Muddy 59
Ruether, Dutch 140
Ruiz, Chico 157
Rush, Bob 91
Ruth, Babe 66
Ryan, Connie 14
Ryan, Nolan 17

Sain, Johnny 71
Scheffing, Bob 92, 94, 129, 130
Schell, Danny 22
Schilling, Chuck 133
Schmidt, Willard 96
Schmitz, Johnny 48
Schoendienst, Red 28, 32
Schofield, Dick 3, 21, 32–*33*, 34–37, 169
Schultz, Joe 80
Schuneman, Al 128
Score, Herb 119
Seghi, Phil 174
Seminick, Andy 21
Shannon, Walter 32
Siebert, Dick 127, 130, 131, 134, 138
Simmons, Curt 1, 11, 13, 16, 28, 144
Sisler, Dick 157
Sisty, Sibby 27, 28
Skowron, Bill 73
Slaughter, Enos 33, 69
Small, Jim 60, 116–*117*, 118–121, 154
Smith, Frank 33
Smith, Mayo 17, 18
Snider, Duke 93, 170
Snyder, Russ 52
Souchock, Steve 6
Spahn, Warren 15, 22, 23, 27, 146, 163
Speake, Bob 92, 129
Spencer, Daryl 28, 30
Stanky, Eddie 14, 33
Stargell, Willie 109
Stengel, Casey 66, 71, 72, 73, 163, 164
Stephenson, Jerry 105
Stephenson, Joe 105
Stoneham, Horace 143
Streuli, Walt 118
Sturdivant, Tom 69, 154

Swango, Bruce 55, 77–78, 79, 112
Swanson, Art 76, 183

Tallis, Cedric 81
Tanner, Chuck 161
Taylor, Bib "Hawk" 28, 149
Taylor, Bob 161, 162
Tebbetts, Birdie 175
Thomas, Frank 29
Thomas, George 6, 59, 118, 154, 155–156
Thompson, Hank 143
Thurston, Hollis 84
Tiant, Luis 187
Tighe, Jack 61, 117, 119–120, 154
Torgeson, Earl 7, 13
Triandos, Gus 185, 193
Tuckey, Russ 52
Turley, Bob 72
Turner, Jim 70, 71
Tuttle, Bill 44, 117

Umphlett, Tom 108

Valdevielso, Jose 43
Veale, Bob 109
Vincent, Al 78, 79

Wagner, Leon 43
Waitkus, Eddie 16
Walker, Harry 35, 96–97
Walker, Jerry 149, 185–*186*, 187–190

Walters, Bucky 142, 143
Weaver, Earl 194, 196, 197
Weiss, George 72, 164
Werts, Don 8
Westrum, Wes 142
Wilber, Del 113
Willen, Carlton 94
Williams, Billy 109
Williams, Dick 34, 158, 193
Williams, Frank 120
Williams, Ted 19, 20, 106, 107, 109, 113, 114, 118, 189
Wills, Maury 135
Wilson, Jim 196
Wilson, Red 19
Wimpy, Howard 58, 60
Winceniak, Eddie 128
Wise, Casey 129
Witt, George 44
Woodling, Gene 71
Wyatt, Whitlow 20
Wynn, Early 185
Wyrostek, Johnny 13

Yawkey, Tom 57, 108
York, Rudy 107
Yost, Eddie 48, 50, 52

Zimmer, Don 29, 131
Zupo, Frank 191–*192*, 193–197

www.ingramcontent.com/pod-product-compliance
Ingram Content Group UK Ltd.
Pitfield, Milton Keynes, MK11 3LW, UK
UKHW042003140426
5217IPUK00015B/961